Meanings into Words
Intermediate

Teacher's Book

Meanings into Words

Intermediate

An integrated course for students of English

Teacher's Book

Adrian Doff, Christopher Jones and Keith Mitchell

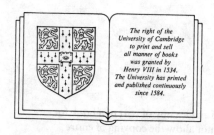

The right of the
University of Cambridge
to print and sell
all manner of books
was granted by
Henry VIII in 1534.
The University has printed
and published continuously
since 1584.

Cambridge University Press

Cambridge
London   New York   New Rochelle
Melbourne   Sydney

Published by the Press Syndicate of the University of Cambridge
The Pitt Building, Trumpington Street, Cambridge CB2 1RP
32 East 57th Street, New York, NY 10022, USA
10 Stamford Road, Oakleigh, Melbourne 3166, Australia

© Cambridge University Press 1983

First published 1983
Fifth printing 1986

Printed in Great Britain
at the University Press, Cambridge

ISBN 0 521 28286 1 Teacher's Book
ISBN 0 521 28283 7 Student's Book
ISBN 0 521 28284 5 Workbook
ISBN 0 521 28285 3 Test Book
ISBN 0 521 23887 0 Cassette (Student's Book)
ISBN 0 521 23888 9 Cassette (Drills)

MX

Contents

Part 1: Contents and organisation

1.1   Meanings into Words

Meanings into Words is an integrated course in general English which takes students from intermediate level to the level of the Cambridge First Certificate examination. It is divided into two parts: an *Intermediate Course* and an *Upper-Intermediate Course*. The two parts can either be used together as a single continuous course, or separately as two independent courses.

The *Intermediate Course* contains 24 units and provides material for 100–130 classroom hours.

The *Upper-Intermediate Course* contains 15 units and provides material for 80–100 classroom hours.

At each level, in addition to the Teacher's Book, *Meanings into Words* consists of:

Student's Book
Workbook
Test Book
Cassette (Student's Book)
Cassette (Drills)

1.2   The Intermediate Course

The Student's Book

The Student's Book contains 24 units, each providing between four and five classroom hours.

Each unit contains presentation and practice material, free oral practice and writing activities, and an extended piece of either reading or listening.

At the end of each unit there is a Language Summary, which lists the main language points covered in the unit.

From Unit 4 onwards, every other unit is followed by an Activities page, which contains two or three free activities. These activities combine and recycle language learnt in earlier units.

The Workbook

The Workbook contains homework exercises which provide extra written practice of the main language points taught in the Student's Book. Each Workbook unit contains four or five exercises, usually including a guided composition.

Every eight units there is a Revision Crossword.

The Test Book

The Test Book contains six short Progress Tests (45–50 minutes each) and one longer Final Achievement Test (90 minutes).

The Progress Tests occur after every four units, and test only the language of those four units. The Final Achievement Test deals with all the main language points covered in the course.

The Drills

To be used in the language laboratory, the Drills give intensive manipulation practice of key structures introduced in the units.

The Drills are divided into 12 Lab Sessions, occurring every two units. Each Lab Session consists of three or four drills, and lasts between 20 and 30 minutes.

Listening material

The Student's Book cassette contains:
   Listening Presentation material
   Listening Models for student interaction
   Extended Listening Comprehension material
   Recorded examples of Practice material

1.3   The syllabus

Meanings into Words covers seven broad functional areas of language:

1 *Action*
   This area consists of language used for talking about the desirability and possibility of action: initiating action in oneself and other people, and commenting on one's own actions and the actions of other people.

2 *Description*
   This area consists of language used for 'physical' description of places, things and people: their appearance, their features, and their location.

3 *Personal information*
   This area consists of language used for giving information about yourself and other people: who you are, what you do, and what kind of person you are.

4 *Narration*
   This area consists of language used for talking about past events, and telling stories in the past. This includes information about when events took place, their sequence, their duration, and their circumstances.

5 *Past and present*
   This area consists of language used for relating the past and the present: present situations and their past origins, past events and their connection with the present, and actions and activities during the period 'up to now'.

6 *Comparison*
   This area consists of language used for comparing and evaluating: talking about similarities and differences, measuring differences, and assessing advantages and disadvantages.

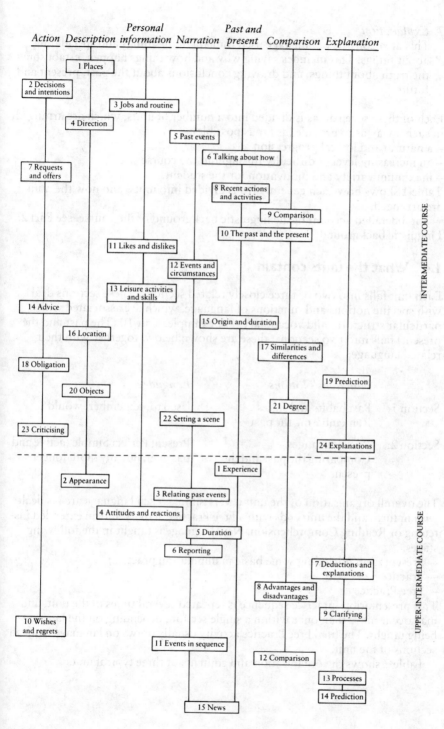

Table 1

7   *Explanation*
This area consists of language used for explaining things and speculating about things. This includes saying why and how things happen, establishing the truth about things, and drawing conclusions about the past, present and future.

Each of these seven areas is divided into a number of units, which are arranged in such a way as to provide (as far as possible):
– a natural and logical progression
– an increasing level of difficulty throughout the course
– maximum variety and motivation for the student.
Table 1 shows how each general area is divided into units, and how the units are arranged.

For a detailed account of the linguistic background of the course, see **Part 2: Linguistic background**.

1.4   What the units contain

Each unit falls into two or three closely related sections. These sections deal with specific notions and functions of language, which are associated with particular structures and vocabulary. For example, Unit 10 (The past and the present) falls into two sections; these are shown below, together with their related language:

	Functions/Notions	*Language*
Section 1:	Past habits and states Remembering the past	Used to; remember; would
Section 2:	Recent changes Comparing the past and the present	Present Perfect Simple (active and passive); not any more/longer

The overall organisation of the unit is very simple: each language area is dealt with in turn, and the unit ends with a Free Practice activity and an extended Listening or Reading Comprehension. New language is taught in the following stages:
– Presentation (including some basic manipulation practice)
– Practice
– Free Practice
This presentation–practice sequence is repeated several times in the unit, and may occur more than once within a single section, depending on the language being taught. The final Free Practice activity usually draws on language from all sections of the unit.

Table 2 shows the organisation and contents of three typical units.

Unit 1
Places

1.1 ROOMS AND FURNITURE
Presentation of: there is / are; have(got); vocabulary; location prepositions
Practice

1.2 WHERE THINGS ARE
Practice

1.3 YOUR OWN ROOM
Free practice
Writing

1.4 SERVICES
Presentation of: have something done.
vocabulary
Practice

1.5 ASKING ABOUT SERVICES
Practice

1.6 AMENITIES
Presentation of: relative clauses with 'which' & 'where'; vocabulary.
Practice

1.7 TALKING ABOUT AMENITIES
Free practice

1.8 ALONG THE COAST
Reading
Writing

Unit 10
The past and the present

10.1 USED TO
Presentation of: used to
Practice

10.2 LIFE IN THE PAST
Practice
Writing

10.3 REMEMBERING THE PAST
Presentation of: remember; used to; would
Free practice

10.4 THINGS HAVE CHANGED
Presentation and practice of: Present Perfect; not... any more / longer

10.5 PRESENT PERFECT PASSIVE
Presentation of: Present Perfect Passive
Practice

10.6 CHANGES OF HABIT
Practice

10.7 MODERN DEVELOPMENTS
Free practice
Writing

10.8 HALLOWE'EN
Reading
Writing

Unit 14
Advice

14.1 SUGGESTIONS & ADVICE
Presentation of: advice / suggestion structures; reporting advice
Practice

14.2 ALTERNATIVE SOLUTIONS
Practice

14.3 PROBLEMS
Free practice

14.4 TAKING PRECAUTIONS
Presentation and practice of: general advice structures; might; otherwise; in case; so that
Practice

14.5 JUST IN CASE
Practice

14.6 ROAD SIGNS: WARNINGS
Practice

14.7 GENERAL ADVICE
Free practice
Writing

14.8 VISITING BRITAIN
Listening
Writing

Table 2

5

1.5 Stages in a unit

Here is a brief description of the stages of the presentation–practice sequence, as well as writing, listening comprehension and reading comprehension.

Presentation

Presentation techniques in the course are designed to suit the requirements of the language being taught, and to involve students as much as possible. There is therefore a wide variety of presentation material: language may be presented by reading, by listening, or by written examples, and the presentation often involves interpretation and class discussion.

The Presentation stage may include some basic manipulation practice of new structures.

Practice

This stage is concerned with controlled practice of new language. It ranges from simple manipulation of structures to more imaginative practice in which students use language in realistic situations.

Practice is usually done in pairs or small groups, and is concerned with appropriate use of language as well as with accuracy.

Free practice

At this stage students are not limited to using particular language. Practice may take the form of role-play, group discussion, or students talking about themselves, and gives them a chance to practise the language they have learnt in a wider context.

Writing

Practice in writing is provided at any stage of the unit where it is appropriate. It usually takes the form of paragraph writing, either based on classroom discussion or as a follow-up to listening or reading comprehension.

Listening/Reading

Each unit ends with a reading or a listening passage which features (but goes beyond) the language of the unit. These passages are followed by comprehension questions, but may also be used as a basis for note-taking, writing, discussion or role-play.

1.6 How the units work

Here is a more detailed picture of a typical unit, showing what happens in the classroom at each stage:

Unit 10   The past and the present

10.1–10.3 Language functions:	talking about past habits and states remembering the past

10.1   USED TO

Presentation Forms of 'used to': positive, negative and questions	Students read a short passage about Eskimos and how their lives have changed. Teacher presents forms of 'used to'. Students make sentences about the passage using 'used to'.
Practice	Students change sentences using forms of 'used to'.

10.2   LIFE IN THE PAST

Practice used to Past Simple (introduced in Unit 5)	In groups, students look at pictures of Victorian Britain and discuss what they think life used to be like.
Writing	They write a paragraph based on their discussion.

10.3   REMEMBERING THE PAST

Presentation I remember + ...-ing I remember + clause	Students listen to a short passage in which someone talks about how she spent her time when she was a child. They answer questions about the passage, to establish how 'I remember' and 'would' are used.
Free practice	In groups, students talk about their own childhood.

10.4–10.6 Language functions:	talking about recent changes comparing the past and the present

10.4   THINGS HAVE CHANGED

Presentation and practice not any more/longer Present Perfect Simple (introduced in Unit 8)	Teacher presents 'not... any more/longer'. In pairs, students have short conversations based on an example. They write sentences summarising each conversation.

10.5   THE PRESENT PERFECT PASSIVE

Presentation Present Perfect Passive verbs of 'change'	Students read a short passage about how a village has changed. Teacher presents the Present Perfect Passive. Students make sentences about the passage using the Passive.
Practice	In pairs, students look at two pictures which

show how a street has changed. They ask each other what changes have taken place.

10.6 CHANGES OF HABIT

Practice
more...than...used to
not as...as...used to
(Comparison introduced in Unit 9)

Teacher reminds students of comparison structures. In pairs, students interview each other about how they have changed, using time comparison structures.

In groups, students talk about other ways in which they have changed over the past few years.

10.7 MODERN DEVELOPMENTS

Free practice
This activity uses language from the whole unit.

In groups, students look at a list of modern developments (e.g. pocket calculators), and discuss how they have changed people's everyday lives.

Writing

Students write a short article about one of the developments they discussed.

10.8 HALLOWE'EN

Reading

Students read an extended passage about what people used to do during the festival of Hallowe'en and what they do now. In groups, they answer comprehension questions.

Writing

Students write a description of Hallowe'en based on the passage.

1.7 The Activities pages

The Activities pages occur after every two units, from Unit 4 onwards. These recycle and combine language learnt in previous units, and provide an opportunity for extended free speaking and writing.

Activities pages contain either two or three activities:

1 A free oral activity. This may take the form of a role-play, a discussion or a game.
2 A free writing activity. Students are given a choice of composition titles, which may be related to the oral activity.
3 Situations (every four units only). These draw on interactional language from the units. They are an oral equivalent of the written Progress tests.

The Activities page following Unit 24 contains extra activities which recycle language from the whole course, and may be used for end-of-course revision.

1.8 Other components

The other components of the course are the Workbook, the Drills and the Test Book. These are all supplementary material, and are intended to be used throughout the course at the teacher's discretion.

The table below shows how material from the Student's Book, the Workbook, the Drills cassette and the Test Book fit together over a four-unit cycle:

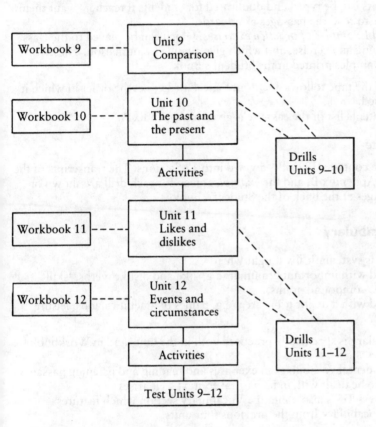

1.9 The recorded material

The *Intermediate Course* is accompanied by two cassettes. These are:
Student's Book cassette
Drills cassette

Student's Book cassette

This cassette contains four kinds of material:

1 *Listening Presentations*, which are used to present new language. Transcripts are given in the appropriate place in Part 4, and in the back of the Student's Book for reference.

2 *Short Listening Models*, which show students the kind of language they are expected to use. Transcripts are given in the appropriate place in Part 4, and in the back of the Student's Book, for reference.
3 *Listening Comprehension Passages*, which are used for comprehension and as a basis for writing and discussion activities. Transcripts are given in the appropriate place in Part 4, but not in the Student's Book, as it is important that students do not read them before doing the comprehension exercise. Transcripts can be typed and duplicated for students if teachers want them to be able to read the passages afterwards.
4 *Recorded Examples of practice exercises*, which can be played to the class before doing an exercise, and which give a guide to intonation. These follow examples printed in the Student's Book.

Material on the tape follows a 'chronological' order, i.e. the order in which it would be used.

A full contents list of the cassette is given in Appendix A.

Drills cassette

This cassette contains 38 drills, divided into 12 Sessions. The transcripts of the drills are in Appendix B, and the *examples* given for each drill are shown on the Drills pages at the back of the Student's Book. .

1.10 Vocabulary

Vocabulary is systematically taught when:
1 it is linked with important grammar (e.g. 'like and dislike' verbs, 'skill' adjectives, compound nouns).
2 it is linked with a major topic area (e.g. names of amenities, jobs, leisure activities).

Such vocabulary is specifically practised both in the units and in Workbook exercises.

Other incidental vocabulary in exercises and reading and listening passages is intended to be dealt with in its natural context as it arises.

The Progress Tests also contain a Vocabulary section which features important vocabulary from the previous four units.

1.11 Pronunciation and intonation

The course does not include any formal teaching of pronunciation or intonation. However, students are given plenty of exposure to spoken English in the form of listening comprehension passages, listening models, recorded examples and the drills. It is assumed that teachers can deal with any particular pronunciation and intonation problems as they arise.

1.12 Examinations

Together, the *Intermediate Course* and the *Upper-Intermediate Course* take students from an intermediate level to the level of the Cambridge First Certificate Examination, and can be used as a preparation for this and other examinations at this level. *Meanings into Words* develops all the language skills needed for FCE, and also gives practice in some of the examination skills. However, the course is not intended primarily to develop specific examination techniques, and students going on to take FCE are recommended to work with past FCE papers as a final preparation for the examination.

The table below shows how *Meanings into Words* would lead up to FCE (a) on a non-intensive five-hour-a-week course (b) on an intensive 15-hour-a-week course.

Five hours a week		*15 hours a week*
Term 1 Term 2 Term 3	*Meanings into Words* *Intermediate*	Term 1
Term 4 Term 5	*Meanings into Words* *Upper-Intermediate*	Term 2
Term 6	Final revision (past papers)	

Part 2: Linguistic background

Meanings into Words is a course in grammar and its use in communication. It sets out to teach the grammatical system of English in relation to the uses to which the learner will predictably want to put it. As the title indicates, we present the grammar of English as a means for putting into words many of the meanings that the learner will want to express in the process of using language for various communicative purposes.

We are concerned, therefore, with getting the student to develop an understanding and command of grammar in terms of *form, meaning* and *use*. This involves teaching the relations between form and meaning (the rules of the grammatical system itself) and also the relations between meaning and use (which Widdowson has called the 'rules of use'). In other words, it is important that the student learns to associate the choice of grammatical form or structure with the expression of a conceptual choice; we must also be sure that he can associate the making of conceptual choices with the performance of various types of communicative activity.

The general aims of the course are perhaps best seen as a concern to integrate traditional and communicative approaches to language teaching. We are convinced that there is an urgent need for materials which draw together and synthesise what is of value in 'structural' courses and in 'functional' courses, reconciling their different aims, supplementing them where they are deficient, and thus reducing the discrepancy between what they cover.

Materials derived from a structural syllabus have been justly criticised for failing to make explicit how their content relates to the student's communicative needs. Such courses seek primarily to ensure coverage of the major grammatical structures of English. They focus on teaching the accurate formation of the structures themselves, and on teaching how contrasts in grammatical form serve to express contrasts of meaning – conceptual distinctions. However, they tend to leave the student to work out for himself when he will have a *use* for the expression of these conceptual distinctions. Structural courses tend to teach form and meaning, but not use.

Many functional courses, on the other hand, have come under criticism for erring in the opposite direction. They start from categories of language use – communicative functions – and present the student with the language forms required for conveying them. However, they often fail to present those language forms as belonging to a coherent system of grammatical choices related to conceptual contrasts. There is nothing to explain how it comes about that particular forms realise certain functions – the student is simply presented with pairings of function and form which he can only commit to memory. This weakness results from an exaggerated preoccupation with 'functions' at the expense of 'notions' – an overemphasis on language as an instrument of social interaction and a neglect of its equally important conceptualising function. For a conceptual as well as a functional element is present in every language act. Functional courses, then, teach form and use, but tend to leave out meaning.

We have tried to ensure that our approach avoids the shortcomings of both types of course by checking whether the relations between form, meaning and use are perceptible to the student at every stage. This has involved the following procedures:

1 In the case of grammatical areas normally only dealt with in terms of form and meaning we have introduced contexts of use. This is especially important where the grammar of English draws conceptual distinctions which are not made in the grammar of the student's own language. Information about use is important here not just for its own sake but also because it helps to clarify and reinforce the student's understanding of the meaning-distinction. We assume, for instance, that when the student sees the Present Perfect tense presented and practised for such purposes as stating one's previous experience, announcing news, describing changes, etc., he will more readily grasp its function as a verb form for referring to 'past events of current relevance'.

2 Even in the case of areas where form rather than meaning is the student's greatest difficulty (e.g. relative clauses) we have sought to ensure that structural practice takes place in contexts which illustrate use (e.g. differentiating between types of object).

3 In dealing with functions, we have tried to offer the student a better understanding of how they and their exponents are related through meaning by grouping them together in conceptually related sets. For instance obligation, permission, exemption and prohibition are systematically related to each other through the concepts of necessity and possibility, which are in turn typically expressed by certain modal auxiliary verbs.

4 Having once identified the major uses of key grammatical structures, we have subjected these uses of language to closer analysis to see what other grammatical material regularly occurs in the same type of context to express either the same meaning or a related meaning. For example, in considering the category 'describing people (function) by reference to their characteristic activities (concept)' as a typical use of the present simple tense, we found that in actual instances of this use speakers commonly add further conceptual information such as 'frequency / intensity' or 'proficiency'. This has led us to invite the student to go beyond simple statements like *She knits* and *He plays tennis* and to tackle sentence types like *She does a lot of knitting* and *He's not a bad tennis player*. Similarly, *be used to + -ing* is introduced into the same unit as the present perfect tense because both structures are used to state previous experience.

Part 3: How to use the course

3.1 Time considerations

Meanings into Words is a complete, self-contained course, which should be worked through unit by unit. The *Intermediate Course* is designed to last between 100 and 130 teaching hours, but the exact time it takes to complete will depend on various factors, such as the level of the class and the intensity of the course.

If the teacher finds that there is not sufficient time to cover all the material, it is of course possible to leave out certain exercises without disrupting the continuity of the course. We have not marked any particular exercises as 'optional' as we feel that this should be left to the individual teacher to decide: the choice of which exercises can be left out will naturally depend on the needs of the students (for example, the class as a whole may be very good at reading or may have already fully mastered certain structures).

If, on the other hand, there is time to spare, the teacher may want to supplement the course with extra listening, reading, writing or discussion material.

3.2 The Workbook, Drills and Test Book

The Workbook

The Workbook is designed to be used parallel to the units, and provides homework material for the students, covering the main points of each unit.

In the Teaching Notes, there are cross-references indicating appropriate times to set individual Workbook exercises.

Workbooks can be taken in for correction, or answers may be gone through in class.

The Drills

The Drills can be used in two ways:
1 with the whole class in language laboratory lessons
2 by individual students as self-access material.
Each Lab Session covers important structures from two units, and should be used towards the end of the second unit, or afterwards for revision.

On the tape, each drill begins with at least two examples, and these examples are given in the Drills pages at the back of the Student's Book, so that students can refer to them while they are doing the Drills.

The Test Book

The Progress Tests are designed to check students' progress every four units, and can be used in two ways:
1 as formal classroom tests, which are taken away and marked
2 as informal 'round the class' tests, or as revision material.
The Test Books are intended to be reusable, and kept by the teacher in class sets, and there is no space provided for students to write their answers. When using the book for formal tests, students should write their answers on pieces of paper, or answer sheets can be typed and duplicated for them.

The Final Achievement Test covers the whole of the *Intermediate Course*, and can be used either as revision material or as part of an end-of-course examination.

A guide to the answers can be found in Appendix C.

3.3 Elicitation

Elicitation plays an important part in presenting new language in the units. Instead of just 'presenting' the language to the students (e.g. by telling them or writing it on the board), the teacher elicits the relevant information from the students by asking questions. The presentation material may take the form of examples, a listening dialogue or reading passage, or even pictures, and the teacher uses this and his* own questions to establish the teaching point or to introduce new items of language.

An example of this is the presentation in Unit 2.1, shown on page 16. The pictures and 'bubbles' demonstrate the difference in usage between *I'll* and *I'm going to*, without actually saying what that difference is. By asking questions (e.g. 'What are they doing in each picture?', 'Are they actually deciding what to do in the second picture? Or have they already decided?') the teacher establishes that *I'll* is used when actually deciding to do something whereas *I'm going to* = 'I've already decided to', and is used for talking about intentions. Once the students have got the main point, the teacher may then present the language formally before going on to the practice stage.

By eliciting, rather than giving a 'straight' presentation, the teacher is able to involve the students much more and focus their attention on the language being presented; he can also see more clearly what students know and do not know, and adapt his presentation accordingly.

---

* We refer to the teacher and student throughout this book as 'he' – this is not because we assume that all teachers and students are male but because the English pronoun system forces us to choose between 'he' and 'she'.

2.1 WILL & GOING TO

Presentation

Four friends have just won £800,000 on the football pools. They celebrate in a restaurant:

Later, a reporter interviews them:

Why do the friends use **I'll** in the restaurant, and **I'm going to** in the interview?

Practice

Work in groups.
1 You have just won £800,000 between you on the football pools. Decide what to do with the money. Use **I think I'll** and **I don't think I'll**.
2 Tell other people in the class about your decisions, using **I'm going to**.

3.4 Pairwork and groupwork

Many of the exercises at the Practice and Free practice stages are designed to be done in pairs or small groups (four or five students). A typical pairwork or groupwork exercise has two or three stages:

1 A *preparation stage*, in which the teacher introduces the exercise and demonstrates the activity (e.g. by going through the examples, or doing the first one or two items with the whole class).

2 An *activity stage*, in which students do the exercise in pairs or groups. During this stage, all the pairs or groups work simultaneously and independently, with the teacher going round the class listening, and giving help where necessary.

3 (optional) A brief *round-up stage*, where the teacher may ask individuals what answers they gave, or, after a discussion activity, what conclusions they came to.

The main advantages of conducting an activity in pairs or groups are:
- It gives more opportunity to students to practise language intensively and develop oral fluency.
- It provides a more 'natural' setting for students to use language – that is, face to face, and 'privately', rather than in front of the whole class.
- It encourages students to use English for real communication with one another.

Pairwork and groupwork can be used for a variety of activity types at different stages in a unit. At an early practice stage, they can be used for simple practice of structures in a situation or for a simple exchange of personal information. At freer practice stages, they can be used for role-playing, discussing topics of general interest, conducting interviews, and more extended exchanges of personal information.

The three examples below show:
1 A pairwork exercise giving simple practice in 'like/dislike' verbs + -ing.
2 A free pairwork activity in which students exchange personal information using the language of Unit 13 (Leisure activities and skills).
3 A free groupwork activity in which students discuss a topic using the language of Unit 10 (The past and the present).

11.2 RESPONDING TO SUGGESTIONS   Practice

Work in pairs. Find out how much your partner likes doing the things below, by making *particular suggestions*, as in the examples. Choose activities in any order you like.

Examples: *flying*
       A: Would you like to come to the States with me?
       B: No thanks – I can't stand flying.

       watching horror films
       A: Let's go and see *Son of Frankenstein*.
       B: That's a good idea – I love watching horror films.

sitting in the sun	eating spicy food
skiing	learning languages
dancing	getting up early
looking after children	cooking
sitting in crowded places	going for long walks
dressing up	talking to foreigners

17

13.8   YOUR OWN LEISURE ACTIVITIES AND SKILLS

Free practice

Work in pairs.
Find out as much as you can about your partner's leisure activities.
Find out *how much* he/she does of each activity, and *how good* he/she is at it. Ask
about:

sports   reading
hobbies   other activities
social life

Write the information down in the form of notes.

10.7   MODERN DEVELOPMENTS

Free practice

Work in groups. Discuss how these modern developments have changed people's
everyday lives. For each one, talk about:
1 what things used to be like
2 what things are like now
3 how things have changed

television   cassette tapes
pocket calculators   supersonic airliners
the telephone   convenience foods

3.5   Dealing with reading

Throughout the course there are reading texts (either Presentation Texts or
Comprehension Passages) which the teacher reads with the class. There are
various ways of doing this:
– The teacher reads the text while the students follow in their books.
– Students read the text silently.
– Individual students read the text aloud.
– (with longer texts) Students read the passage beforehand at home.

None of these is 'right' or 'wrong', and the choice should depend on what the
teacher and students feel is best. In general, a varied approach is likely to be
the most satisfactory.

The main purpose of *Presentation Texts* is to show how particular language is used in context or to provide a stimulus for language practice. Because of this, comprehension of the passage is only a preliminary stage, and is dealt with quite quickly.

In *Reading Comprehension Passages*, on the other hand, comprehension of the passage is the main purpose of the activity, and any role-play, discussion or writing that may follow it can be regarded as an extension.

The questions that follow a comprehension passage are varied in type, both to provide interest and to suit the needs of the passage. As well as straight factual questions, there are also 'implication' questions, and questions for discussion. For this reason, it is usually best to divide the class into small groups to answer the questions, and to go through the answers with the whole class afterwards.

3.6 Dealing with listening

There are four kinds of listening material in the units. These are:
Listening Presentations
Listening Models
Listening Comprehension Passages
Recorded Examples

Listening Presentations

The main purpose of *Listening Presentations* is to focus students' attention on new language items. Because of this, as with Reading Presentations, general comprehension is only a preliminary stage. In general, the procedure is as follows:
1 The teacher plays the tape once, and asks general comprehension questions.
2 The teacher plays the tape again, pausing where necessary, and asks questions about specific language points. It may be necessary to play the tape more than once at this stage.

Listening Models

Listening Models are dealt with in a similar way to Listening Presentations, but their function is rather different: they occur at the Practice stage, and act as loose models of the kind of language that students are expected to use in an activity. The activity might take the form of a discussion, an exchange of personal information or a role-play. In general, the procedure is as follows:
1 The teacher plays the tape once, and deals quickly with any new language items.
2 The teacher plays it a second time.
3 The teacher divides the class into pairs or groups for the activity.

Listening Comprehension Passages

As with Reading Comprehension Passages, *Listening Comprehension Passages* are intended to develop comprehension skills. The way Listening Comprehension passages are dealt with depends on whether they are used in the classroom with the teacher playing the tape recorder, or in the language laboratory.

In the classroom

1 *either* The teacher plays the whole passage once and asks a few general comprehension questions.

   or The teacher stops the tape periodically, and asks general questions as he goes along.

2 The teacher plays the passage again. This time he stops frequently and repeats sections of the passage (and even phrases) where necessary, and deals with each question in turn.

3 When all the questions have been dealt with, the teacher plays the tape once more straight through, as a round-up. At this point, duplicated copies of the passage can be given out to the students.

In the language laboratory

In many ways, the language laboratory is the ideal place to conduct a listening comprehension: students can work individually at their own speed, and the teacher is free to give help to individual students as they need it. The procedure is as follows:

1 The passage is recorded onto students' machines, and the machines are then put on student control.

2 Students work through the questions at their own speed. They listen to the tape, pause, and repeat sections as they need to.

3 When most students are coming towards the end, the teacher stops the machines, and discusses the answers with the class.

Recorded Examples

The *Recorded Examples* are an 'optional extra', and may be played once through to introduce an exercise at the Practice stage, while students follow in their books. They are particularly useful where intonation plays an important part in an exercise, e.g. 17.1 A: My parents never write to me.

B: Nor do mine.

C: Mine don't write to me, either.

Part 4: Teaching notes

The teaching notes for each unit begin with a summary of what the unit contains, in the form of a description accompanied by a diagram.

Notes for each exercise contain:

1 A description of the *language* introduced in the exercise (intended mainly for the teacher's own information) e.g. in 1.6:

> **Language:** Vocabulary: names of amenities that might interest a visitor.
> Use of 'non-defining' relative clauses with *which* and *where* for giving additional information.
>
> *Note:* Other relative clause types are introduced in later units.

2 Notes on suggested *procedure* for conducting the exercise (including ideas for presentation and practice). Numbers in brackets refer to questions in the Student's Book.

   Language in boxes is intended as presentation material that the teacher can write on the board, or build up by eliciting information from the students e.g. in 1.6:

> There are night clubs. They stay open till 4 o'clock in the morning.
> There are nightclubs, <u>which</u> stay open till 4 o'clock in the morning.
>
> There are pubs. You can sit in them and have a glass of beer.
> There are pubs, <u>where</u> you can sit and have a glass of beer.

Answers to some exercises are given. Numbers in brackets refer to questions in the Student's Book.

Remedial presentation and practice

Language points which are presented as 'new language' are dealt with in detail in the unit-by-unit notes; there are, however, some more elementary language points (e.g. basic comparative forms, Present Simple Passive) which students are expected to have covered, but which may need some remedial practice. Ideas for presentation and practice of this language are given in a separate 'Remedial presentation and practice' section following the main unit-by-unit notes. Points at which teachers should refer to this section are indicated by the symbol ▶ RP ◀.

Part 4:   Teaching notes

Cross-references to the Workbook

At the end of the notes to individual exercises there may be a cross-reference which indicates an appropriate point to set Workbook homework exercises, e.g. ▶ **W2 Ex 3** ◀ refers to Workbook Unit 2, Exercise 3.

Listening symbols

The symbol 📼 indicates that the exercise is accompanied by an essential piece of listening (Listening Presentation, Listening Model or Listening Comprehension). The text of the recorded material is included in the notes for that exercise.

The symbol 📼 indicates that the written example in the Student's Book is also recorded on the tape, and can be played to the class before they do the exercise. The texts of the Recorded Examples are not included in the teaching notes.

Unit 1   Places

This is the first of a series of units concerned with physical *description* of places, things and people. It deals with various aspects of describing places: what there is in places, where things are, and what you can do in them.

The unit falls into three sections, followed by a Reading Comprehension. The first section is concerned with describing rooms and their contents; the second section is concerned with services, and introduces *have something done*; the third section is concerned with describing what amenities there are in towns, and what you can do there.

As this is an 'introductory' unit, it brings together a range of structures and vocabulary that students should already have come across at a lower level: *there is/are, have (got)*, location prepositions and simple relative clauses.

1.1 ROOMS AND FURNITURE
Presentation of: there is / are; have(got); vocabulary; location prepositions.
Practice

1.2 WHERE THINGS ARE
Practice

1.3 YOUR OWN ROOM
Free practice
Writing

1.4 SERVICES
Presentation of: have something done; vocabulary.
Practice

1.5 ASKING ABOUT SERVICES
Practice

1.6 AMENITIES
Presentation of: relative clauses with 'which' & 'where'; vocabulary.
Practice

1.7 TALKING ABOUT AMENITIES
Free practice

1.8 ALONG THE COAST
Reading
Writing

23

1.1 ROOMS AND FURNITURE

> **Language:** *There is / are* and *have / have got.*
> Vocabulary: rooms and furniture.
> Location prepositions.
>
> *Note:* This language should be partly known already, and is
> introduced here for revision.

Presentation

This is a Listening Presentation. (For procedure, see 'Dealing with listening' in
Part 3.)

Landlady: 447 4716

Student: Hello. Is that Mrs Davies?

Landlady: Speaking.

Student: Good afternoon. My name's
Stephen Brent. I was given your
address by the student accommodation agency. I understand you have
a room to let.

Landlady: Yes, that's right. I've just got
one room still vacant. It's an attic
room, on the second floor. It's rather
small, but I'm sure you'll find it's very
comfortable.

Student: I see. And how much do you
charge for it?

Landlady: The rent's £25 a week. That
includes electricity, but not gas.

Student: Has the room got central
heating?

Landlady: No, it's got a gas fire which
keeps the room very warm.

Student: I see...And what about
furniture? It is furnished, isn't it?

Landlady: Oh yes...There's a divan bed
in the corner with a new mattress on
it...Let me see... There's a small
wardrobe, an armchair, a coffee table,
a bookshelf...

Student: Is there a desk?

Landlady: Yes, there's one under the
window. It's got plenty of drawers
and there's a lamp on it.

Student: Oh good...Is there a washbasin in the room?

Landlady: No, I'm afraid there isn't a
washbasin. But there's a bathroom

just across the corridor, and that's got
a washbasin and a shower as well as a
bath. You share the bathroom with
the people in the other rooms. The
toilet is separate, but unfortunately
it's on the floor below.

Student: Oh, that's all right...What
about cooking? Can I cook my own
meals?

Landlady: Well, there's a little kitchen-
ette next to your room. It hasn't got a
proper cooker in it, but there's a gas
ring and an electric kettle by the sink.
I find my students prefer to eat at the
university.

Student: I see. And is the room fairly
quiet?

Landlady: Oh yes. It's at the back of the
house. It looks onto the garden and it
faces south, so it's bright and sunny,
too. It's very attractive, really. And it's
just under the roof, so it's got a low,
sloping ceiling. Would you like to
come and see it? I'll be in for the rest of
the day.

Student: Yes, I'm very interested. It
sounds like the kind of room I'm
looking for. Can you tell me how to
get there?

Landlady: Oh, it's very easy. The house
is only five minutes' walk from
Finchley Road tube station. Turn
right outside the station, and then it's
the third street on the left. You can't
miss it. It's got the number on the gate.
It's exactly opposite the cemetery.

1 Before you play the tape, let students look quickly at the pictures and map.
2 Play the tape. Students answer (1) – (3), which check general comprehension of where the room is, what furniture it has, and how to get to the house. Ask students what the landlady actually says in each case.
  Answers: (1) The window in the roof ('attic room on the second floor', 'at the back of the house').
             Note: The three floors are the ground floor, the first floor and the second floor.
          (2) Picture 4. (Lamp on desk, gas fire, sloping ceiling, no washbasin in the room.)
          (3) Blake Road. ('Turn right outside the station, then it's the third street on the left.')
3 Play the tape again. Students answer (4), which checks comprehension of exactly what there is and where things are.
  Answers: (4) (a) On the second floor, at the back of the house, just under the roof.
              (b) In the corner of the room.
              (c) Under the window.
              (d) On the desk.
              (e) Across the corridor.
              (f) On the floor below.
              (g) Next to the room.
              (h) By the sink, in the kitchenette.
4 If you like, check students' knowledge of other words and expressions from the dialogue by asking questions of your own:
  e.g. What kind of bed has the room got?
        What is there in the bathroom?
        How much is the rent?

Practice

1 Before you begin the pairwork, remind students of the forms of *there is / are* and *have / have got*. Point out that *have* and *have got* have the same meaning but different forms. If necessary, present them on the board and do some basic practice. ▶ RP ◀
2 Divide the class into pairs to improvise the conversation.

1.2 WHERE THINGS ARE   Practice

Language: Location prepositions.
      Practice of language introduced in 1.1.

Note: Students should already know many of these prepositions. Concentrate on those that are new or cause difficulty.

Part 4: Teaching notes

1 Look at the list of prepositions, and check that students know what they mean by using objects (and people) in the classroom.
2 Look at the pictures with the class, and ask students questions of two kinds:
 e.g. Where is the coffee table?
   What is there next to the armchair?
 Present any new vocabulary as you go along.
3 Ask similar questions about the room you are in.
▶ W1 Ex 1 ◀

1.3 YOUR OWN ROOM

> **Language:** Free practice of language introduced so far in this unit.

Free practice

1 Demonstrate the pairwork by describing a room in your own flat / house.
2 Divide the class into pairs. Point out that they should all take notes, as they will later have to write about their *partner's* room. They take it in turns to describe their room.

Writing

The writing can be done in class or for homework.
▶ W1 Ex 2 ◀

1.4 SERVICES

> **Language:** *Have something done.*
>   Vocabulary: i) places that provide services
>   ii) associated verbs.
>
> *Note:* The structure *have something done* is a special form of the Passive (often called the 'have-passive'). Different forms and uses of this structure are introduced in later units – in this unit it is introduced in its basic (infinitive) form and in the Present Simple, and can be treated simply as a formula.

Presentation

1 Read the text (see 'Dealing with reading' in Part 3.) Check general comprehension by asking questions round the class:
 e.g. What kind of hotel is the Supercontinental?

26

What three services does it offer?
What exactly will they do for you at the hairdressing salon?
Explain any new vocabulary.
2 Present *have something done* by comparing things you do at home and
things people do for you at a hotel, and write this table on the board:

At home:	At a hotel:
You make your own bed.	Someone makes your bed for you. – You <u>have</u> your bed <u>made</u>.
You wash your own clothes.	Someone washes your clothes for you. – You <u>have</u> your clothes wash<u>ed</u>.

Point out the form and sequence of the structure:
   have + Noun + Past Participle.
Point out that it is *not* the Present Perfect or any other tense!
3 Give other sentences from the text, and ask students to change them into
have something done forms:
   e.g. You: They clean your shoes for you, so...
         Student: ...You can have your shoes cleaned.
4 If you think they need more practice, ask students to go through the text
again, working in pairs.

Practice

1 Look at the pictures with the class, and ask them to tell you the names of
the places.
2 Ask students to suggest as many things as possible that you can have done
at each place.
   Answers: Hairdresser's: hair washed, trimmed, dyed, cut; beard trimmed.
               Optician's: eyes tested, eyesight checked; glasses mended.
               Dentist's: teeth cleaned, filled; a tooth taken out.
               Photographer's: film developed, printed, processed; camera repaired;
                  photograph taken.
               Garage: car repaired, serviced, washed; oil changed; tyres pumped up.
               Laundry / Dry-cleaner: clothes washed, ironed, (dry-)cleaned.

1.5 ASKING ABOUT SERVICES   Practice

> **Language:** Practice of language introduced in 1.4.
> Practice of location prepositions.

1 Play the example on the tape. Then demonstrate the pairwork by doing
(1) with the whole class:
   e.g. You: Your sheets are dirty.
         Student 1: I want to have my sheets washed. Do you know a good
                    laundry around here?
         Student 2: I usually have mine washed at the Express Laundry.

Student 3: The Express Laundry? Where's that exactly?
Student 4: It's in Bridge Street, next to the bank.
2 Students have other conversations in pairs.
▶ W1 Ex 3 ◀

1.6   AMENITIES

> **Language:**   Vocabulary: names of amenities that might
>   interest a visitor.
>   Use of 'non-defining' relative clauses with *which*
>   and *where* for giving additional information.
>
> *Note:* Other relative clause types are introduced in later
> units.

Presentation

Ask students to suggest as many places as they can for each category, writing
new items on the board.
Possible answers: (1) Hotel, guesthouse, bed and breakfast place, youth hostel,
camping site.
(2) Library, bookshop, newsagent's, bookstall.
(3) Park, public gardens, beach; football ground, tennis court, swimming
pool.
(4) Zoo, circus; funfair, children's playground.
(5) Museum, art gallery, exhibitions.
(6) Pub, restaurant, discotheque, nightclub; theatre, cinema, opera
house.
▶ W1 Ex 4 ◀ (Students can write their answers in the table.)

Practice

1 Show how *which* and *where* are used to give additional information *in a
single sentence*, by writing these sentences on the board:

> There are night clubs. They stay open till 4 o'clock in the morning.
> There are nightclubs, <u>which</u> stay open till 4 o'clock in the morning.
>
> There are pubs. You can sit in them and have a glass of beer.
> There are pubs, <u>where</u> you can sit and have a glass of beer.

2 Ask students to make sentences with *which* or *where* about the other places
where you can spend a night out:
e.g. There are cinemas, which show a different film each week.
3 Divide the class into groups. Working together, they make similar sentences
about the other places.
Note: There is no need to continue this for too long, as these structures are
practised in the next exercise.
▶ W1 Ex 4 ◀

1.7 TALKING ABOUT AMENITIES   Free practice

> **Language:** Free practice of language introduced in 1.6.

This exercise begins with a Listening Model. (See 'Dealing with listening' in Part 3.)

1 Play the tape. Students write the answers to (1) and (2) in the table.
2 Using the topics in their books, students interview each other in pairs, conducting two interviews each.
3 As a round-up, ask individual students to tell you what they said.

▶ W1 Ex 5 ◀

Visitor: Where can I stay in this town?
Resident: There are lots of hotels, but they tend to be fairly expensive. And then there are bed and breakfast places, which are much cheaper – and you can find out about them through looking in the paper, or else just walking around the streets, and they have signs in the window saying 'Bed & Breakfast'. And then there are youth hostels.
Visitor: What are the youth hostels like?
Resident: The youth hostels are OK. All you get is a bed, but they do tend to be very cheap.
Visitor: Do I have to become a member?
Resident: Yes, you do, in fact. But it's very easy to join, and there's an office along the road, where you can go and sign on.

1.8 ALONG THE COAST

Reading

For procedure, see 'Dealing with reading' in Part 3.
Answers: (1) (b)
(2) (a) There are luxury hotels, less expensive guest houses, bed and breakfast places, camping sites.
(b) There are secluded coves and large sandy beaches.
(c) The cliffs are winding, and you can walk for miles along them.
(d) Lots of it, sophisticated, varied: discos, opera, ballet, variety shows, theatre.
(e) It's good for fishing and water-skiing.
(3) (a) Go walking along the cliffs or go to the coves.
(b) Dartmoor National Park.
(4) It has a model railway, and lights up at night.
(5) (a) Small sheltered bay.
(b) Sandwiches, drinks, ice cream, etc.

(c) Folding chair with a cloth seat.
(d) Small hut behind the beach which you can rent, and use for changing, keeping your clothes in, etc.
(e) A show with many short performances (e.g. singing, dancing, jokes).
(6) Torquay harbour. There are boats, yachts, a cliff, hotels, etc.
(7) (This is a discussion question.)

Writing

The writing can be done in class or for homework.

Unit 2   Decisions and intentions

This is the first of a series of units concerned with taking, initiating and commenting on *action*. It deals with language used for making decisions and for talking about decisions and arrangements you have made.

The unit falls into three sections, followed by a Listening Comprehension. The first section is concerned with making decisions, and practises the Future tense; the second section is concerned with intentions and plans, and practises *going to* and other related structures; the third section is concerned with definite arrangements that have been made for the future, and practises the Present Continuous tense.

2.1 WILL & GOING TO
Presentation of: will versus going to; I(don't) think I'll.
Practice

2.2 MAKING DECISIONS
Practice

2.3 CHANGING YOUR MIND
Practice

2.4 INTENTIONS AND PLANS
Presentation of: going to; planning to; intending to; thinking of + -ing.
Practice

2.5 MAKING MONEY
Free practice
Writing

2.6 ARRANGEMENTS
Presentation of: Present Continuous for future arrangements.
Practice

2.7 YOUR OWN PLANS
Free practice

2.8 A CELEBRATION
Listening

2.1 WILL & GOING TO

> **Language:** Use of:
> *I'll* for making *spontaneous decisions* (i.e.
> announcing your decision to do something as
> you decide it).
> *I'm going to* for expressing *intention* (i.e.
> saying what you have already decided to do or
> not to do).
>
> *Note: Will* and *going to* are also used in making predictions –
> see Unit 19.
> In making decisions, *I'll* is usually preceded by *I think, maybe,*
> or *perhaps* – this has the effect of making the decisions more
> 'tentative' and therefore more 'polite'. These forms are
> practised in this exercise and in 2.2.

Presentation

1 ▢ Look at the two pictures with the class, and play the captions on the
  tape.
2 Elicit from the class why the friends use *I'll* in one picture and *I'm going to*
  in the other. Help them by asking what the people are doing in each picture.
  (Picture 1: they're having a meal, celebrating, and *deciding* how to spend
  the money. Picture 2: they're talking to a reporter and telling him *what
  they've decided*.)
3 Point out the negative forms:
  I *don't think* I'll...
  I'm *not* going to...

Practice

1 Divide the class into groups. Each student should make a different decision.
2 Ask one person from each group to tell the class what each person in his
  group has decided:
  e.g. I'm going to buy a house.

2.2 MAKING DECISIONS   Practice

> **Language:** Practice in making spontaneous decisions
> (positive and negative forms).

1 Go through the examples, and point out the different negative forms:
  Perhaps / Maybe I *won't*...
  I don't think *I'll*...
2 Students make decisions round the class, adding a reason each time;
  e.g. I think I'll have a beer. I'm thirsty.

3 Either do the second part of the exercise with the whole class, or let them do
it in groups and go through the answers afterwards. Different decisions can
be added to each remark:
e.g. I'm getting much too fat. I think I'll go on a diet.
                     I don't think I'll eat today.
                     Perhaps I won't have an ice cream.
▶ W2 Ex 1 ◀

2.3 CHANGING YOUR MIND   Practice

> **Language:** Practice in making spontaneous decisions.
> Use of *in that case* for making an alternative
> decision.

1 🎞 Play the example on the tape. Ask students to suggest how D might continue:
e.g. 'Hitchhike? Don't do that – it's terribly dangerous.'
Point out the use of *in that case*.
2 Demonstrate the groupwork by doing (1) with the whole class, starting the
conversation yourself.
3 Divide the class into groups to do the exercise.
▶ W2 Ex 2 ◀

2.4 INTENTIONS AND PLANS

> **Language:** Practice of *going to*.
> Other verbs for expressing intentions and plans:
> *intending to*
> *planning to*
> *thinking of ...-ing*.

Presentation 🎞

This is a Listening Presentation. (For procedure, see 'Dealing with listening' in
Part 3.)

1st Student: Well, first of all I'm
intending to have a good long
holiday abroad, just travelling round
Europe, and then when I get tired of
travelling I'm going to – well, come
back and start looking for a job. I
haven't quite decided yet what job,
but I'm probably going to try and get
a job in advertising of some kind.
2nd Student: Well eventually I'm
planning to open my own restaurant.
Only I haven't got enough money to
do that at the moment of course, so
I've decided to get a temporary job
for a year or so, and I'm going to
work really hard and try and save as
much money as possible. Actually,
I'm thinking of working as a waiter,
or some job in a restaurant anyway...

33

1 Play the tape. Students answer (1), which checks general comprehension.
2 Play the tape again. Students answer (2), (3) and (4), which focus on structures for expressing intentions / plans.
   Answers to (4): (a) She's not sure what permanent job she's going to look for.
   (b) He's not sure exactly what temporary job he's going to do.
   (*Note:* The purpose of this question is to establish the meaning of 'I'm thinking of working...' – see below.)
3 Establish that '*I'm thinking of...*' is followed by a *gerund* (-ing form), and that it means 'I'm *probably* going to... (but I'm not sure)'.

Practice

1 Either do the exercise round the class or in groups. Several answers are possible for each situation:
   e.g. (1) He's going to look for a better job.
   He's thinking of speaking to his boss about it.
   He's planning to do a second job in the evenings.
2 The pictures are deliberately ambiguous, so that there are several possible interpretations.
   ► W2 Ex 4 ◄

2.5 MAKING MONEY

> **Language:** Structures used in coming to a decision with someone else:
> *Shall we...?*
> *Wh-...shall we...?*
> *Let's...*
> *Why don't we...?*
> Free practice of language introduced in 2.4.

Free practice

1 Before you begin, make sure students are familiar with the expressions given in the box in their books. If necessary, do some basic practice of questions with *shall we?* ► RP ◄
2 Briefly demonstrate the pairwork by choosing one student as your 'partner' and beginning a discussion with him about what you might do to make money.
3 Divide the class into pairs. Students discuss with their partners what they will do.
4 Students form new pairs to interview each other about what they are planning to do.

Writing

The writing can be done in class or for homework.
▶ W2 Ex 3 ◀ (for questions with *shall I?*)

2.6   ARRANGEMENTS

> **Language:**   Use of Present Continuous tense for talking
> about things in the future that have been
> *definitely arranged.*
>
> *Note:* Other uses of the Present Continuous are introduced
> in Unit 6.

Presentation

1 After going through the dialogue, show how the Present Continuous is used
   by giving some contrastive examples of your own:
   e.g. We're going to move to a new house. (=We've decided to move.)
         We're moving to a new house. (=It's already arranged, we've found a
         house and found someone to buy our old one.)
2 Go through the programme. Ask the class to make sentences about what
   the students are doing on Saturday.
   Answers: They're stopping for coffee at Buckingham; they're arriving at Stratford
          at 12; they're having lunch at The Riverside Restaurant; they're going on
          a tour of the town; they're not doing anything special in the afternoon;
          they're seeing *King Lear*; they're leaving at 11; they're arriving back at
          Cambridge at 2.
          (*Note:* It is also possible to use the *Present Simple* for events which are
          clearly part of a fixed timetable, e.g. the coach *leaves* Stratford at 11.)

Practice

1 If necessary, introduce the pairwork by establishing what Samira's questions
   are:
   e.g. (1) What time are we leaving?
2 Students ask and answer questions in pairs.

2.7   YOUR OWN PLANS   Free practice

> **Language:**   Free practice of language introduced in this
> unit.

1 Introduce the activity by telling the class about some of your own arrangements and plans.

2 Divide the class into groups for the activity.
3 As a round-up, ask each group to tell you some of the plans they talked about.
▶ W2 Ex 5 ◀

2.8 A CELEBRATION Listening 📼

This is a Listening Comprehension Passage. For procedure, see 'Dealing with listening' in Part 3.

Alan and Jane: Good evening.
Waiter: Good evening. Would you like to sit here by the window?
Alan: Er, no. A friend's joining us a bit later. We'll need a table for three.
Waiter: Ah, in that case, perhaps you'd like this table.
Jane: Thank you.
Waiter: Shall I wait until your friend comes before taking your order?
Alan: Er, no. I don't think we'll wait, thank you. We'll order now. Can I see the menu?

* * *

Jane: What are you going to have, Alan?
Alan: I'm not sure. The salmon, maybe.
Jane: It's a bit expensive.
Alan: Mmm, yes, it is, isn't it? Well, in that case I think I'll have the steak.
Jane: Perhaps I'll try the steak and kidney pie.
Alan: What wine shall we have?
Jane: None for me. I'm going to have beer.

* * *

Waiter: Have you decided what to order, sir?
Alan: Yes, I'm going to have the steak.
Waiter: How would you like it, sir?
Alan: Er ...I think I'll have it rare ...no, medium.
Jane: And I'd like the steak and kidney pie.

Waiter: Sorry, madam. The steak and kidney pie's off.
Jane: Oh. In that case, I'll have ...er ...mixed grill.
Waiter: With chips?
Jane: Er, no. I don't think I'll have chips. Just some mashed potatoes.
Waiter: Thank you.
Alan: Oh – and two beers, please.

* * *

Charles: Hi. Have you ordered yet?
Jane: Hi, Charles. Yes, we have. I'm having a mixed grill and Alan's having a steak.
Charles: Well, I know what I'm going to have. I'm starving. I'm going to have an enormous steak and kidney pie.
Alan: They haven't got any.
Charles: That's a pity. What wine are we having?
Jane: We're not. We're having beer.
Charles: Beer? But the beer's awful in this place. Right...er...I'll have soup, mixed grill with double chips, apple pie and custard – and a whole bottle of wine. Waiter!

* * *

Jane: Mmm, that was delicious. I think I'll come here again.
Alan: Right, let's get the bill. Shall I pay, or will you, Jane?
Charles: I'm paying. We agreed that yesterday. After all, it's me who's celebrating the end of my diet, not you.

Answers: (1) See Listening Text.
(2) (a) Sit by the window / wait for Charles. (b) Salmon. (c) Chips.
(3) Alan: (a) Medium steak. (b) Beer.
     Jane: (a) Mixed grill and mashed potatoes. (b) Beer.

Charles: (a) Soup, mixed grill with double chips, apple pie and custard.
(b) A whole bottle of wine.
(4) (a) 'What wine shall we have?' (b) 'Shall I pay or will you, Jane?'
(5) (a) No. (She says 'I think I'll come here again.') (b) Yes. (He knows the beer is awful.)
(6) To have a meal together and that Charles would pay.
(7) To celebrate the end of Charles's diet.

Unit 3 Jobs and routine

This is the first of a series of units concerned with giving *personal information* about yourself and other people. It deals with ways of describing what you and other people do: their job, their daily routine, and regular events in their life.

The unit falls into two sections, followed by a Reading Comprehension and Free Practice. The first section is concerned with describing your own and other people's jobs and what they involve; the second section is concerned with describing your daily routine, saying how often you do things, and describing things that often happen to you and other people.

The unit practises the Present Simple active and passive, compound noun phrases, and frequency adverbs and phrases.

3.1 JOBS
Presentation and practice of: compound noun phrases; Present Simple; vocabulary.

3.2 WHAT'S YOUR JOB?
Practice

3.3 PLACES AND PEOPLE
Practice

3.4 YOUR OWN JOB
Free practice

3.5 DAILY ROUTINE
Presentation of: Present Simple question forms; frequency adverbs and phrases.
Practice
Writing

3.6 PRECISE FREQUENCY
Presentation and practice of: precise frequency expressions.
Practice

3.7 ALL IN A DAY'S WORK: THE PASSIVE
Presentation of: Present Simple Passive with 'be' or 'get'.
Practice

3.8 A LIFE IN THE DAY OF...
Reading

3.9 TALKING TO JANET AND WARREN
Free practice

3.1 JOBS   Presentation and practice

> **Language:** Present Simple Tense (revision).
> Vocabulary for names of jobs:
> i) Compound Noun Phrases
> ii) Single Nouns ending in -*er, -or, -ist.*
>
> *Note:* The main purpose of this exercise is to show the
> relationship between nouns, noun phrases and verbs for
> describing what people do.

1 Introduce the exercise by asking what the picture is. (It's the window of a
   'Job Centre' or employment exchange, and the cards are advertising
   available jobs.)
2 Look at the example, and ask students to define the other jobs in the
   window. Check that they use the Present Simple correctly.
3 Establish that:
   i) Names of jobs may be single nouns (often ending in -er, -or, -ist), or
       compound nouns.
   ii) The first noun in compound nouns is *always singular* (e.g. *bus* driver,
       not 'buses driver').
   If you like, write these examples on the board to show the relationship
   between compound nouns and verbs:

He	drives buses. cleans windows. digs graves.	He's a	bus driv<u>er</u>. window clean<u>er</u>. grave dig<u>ger</u>.

4 Do the exercise round the class.
   Answers:
   (1) Watchmender
   (2) Supermarket manager
   (3) Bookseller
   (4) Photographer
   (5) Road sweeper
   (6) Film actor and actress
   (7) TV news reader
   (8) Classical guitarist
5 Explaining what people do: Either do this part round the class, or let
   students discuss it in groups and go through the answers afterwards.
   Note: There are no single 'obvious' definitions of the nouns, so various
   answers are possible.

   Possible answers:

Secretary:	writes letters, keeps records, etc. in an office.
Cashier:	deals with money in a shop, bank, etc.
Mechanic:	repairs machinery or engines.
Plumber:	fits and repairs water pipes, etc.
Nightwatchman:	looks after a building at night.
Gardener:	works in a garden, grows plants and vegetables.
Receptionist:	welcomes guests arriving at a hotel.
Air hostess:	looks after and serves passengers on an aeroplane.

Part 4: Teaching notes

3.2 WHAT'S YOUR JOB? Practice

> **Language:** Practice of language introduced in 3.1.
> Use of *at* for places of work.
> 'Positive' tag questions used for making
> deductions: e.g. 'So you*'re* a doctor, *are you?*'

1 🔊 Play the example on the tape.
  Point out that *at* can be used for all the places shown, although *in* can also be used for buildings (if the person actually works inside them).
2 Point out the use of 'positive' tag questions (You are..., *are* you?), which are used when you realise something or come to a conclusion. Give some examples to show the difference between 'positive' and 'negative' tag questions:
  e.g. You*'re* a doctor, *aren't* you? (Negative tag) = I'm not sure, so I'm checking.
  You*'re* a doctor, *are* you? (Positive tag) = I conclude from what you are saying that you're a doctor. Am I right?

  Note: Tag questions of both types occur in later units. There is no need to deal with them fully at this stage: it is enough for students to be aware that there are two types.

3 Demonstrate the pairwork by doing (1) with the whole class.
4 Students do the exercise in pairs. In (5) – (9), they should think of suitable jobs themselves.
5 As a round-up, ask individual students what answers they gave.

3.3 PLACES AND PEOPLE Practice

> **Language:** Practice of language introduced in 3.1 and 3.2.

1 Ask students to suggest as many jobs as they can for each place, and tell them others you can think of:
  e.g. Airport: pilot, air hostess, barman, porter, ticket clerk, customs officer.
  ▶W3 Ex 1◀ (Students can write their answers in the table.)
2 🔊 Play the example on the tape. Then demonstrate the game by choosing a job yourself and asking students to guess it.
3 Before dividing the class into groups, ask each student (secretly!) to write a place and a job on a piece of paper.
4 Divide the class into groups of four to six. They take it in turns to have their job guessed.
  ▶W3 Ex 1◀

3.4 YOUR OWN JOB   Free practice

> **Language:** Free practice of language introduced so far in
> this unit.

1 Demonstrate the activity by getting the class to interview you.
2 Divide the class into groups to interview each other.
3 As a round-up, ask different students what they found out about others in
   their group.

3.5 DAILY ROUTINE

> **Language:** WH- questions using Present Simple tense.
> Adverbs and phrases expressing general
> frequency.

Presentation

1 Ask students to make questions from the prompts. Present any new items:
   e.g. (2) What do you have *for* breakfast?
      (3) *How long does it take you to* get to work?
      (6) *Who* do you go out *with*?
2 Write the sentence on the board, and ask students to tell you where to put
   each adverb or phrase. Establish that there are three types:
   i)   *always, never* (also *often*, which is not practised here) must come
       immediately before the verb:
       e.g. I *always* have lunch in the office canteen.
   ii) other single-word adverbs (*sometimes, usually, generally, normally,
       occasionally*) come immediately before the verb, or for special emphasis
       may come at the beginning or end of the sentence:
       e.g. I *sometimes* have lunch in the office canteen.
          Normally, I have lunch in the office canteen.
          I have lunch in the office canteen *occasionally*.
   iii) adverb phrases (*as a rule, now and again, from time to time*)
       must come at the beginning or the end of the sentence:
       e.g. *As a rule*, I have lunch in the office canteen.
          I have lunch in the office canteen *now and again*.

Practice

1 Introduce the pairwork by telling the class a few things about your own
   daily routine.
2 Students interview each other in pairs.
3 As a check, ask individual students to tell you about their partner's daily
   routine.

Writing

The writing can be done in class or for homework.
▶ **W3 Ex 2** ◀ for practice of questions.
▶ **W3 Ex 4** ◀ for frequency adverbs.

3.6   PRECISE FREQUENCY

> **Language:** Phrases expressing precise frequency.

Presentation and practice

1 Go through the examples, and then write these tables on the board to show the two types of frequency expression:

once an hour	...
twice an hour	every three hours
three times an hour	every two hours
...	every hour

Point out that the same expressions can be used with seconds, days, years, centuries, etc.

2 If necessary, do some quick practice by giving series of times and asking students to tell you the frequency:
  e.g. You: Monday, Wednesday, Friday.
     Student: Every two days. *or* Three times a week.
     You: 4.00, 4.30, 5.00, 5.30, 6.00 ...
     Student: Twice an hour. *or* Every half hour.

3 Students discuss the questions in groups.
  Answers to factual questions: (1) every four years.
              (3) About 80 times a minute.

4 Ask different students what answers they gave.

Practice

1 🔲 Play the example on the tape. Point out that the two people are trying to sound 'better' than each other all the time.

2 Look at the five remarks with the class, and ask students to suggest a few activities for each:
  e.g. (1) I visit them once a month; I write to them twice a week; I ring them up every evening.

3 Students have conversations in pairs.
▶ **W3 Ex 3** ◀

3.7 ALL IN A DAY'S WORK: THE PASSIVE

Language: Present Simple Passive with *be* or *get*.

Note: Students should already be familiar with the basic *form* of Passive sentences. This exercise concentrates on the *use* of the Present Simple Passive for talking about things that often happen to people.

Presentation

1 Read the passage. Check comprehension by asking students to explain the meaning of some of the key words (e.g. article, cover, demonstration, mistake someone for, arrest).
2 Look at the example. If necessary, show students how to form the Present Simple Passive and do some basic practice. ▶ RP ◀
Make sure students understand the purpose of using the Passive, i.e. to emphasise what *happens to Ron Glib*, rather than what the newspaper or the police *do*.
3 Point out that *get* can be used instead of *be* when talking about *events* in the Passive:
e.g. He *is / gets* woken up early in the morning.
BUT He *is* (not 'gets') liked by everybody.
4 Students make Passive sentences from the passage, using the verbs given.

Practice

1 If you think it is necessary, demonstrate the activity by discussing one of the jobs with the whole class first.
2 Divide the class into groups to talk about the other jobs.
3 Ask each group what ideas they had.
▶ W3 Ex 4 ◀

3.8 A LIFE IN THE DAY OF... Reading

For procedure, see 'Dealing with reading' in Part 3.
Answers: (1) (a) Skating.
  (b) Janet works in a department store and Warren works in a betting office.
  (2) (d)
  (3) (a) At Janet's parents' house.
  (b) Because they need to get up early to skate together so it's convenient; and because they're friends.
  (4) 5.40 – 8.15   9.00 – 12.00
  (5) (a) They sometimes get chased by dogs.
  (b) They don't get paid.

(6) (a) True. (b) True. (c) False. (d) True. (e) False.
(7) Students should write brief notes, *not* complete sentences:
 e.g. 4.30 alarm: Janet wakes Warren.
   5.15 leave house – car.
   5.20 arrive at ice-rink.

The purpose of this question is to check comprehension, to give practice in making notes, and to provide a basis for the role-play in 3.9.

3.9   TALKING TO JANET AND WARREN   Free practice

> **Language:** Free practice of language introduced in this unit.

1 Give each student a role – A, B or C. Give a few minutes for students to prepare what they are going to say. Students B and C should prepare together in pairs.
2 Divide the class into groups of three, so that each group has one A, one B and one C. They conduct the interview.
3 As a possible round-up, ask each 'interviewer' to tell you the most *interesting* things he found out about Janet and Warren.
 ▶ W3 Ex 5 ◀

Unit 4 Direction

This is the second in the series of units concerned with physical *description* of places, things and people. Like Unit 1 it is concerned with describing places. It deals with language for saying what direction things and people move in.

The unit falls into two sections, followed by a Listening Comprehension. The first section is concerned with talking about direction in descriptions and simple instructions, and practises direction prepositions; the second section is concerned with giving street directions, and practises related expressions and vocabulary.

4.1 PREPOSITIONS OF DIRECTION
Presentation of:
direction prepositions.

4.2 WHERE DO THEY GO?
Practice

4.3 HOW DO YOU DO IT?
Practice

4.4 DESCRIBE AND DRAW
Practice

4.5 GIVING DIRECTIONS
Presentation of:
expressions for giving street directions.

4.6 FINDING YOUR WAY
Practice

4.7 YOUR OWN AREA
Free practice

4.8 MAKING PUPPETS
Listening

4.1 PREPOSITIONS OF DIRECTION   Presentation

> **Language:** Prepositions of direction: *in(to), out of;*
> *on(to), off; up to, towards, away from; up,*
> *down; along, through, between; across,*
> *round, past; over, under.*
>
> *Note:* Students should already know many of these
> prepositions. Concentrate on those that are new or cause
> difficulty, especially those that consist of two words: *out of,*
> *up to, away from.*

1 Elicit prepositions from the class, using simple line drawings and arrows on
the board:

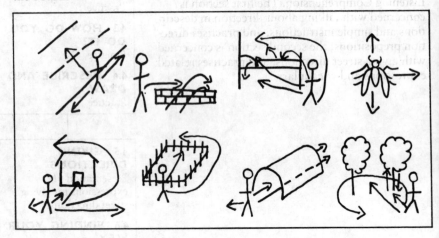

Expected answers: (1) up, down, along, across the street.
(2) (step) over, onto, go along the wall.
(3) (get) onto, off the bed; get into, out of bed; go round, under the bed.
(4) go up, down, across the wall; fly off the wall.
(5) towards, away from, up to, past, round, into the house.
(6) across, through, round the field.
(7) into, out of, through, away from the tunnel.
(8) between, round the trees; go up to, climb up, down, one of the trees.

2 Students write prepositions in the gaps. The purpose of this is to check what
they know.

Answers: (1) towards, over, into.   (2) off / from, on(to), in(to).
(3) along, down.   (4) past, between.
(5) up to, round.   (6) through / out of,
(7) through / down,   down / along / up, in(to).
away from.   (8) over, under.

▶ W4 Ex 1 ◀

4.2 WHERE DO THEY GO? Practice

> **Language:** Practice of language introduced in 4.1.
> Verbs of motion: *climb, swing, crawl, jump, dive, swim.*

Either discuss the pictures with the whole class, or let them discuss them in groups and go through the answers afterwards.

Expected answers: (1) The road goes past the house, over / down the hill, into the valley, through a wood, over a bridge, across a river, through a village, past a lake, round a hill, through / over the mountains.

(2) The burglar went across the road, along the pavement, through the gate, into the garden, up / along the path, up to the front door, round the side of the house, into the house through the back window, out of the house at one side, between two trees, out of the garden through the back gate, round the side, along (the side of) a wall, across the road.

(3) The soldier has to climb up a tree, swing along a rope to another tree, climb down the tree, climb over a wall, crawl under a fence, climb up a ladder onto a wall, jump off the wall, crawl through a tunnel, dive into a river, swim across it and climb out of it onto the other bank.

▶ W4 Ex 2 ◀

4.3 HOW DO YOU DO IT? Practice

> **Language:** Practice of language introduced in 4.1.
> Sequence words.

1 Go through the example, and point out:
i) how *you* is used in giving instructions
ii) how sequence words are used to show what order you do things in.
If you like, write these sequence words on the board:

> First...   Then...
> After that,...
> , and then...

2 Students solve the problems in groups or pairs. Remind them that the purpose of the exercise is not only to solve the problems but to *express the answer* using direction prepositions and sequence words.
3 Go through the answers with the class.

Answers: (2) You put the needles through the matchbox, one at each end, so that they stick out of the sides. Then you cut the candle into four pieces with the knife, and you stick the pieces of candle onto the ends of the needles.

(3) You find two trees, not too far from each other. You tie the rope from one tree to the other. Then you hang the sheet over the rope,

and you stick the pencils through the edges of the sheet into the
ground (three each side).

(5) You know where you've come *from*. So you put up the signpost with
that arm pointing along the road you've just come down.

▶ W4 Ex 4 ◀

4.4   DESCRIBE AND DRAW   Practice

> **Language:** Practice of language introduced in 4.1.

1 Ask students to identify the five objects.
2 Divide the class into pairs, and give each student a letter: A or B. Make sure
only Student B in each pair looks at the complete picture. Student B describes
where the pieces of string go, and Student A draws them in his picture.
3 Go through the answers with the whole class.
4 In their pairs, students discuss exactly how the device works:
e.g. When the burglar picks up the watch, it pulls a piece of string which is
tied to the cat's tail. So the cat jumps on the table, and the burglar
steps back...
5 As a round-up, ask individual students to describe the different things that
happen.

4.5   GIVING DIRECTIONS?   Presentation

> **Language:** Basic expressions for giving street directions.

Go through the exercise with the class, dealing with any language points as
they come up:
e.g. *Go* (straight) along this road.
Keep (straight) *on* along this road.
Turn left / right.
Take the first *turning on* the left / right.
as far as, past
Note: The point of this exercise is to show the variety of expressions that can
be used to give the same directions.

4.6   FINDING YOUR WAY   Practice

> **Language:** Practice of language introduced in 4.5.
> Expressions for asking directions.

1 Look at the street plan with the class, and make sure students understand
what all the places are.
2 Demonstrate the exercise by doing (1) with the whole class.

3 Students do the exercise in pairs, taking it in turns to give directions.
4 As an alternative, the continuation of the exercise can be done as a game, as
follows:

One student in the pair chooses a place on the map, and tells his partner
to start there. He then chooses a destination, and secretly writes it down.
He then gives his partner directions to the destination, without telling
him the name of the place. The partner follows the directions, and then
says where he thinks he is.

If you play this game, you should demonstrate it by choosing a place
yourself and giving directions to the class, who try to guess where it is.
▶ W4 Ex 3 ◀

4.7 YOUR OWN AREA   Free practice

> **Language:** Free practice of language introduced in 4.5.

1 If you think it is necessary, demonstrate the activity by doing (1) with the
whole class.
2 Divide the class into groups. They take it in turns to give directions.

4.8 MAKING PUPPETS   Listening 📼

This is a Listening Comprehension Passage. For procedure, see 'Dealing with
listening' in Part 3.

Interviewer: Do you usually make your own puppets?

Puppeteer: Yes, I do usually make my own puppets, and...er... there are two different ways of doing it. You can either make a rag doll puppet – you make a head exactly as if you were making a rag doll, with an old stocking stuffed, and wool for hair, and the eyes can be embroidered or painted, but you put a little cardboard tube the size of your forefinger into the neck, so that it will support your finger and you can control the puppet's head when you're using it.

Interviewer: What about the dress?

Puppeteer: It's simply a little dress like a doll's dress, only the sleeves, instead of going down from the shoulder, they go up, they point up, and then when you slip it on you are putting on a glove. Your forefinger goes into the neck, and your thumb

and middle finger go into the two sleeves.

Interviewer: I believe you can also make puppets just using a matchbox and a handkerchief. Is that right?

Puppeteer: Yes, they're very useful, because they can be made so quickly – you can do them in a few minutes, really. You take a matchbox first to prepare the head, – just the cover of a matchbox – and you stick paper over the coloured label on the matchbox, and on that you can draw a face with felt-tipped pencils. Now when you've done that, you want to put your puppet together. So you take your handkerchief, and put it over your forefinger, spread out your thumb and third finger, and you anchor the whole thing down by putting the matchbox firmly in place on the forefinger, where the head would be. Then you arrange the handkerchief round so that the tips of your puppet's hands are showing at the edge of the handkerchief and you can secure it at the bottom with an elastic band round the wrist if you wish, and then you can use it for quite a while.

Interviewer: So you can make quick puppets. Can you make a quick theatre as well?

Puppeteer: As a matter of fact, that's just what I did once. I was staying with an artist friend in Cornwall, and she very much wanted to see one of my puppet shows, and I had nothing with me at all. So I made two matchbox puppets, and then, for the theatre I balanced a big gold frame of hers on a chair in a corner of the studio, and draped a sheet over the front. I was all ready to start but I wanted some children, so we both went out into the streets of the village and collected up all the kids we could find, and brought them all in, and we all had a very good time together.

Note: Before you play the tape, look at (1) with the class. Explain any new vocabulary.

Answers: (2) (a) Head: an old stocking stuffed; hair: wool; eyes: embroidered or painted.
(b) Into the neck; to control the puppet's head.
(c) The sleeves point up, not down.
(d) You put your forefinger into the neck, and your thumb and middle finger into the sleeves.

(3) (a)

Material	What it's for
matchbox cover	the puppet's head
paper	the puppet's face
pencils	to draw the face
handkerchief	to cover your hand
elastic band	to secure the puppet

(b) See Listening Text.
(4) (a) Matchbox puppets.
(b) A gold picture frame on a chair, with a sheet over the front.
(c) Children in the street.

Activities (following Unit 4)

ROOM TO LET

> **Language:** This activity draws on language from:
> Unit 1 (describing a room)
> Unit 2 (making decisions)
> Unit 4 (giving street directions).

1 Preparation stage. Divide the class into pairs. Some pairs are *both* the student, other pairs are *both* the owner. Working together, they think what they will say.
2 Students form new pairs, so that each pair consists of one owner and one student. They improvise the conversation.
3 As a round-up, ask students whether the room they asked about sounded suitable, and why / why not.

COMPOSITION

> **Language:** This is an extension of Exercises 3.8 and 3.9, and draws on language from the whole of Unit 3.

The writing can be done in class or for homework.

SITUATIONS

> **Language:** The situations draw on language from Units 1, 2, 3 and 4.

Either: Give a few minutes for students to read and think about the situations, and then do them round the class.
Or: In pairs, students take it in turns to read and respond to the situations. Go through them afterwards with the whole class.

Unit 5   Past events

This is the first of a series of units concerned with *narration* of past events. It deals with language for relating past events and saying when and in what order they happened.

The unit falls into two sections, followed by a Reading Comprehension. The first section is especially concerned with the order in which events took place, and practises a range of 'sequence' structures with the Past Simple; the second section is concerned with giving the history of people and places, and practises the Past Simple active and passive, and past time expressions.

5.1   RELATING PAST EVENTS
Presentation of: later, after that; before / after / while + Past Simple; after + -ing.
Practice

5.2   BEFORE, AFTER & WHILE
Practice

5.3   FIRST EXPERIENCES
Practice

5.4   LIFE STORY
Writing

5.5   PAST TIMES
Presentation of: time expressions with 'in', 'on', 'at', and no preposition.
Practice

5.6   PAST EVENTS: THE PASSIVE
Presentation and practice of: Past Simple Passive.
Writing

5.7   TEST YOUR MEMORY: QUIZ
Free practice

5.8   FAMOUS LIVES
Reading
Writing

5.1   RELATING PAST EVENTS

> **Language:** The listening passage contains various
> expressions that show the sequence of past
> events. These are presented and practised in
> 5.1–5.4. The second part of the exercise
> practises sequence structures using *later, after
> that, after + -ing,* and *after + Past Tense.*

Presentation

This is a Listening Presentation. (See 'Dealing with listening' in Part 3.)

Interviewer: Now let's go back to your first novel, *Rag Doll.* When did you write that?

Writer: Rag Doll, yes. I wrote that in 1960, a year after I left school.

Interviewer: How old were you then?

Writer: Eighteen? Yes eighteen, because a year later I went to Indonesia.

Interviewer: Mm. And of course it was your experience in Indonesia that inspired your film *Eastern Moon.*

Writer: Yes that's right, although I didn't actually make *Eastern Moon* until 1978.

Interviewer: And you worked in television for a time too?

Writer: Yes, I started making documentaries for television in 1973, when I was 30. That was after I gave up farming.

Interviewer: Farming?

Writer: Yes, that's right. You see, I stayed in Indonesia for eight years. I met my wife there in 1965, and after we came back we bought a farm in the West of England, in 1970. A kind of experiment, really.

Interviewer: But you gave it up three years later.

Writer: Well yes you see it was very hard work, and I was also very busy working on my second novel, *The Cold Earth,* which came out in 1975.

Interviewer: Yes, that was a best-seller, wasn't it?

Writer: Yes it was, and that's why only two years after that I was able to give up television work and concentrate on films...

1 Play the tape. Students answer (1) – (5), which check comprehension of the main events in the passage.

    Answers: (1) Wrote his first novel, *Rag Doll.*
               (2) Met his wife.
               (3) Bought a farm in the West of England.
               (4) Gave up the farm.
               (5) Gave up TV work and concentrated on films.

2 Play the tape again, pausing where necessary. This time students make notes in the table. Either go through the answers straight away, or use the Practice stage (below) for this purpose.

Answers:

1959 – left school	1970 – bought a farm
1960 – wrote *Rag Doll*	1973 – started making TV documentaries
1961 – went to Indonesia	1975 – *The Cold Earth* was published
1965 – met his wife	1977 – gave up TV work
1969 – left Indonesia	1978 – made film *Eastern Moon*

Practice

1 Go through the first example, and ask students to continue it round the class:
   e.g. A year after that he went to Indonesia. Four years later he met his wife,...etc.
   This exercise can be used as a check on the answers in the table.
2 Go through the second example, and point out that *after* can be followed by -ing or the Past tense, with no difference in meaning. Ask students to continue it, either round the class or in pairs:
   e.g. A year after writing his first novel, he went to Indonesia. Four years after he went to Indonesia, he met his wife,...etc.
▶ W5 Ex 1 ◀

5.2 BEFORE, AFTER & WHILE   Practice

> **Language:** *Before / after / while* + Past Simple.
> *When?* questions using the Past Simple.

1 Look at the pictures with the class, and ask students what events the arrows above point to.
   Note: In most cases the arrows represent *two* events: one marking the end of the preceding period, the other marking the beginning of the next period.
   Answers: Left / finished school; went to college.
   Left / graduated from college; joined the army / became an army captain. Was promoted to general.
   Left / retired from the army; went into / became involved in politics. Was arrested / was sent to prison.
   Came out of prison / was released; retired / went to live in the Bahamas.

2 Look at (2). Make sure students can distinguish between:
   i) single events (e.g. he *went* to college)
   ii) activities / states extending over a period (e.g. he *was* at college).
   Before and *after* are used with *events*:
   e.g. He met Angeline *before* he *became* a captain.

While is used with *activities / states*:
e.g. He married Angeline *while* he *was* a captain.
3 After going through the example, ask what the other questions will be:
e.g. When did he marry Angeline?
4 Divide the class into groups of four to do the exercise.
▶ W5 Ex 2 ◀

5.3 FIRST EXPERIENCES   Practice

> **Language:** *When* + Past Simple tense.
> *Not...until* + Past Simple tense.
>
> *Note: Didn't...until* has the meaning 'it happened later than
> you'd expect'. There is no simple structure in English that
> gives the opposite meaning, 'it happened earlier than you'd
> expect'. This meaning can, however, be expressed by stress
> and intonation: e.g. '*I* learnt to drive when I was *16*'.

1 ▣ Play the example on the tape. Check that students can form Past Simple
negatives correctly, and that they understand the meaning of *not ... until*.
2 If necessary, go through the exercise asking students to give just the verb
forms of the answers:
e.g. I learnt.., I first wore.., I first went...
3 Demonstrate the pairwork by doing (1) with one student.
4 Students have conversations in pairs.
5 As a round-up, ask different students what answers they gave.

5.4 LIFE STORY   Writing

> **Language:** Free practice of language introduced so far in
> this unit.

1 Remind students of the range of linking devices they should use by writing
this list on the board:

> ...years later,...
> after that,...
> before / after...
> while...
> when...
> not...until...

Point out that they should use as many different expressions as possible, for
variety.
2 The writing can be done in class or for homework.

5.5   PAST TIMES

> **Language:**   Past time phrases with *in, on, at,* and no
>   preposition.
>
> *Note:*   Students should already know many of these phrases.
> Concentrate on those that are new or cause difficulty.

Presentation

1 Check students' knowledge of time phrase prepositions by asking them to
   complete the expressions round the class.
2 If necessary, give these rules for time preposition usage:

at:	points of time (at 4 o'clock, at the end of May)
	names of holiday periods (at Christmas)
on:	days (on Tuesday, on 14 May)
	parts of specific days (on Tuesday morning)
in:	parts of days (in the morning)
	periods longer than a day (in May, in the summer, in 1945)
no preposition:	before phrases with *ago* (three weeks ago)
	before phrases with *last* (last Tuesday)
	before *yesterday* and *the day before yesterday*
	(Also, of course, before *tomorrow, the day after tomorrow,* and phrases with *next* – these are not dealt with here as they are not *past* time phrases.)

Practice

1 Prepare for the groupwork by asking students to give questions from the
   prompts. Point out that they must be *When?* questions about the *past*:
   e.g. When did you get up this morning?
2 Divide the class into groups. Students take it in turns to ask the others questions.
3 As a round-up, ask some of the questions round the class.
▶ W5 Ex 3 ◀

5.6 PAST EVENTS: THE PASSIVE

> **Language:** Past Simple Passive.
>
> *Note:* Students should already be familiar with the form of the Past Simple Passive. This exercise concentrates on its use for:
> i) talking about the origins of things (e.g. where things were made)
> ii) giving information about historical events.

Presentation and practice

1 Check that students know how to form the Past Simple Passive. If necessary present it by referring to the Present Simple Passive (see Unit 3.7):

> Verb: be paid
> PRESENT The workers <u>are paid</u> once a month.
> PAST   The workers <u>were paid</u> last Friday.
>
> Verb: be sent
> PRESENT Ron Glib <u>is sent</u> to many countries.
> PAST   Last month he <u>was sent</u> to Mexico.

2 Read the example, and ask what else the record catalogue entry tells you.
   Answers: That it *was played / performed* by the London Philharmonic Orchestra, and that the record *was made / produced* by Decca.
3 Either go through the exercise with the whole class, or let students discuss the information in groups and go through the answers afterwards.
   Important verbs: painted; worn; translated; used, invented; bottled; killed; produced, grown, canned; founded; written, published; born.

Writing

1 Look at the pictures, and ask students to tell you what happened.
   Important verbs: built; attacked, burnt down / destroyed; re-built; extended, added; modernised, installed; opened; sold / bought; turned into / converted into.
2 The writing can be done in class or for homework.
▶ W5 Ex 4 ◀

5.7 TEST YOUR MEMORY: QUIZ   Free practice

> **Language:** Free practice of language introduced in this unit.

1 Ask the questions round the class or get students to answer them in groups.
   Answers: (1) Julius Caesar was assassinated.

    (2) (a) It was discovered by Alexander Fleming in 1929.
       (b) It was discovered by Christopher Columbus in 1492. (or by the Vikings in 1000!)
    (3) They were built by the Ancient Egyptians, in about 3000 BC.
    (4) (a) 1969 (Neil Armstrong) (b) 1903 (Wright brothers) (c) 1979 (Margaret Thatcher).

Note: The importance of this quiz, like others in later units, is not in getting the correct answers, but in the language practised while answering the questions.

2 Each student writes three questions. They can choose any question they like as long as the question or the answer (or both) is about the *past*. Encourage students to think of questions using language they have practised (e.g. when, after, time phrases).
3 Divide the class into groups for the first part of the quiz.
4 Give a few minutes for each group to choose their 'best' questions. For the second part of the quiz, one student from each group asks their three questions to the rest of the class.

5.8 FAMOUS LIVES

> **Language:** As the reading passages are retold by the students, they give further free practice of language introduced in this unit.

Reading

1 Divide the class into three groups, and give each group a letter: A, B or C. (If the class is very large, divide it into six groups to form two Group A's, two Group B's and two Group C's.)
2 Explain that:
   i) Each passage is a biography of a famous person, but the best-known fact about them is left out in each case.
   ii) Each group should read their own passage only.
   iii) Everyone in the group must be sure they understand the passage, as they will all have to retell it.
   iv) When they retell their passage, other students will try to guess who the famous person is.
3 Give time for each group to read their passage and practise retelling it among themselves. Let students make brief notes if they like. Go from group to group, giving help where necessary, and quietly tell each group who their famous person is.
  Answers: (A) Ernest Hemingway (the fact that he is a writer is not mentioned).
      (B) Princess Grace / Grace Kelly (the fact that she is a princess is not mentioned).
      (C) Agatha Christie (the fact that she wrote detective stories is not mentioned).

4 Students close their books and form new groups. Each new group should contain at least one person from each original group. They take it in turns to tell their story and the others try to guess who the person is.

Writing

The writing can be done in class or for homework.
▶ W5 Ex 5 ◀

Unit 6 Talking about now

This is the first of a series of units concerned with
relating *the past and the present*. It deals with
language for describing present situations and
activities.

The unit begins with a general Presentation, and
then falls into two sections, followed by a Listening
Comprehension. The first section is concerned
with things that are happening at the moment of
speaking, and with long-term developments and
processes; the second section is concerned with
activities taking place during a current period.

The unit practises the Present Continuous active
and passive, and structures with *there* + Present
Continuous.

6.1 USES OF THE PRESENT CONTINUOUS
Presentation of: Present
Continuous used for (a)
activities 'at the
moment'; (b) long-term
changes; (c) activities
during a current period.

6.2 WHAT ARE THEY DOING?
Practice

6.3 SEE FOR YOURSELF
Presentation of: there's
someone + -ing; Present
Continuous Passive.
Practice

6.4 DESCRIBE AND CHOOSE
Practice

6.5 LONG-TERM CHANGES
Free practice

6.6 CURRENT ACTIVITIES
Practice

6.7 READING GAME: THE PRESENT CONTINUOUS PASSIVE
Practice

6.8 WHAT'S GOING ON?
Free practice
Writing

6.9 A TELEPHONE CALL
Listening
Writing

6.1 USES OF THE PRESENT CONTINUOUS Presentation

> **Language:** This exercise presents three main uses of the
> Present Continuous:
> i) To describe an activity which is taking
> place *at the moment of speaking*. (This
> use is practised in 6.2, 6.3 and 6.4.)
> ii) To talk about *long-term developments
> and processes*, which are going on all the
> time. (This use is practised in 6.5.)
> iii) To talk about activities *during a current
> period*, but which are not necessarily
> happening at the moment of speaking.
> (This use is practised in 6.6, 6.7 and 6.8.)

1 Read the passages. After each passage, ask students to tell you:
  i) where they might see or hear the passage
  ii) briefly what it's about.
  Expected answers: (A) Radio or TV commentary; describing a royal procession.
             (B) In a pamphlet or book; describing gradual changes in the British
                 Isles, and why London is in danger of flooding.
             (C) Part of a postcard or letter; describing how two people are spending
                 their time in London.
2 Discuss the three different uses of the Present Continuous in the passages
  (see Language notes above). If necessary, give other examples of your own
  to check that students understand the three uses:
  e.g. He's waiting at the bus stop (= just at this moment).
       Oil is gradually running out (= long-term process).
       He's going to lots of parties (= during this period).

6.2 WHAT ARE THEY DOING? Practice

> **Language:** Present Continuous for describing what is
>   happening at the moment of speaking. (revision)
> Telephone formulae: *Could I*
>   *I'd like to* speak to...

1 Before you begin the exercise, make sure students know how to form the
  Present Continuous tense correctly.
2 ⊟ Play the example on the tape, and ask students to think of alternative
  replies for the last remark:
  e.g. She's talking to a customer, doing some shopping, etc.
3 Demonstrate the pairwork by doing (1) with the whole class.
4 Students have conversations in pairs.

6.3 SEE FOR YOURSELF

> **Language:** Describing what is happening at the moment
> of speaking, using:
>   i)   Present Continuous Active
>   ii) *There* + Present Continuous
>   iii) Present Continuous Passive.
>
> *Note:* These forms are not simply alternatives. 'There' and the
> Passive are used to avoid an indefinite noun or pronoun as the
> subject of the sentence.
>
> *That* dog is following us. BUT There's *a* dog following us.
>   We're being followed by *a* dog.
>   (We don't say: 'A dog is
>   following us.')
> (cf. Unit 1: There is a desk in the room, *not* A desk is in the
> room.)

Presentation

1 Present *there* + Present Continuous by referring to *there is / are* structures
in Unit 1. Write these sentences on the board:

Someone <u>is</u> at the door.	Some people <u>are</u> at the door.
→ <u>There is</u> someone at the door.	→ <u>There are</u> some people at the door.

Now write similar pairs, using the Present Continuous:

Someone <u>is</u> stand<u>ing</u> at the door.	Some people <u>are</u> stand<u>ing</u> at the door.
→ <u>There is</u> someone stand<u>ing</u> at the door.	→ <u>There are</u> some people standing at the door.

2 Present the Present Continuous Passive by referring to the Present Simple
Passive (Unit 3) and the Past Simple Passive (Unit 5). Write these forms on
the board:

Passive: BE + Past participle	Example: be paid
Present Simple IS / ARE + p.p.	The workers <u>are</u> paid every Friday.
Past Simple WAS / WERE + p.p.	The workers <u>were</u> paid last Friday.
Present Continuous IS / ARE BEING + p.p.	The workers <u>are being</u> paid now.

3 Do the exercise round the class. Point out the negative, (7) and (8), and
question forms, (9) and (10).
4 If necessary, students can go through the exercise again, working in groups
of three.

Practice

Either do the exercise with the whole class, or let them do it in groups and go through the answers afterwards. Point out that more than one continuation is possible in each case.

Possible answers: (1) I'm listening to it / there's someone talking about my town.
(2) it's melting / it's running down your shirt.
(3) it's leaking / there's water coming in.
(4) my nose is running / my finger's bleeding.
(5) it's being redecorated / there's someone changing in it.
(6) it's peeling / it's going red.
(7) they're being looked after / they're watching TV.
(8) there's someone coming up the stairs / my husband's coming back.

6.4 DESCRIBE AND CHOOSE   Practice

> **Language:** *There* + Present Continuous.
> Questions with *is / are there* + Present Continuous.
>
> *Note:* These structures are particularly important for
> describing scenes in pictures. (See the use of *there is / are*
> for static description in Unit 1.)

1 Explain that:
  i)   This is a guessing game: one student describes a picture, the other student guesses which one it is.
  ii) The first student should only describe what *is happening* (not what buildings there are, etc).
  iii) When the second student thinks he knows which is the right picture, he should check by asking questions about it.
2 Demonstrate the pairwork by choosing a picture yourself and describing it. The class tries to guess which one it is.
3 Students play the game in pairs. When a student has guessed a picture, he chooses another one and describes it.
▶ W6 Ex 1 ◀

6.5 LONG-TERM CHANGES   Free practice

> **Language:** Free practice of Present Continuous Active and
> Passive, to describe long-term processes and
> developments (see 6.1 passage B).
>
> *Note:* This exercise also involves the use of 'change of state'
> verbs and comparative adjectives: e.g. '...is getting cooler',
> '...is becoming bigger', '...are becoming more sophisticated'.
> These structures are presented and practised in Units 8, 9 and
> 10.

1 Introduce the activity by talking about one of the topics yourself:
  e.g. The Sahara is slowly getting bigger, sand is covering fertile land, and
    people are moving further south because there isn't enough food for
    their animals...
2 Either discuss the topics with the whole class, or let students discuss them in
  groups, and ask them afterwards what they said about each.

Possible answers: (1) Venice is slowly sinking into the sea; the buildings are
    decaying because pollution is damaging the foundations.
  (2) The Sun is gradually cooling down, and its pull is getting weaker.
  (3) Fossil fuels (coal, oil, gas) are being used up, and people are searching
    for new sources of energy, e.g. from the sun, the wind, the waves.
  (4) See example.
  (5) People are living longer because more diseases are being cured by
    modern medicine, and doctors are discovering new drugs.
  (6) The Mediterranean is getting more polluted because the countries
    round it are pouring industrial waste into their rivers; fish are
    disappearing; it's becoming dangerous for swimmers.
  (7) The population of the world is increasing, because fewer people are
    dying young and more babies are surviving.

6.6 CURRENT ACTIVITIES   Practice

> **Language:** Present Continuous for talking about activities
> during a current period (see 6.1 passage C).
> Present Simple for talking about jobs and
> activities in general (see Unit 3).

1 Establish the difference between:
  i) what you *are* (i.e. the name of your job)
  ii) what you *do* (i.e. what your job involves in general)
  iii) what you *are doing* (i.e. current, temporary activities).
  Illustrate this by telling the class about yourself.
2 🔊 Play the example on the tape. Demonstrate the pairwork by interviewing
  one student.
3 Students interview each other in pairs, taking on the roles given.
4 Introduce the second part of the exercise by telling the class some of the
  things you are doing these days, e.g. I'm working very hard, I'm going to
  evening classes.
5 Students talk to each other in groups.
6 As a round-up, ask individual students what others in their group are doing.
► W6 Ex 2 ◄

6.7 READING GAME: THE PRESENT CONTINUOUS PASSIVE   Practice

> **Language:** Practice of the Present Continuous Passive for talking about current activities.

1 Read the sentences and 'continuations' with the class. Where appropriate, ask students to say what they mean, and explain any new words and phrases.
2 Either read out the sentences yourself and ask students to add continuations in the Passive, or let students read out the sentences in groups, and go through the answers afterwards.

Answers: (continuations only)

    (1) (As example.)
    (2) : she's being taken out to nightclubs and she's being bought bouquets of roses.
    (3) : the crops are being destroyed by troops and all the villages are being burnt down by the invading army.
    (4) : a new exhaust pipe is being fitted and the brakes are being tightened.
    (5) : most students are being sent home at 5 o'clock and evening classes are being held by gas light.
    (6) : coloured lights are being put up in the High Street and Christmas trees are being sold in all the shops.
    (7) : their telephone is being tapped and the house is being watched from across the street.

▶ W6 Ex 3 ◀

6.8 WHAT'S GOING ON?

> **Language:** Free practice of Present Continuous Active and Passive and with *there*, for talking about activities during a current period.

Free practice

1 Read the letter, and point out how the writer develops the paragraph by giving details that describe 'signs' or 'consequences' of the hot weather.
2 In groups, students construct similar 'oral' paragraphs on the other four topics.
3 Ask different groups what ideas they had for each topic.

Writing

The writing can be done in class or for homework.
▶ W6 Ex 4 ◀

6.9 A TELEPHONE CALL

Listening 📼

This is a Listening Comprehension Passage. For procedure, see 'Dealing with listening' in Part 3.

Mike: Hello?
Sue: Hello, Mike. I'm ringing you up to wish you a happy birthday.
Mike: Sue, what a fantastic surprise! Where are you phoning from? I can hear you so clearly. I thought you were in Spain.
Sue: Yes, I am. And I'm having a marvellous time here.
Mike: What's the weather like? It's pouring with rain here.
Sue: Oh, here it's absolutely boiling. I'm living in my bikini, and getting really brown.
Mike: Lucky you. Hey, where are you ringing from? I can hear people laughing and talking in the background.
Sue: Ah, that's because I'm in a café by the beach. Jill and I are having a drink here and writing our postcards. I'm sending you one, so that you can see what it looks like here. I wish you were here, Mike. I can see the beach from where I'm standing. There are thousands of people sunbathing, and there's...

Mike: Hey, stop. You're making me jealous. There's nothing interesting happening here. Everybody's complaining and saying what an awful summer we're having.
Sue: Oh dear – still, I expect you're getting a lot of work done. How's it going?
Mike: Oh, fine. I'm working on the last article now. Actually, at this very moment I'm having a break and making myself some coffee. Good God, that reminds me. Can you hold on a moment? The kettle's probably boiling. Just a tick.
Sue: Hey, Mike, don't go. I'd better ring off now. This is costing me a fortune. I'll ring you again in a few days, OK?
Mike: Right. Thanks for remembering my birthday. I'm feeling better already. Look after yourself. Miss you.
Sue: Me too. Goodbye.
Mike: Bye.

Answers: (1) Sue is on holiday in *Spain* with her *sister*. She is ringing up her *boyfriend*, Mike, because it's *his* birthday. Mike has stayed at home because *he's working*. When she phones, he is just *making coffee*.
(2) Pouring with rain.
(3) (a) It's very hot.
    (b) She's spending nearly all the time sunbathing.
(4) So that he can see what it looks like where she is.
(5) Sunbathing.
(6) Complaining about the weather.
(7) A journalist (he writes articles).
(8) See Listening Text.

Writing

For the first stage, students should listen to the tape again and make notes. The postcard can be written straight away or left for homework.

Activities (following Unit 6)

INTERVIEWING FAMOUS PEOPLE

> **Language:** This activity draws on language from:
> Unit 3 (describing jobs)
> Unit 5 (giving personal history)
> Unit 6 (talking about current activities).

1 Before dividing the class into groups, give time for each student to think (secretly) of a famous person.
2 Divide the class into groups of four. In turn, each student is interviewed by the others, who try and guess who he is.
3 As a possible follow-up to the activity, each group can choose the most interesting of their famous people, who can then be interviewed by the rest of the class.

COMPOSITION

> **Language:** The compositions draw on language from Unit 5.

The writing can be done in class or for homework.

Unit 7   Requests and offers

This is the second in the series of units concerned with taking, initiating and commenting on *action*. It deals with language used for making and reporting requests and offers.

The unit falls into two sections, followed by a general Free Practice exercise and a Reading Comprehension. The first section is concerned with making and reporting two kinds of request – asking other people to do things and asking their permission to do things yourself; the second section is concerned with making and reporting two kinds of offer – offering to do things for other people and offering to let them do things.

This unit brings together a number of different structures and expressions, some of which students should have come across before; it focusses both on structural features and on features of appropriateness.

7.1   ASKING PEOPLE TO DO THINGS
Presentation of: 'request' expressions; 'reporting' expressions.
Practice

7.2   GETTING PEOPLE TO STOP
Presentation and practice of: stop / would you mind not + -ing; I thought / didn't realise + past.

7.3   REQUEST NOTES
Writing

7.4   ASKING FOR PERMISSION
Presentation and practice of: 'requests for permission' expressions; 'reporting' expressions.
Practice

7.5   MAKING OFFERS
Presentation of: 'offers' expressions.
Practice

7.6   REPORTING OFFERS
Presentation of: offer someone something; offer to do something; offer to let someone do something.
Practice
Writing

7.7   PROBLEMS
Free practice

7.8   GREAT BORES OF TODAY
Reading
Writing

7.1 ASKING PEOPLE TO DO THINGS

> **Language:** A range of structures for making requests,
> from 'casual' to 'careful'.
> Structures for reporting requests.
>
> *Note:* How a request is made in any situation can depend
> on a number of factors; this exercise focusses on one of them,
> namely how *difficult* or *inconvenient* it would be to carry out
> the task. Notice that the relationship between the speakers,
> and the task itself, are the same in each picture.

Presentation

1 ⊟ Look at the pictures and play the remarks on the tape. Elicit from the class:
   i) in what ways the three situations are the same
   ii) in what ways the three situations are different.
   Establish that:
   – In the first picture the request causes the listener very little inconvenience; it is a routine thing to ask, so the request can be casual.
   – In the second picture, it is slightly inconvenient, as the listener is watching TV; so the speaker must be more careful how he asks.
   – In the third picture, it is very inconvenient, as the listener is with her boyfriend; so the speaker must make her request *very carefully*.
2 If you like, you can use (2) as a basis for a more general discussion of 'appropriateness'. An 'elaborate' request like the one given could be used whenever the request must be more than casual:
   e.g. – When asking a complete stranger, or an important guest.
   – If it is snowing outside, and so very unpleasant to go out.
   – If there is a very large quantity of washing.
   – If the listener is feeling very tired.

Practice

1 Look at the structures in the box. Point out that the structures in the left-hand column are 'casual', those in the middle are 'fairly careful', those in the right-hand column are 'very careful'.
2 Ask students to make requests with each of the structures for 'help me get the washing in':
   e.g. Could you help me get the washing in?
   Would you help me get the washing in? etc.
   If necessary, do some basic practice of these structures round the class.
   ▶RP◀
3 Ask students to suggest suitable replies, i.e. ways of agreeing or refusing:
   e.g. 'Of course I will', 'Well, all right', 'Actually, I'd rather not', 'Can't you do it yourself?'.

4 Make sure students understand the situation, and demonstrate the exercise by doing (1) and (2) with the whole class:
    e.g. A: Would you lend me your bike?
          B: Sorry, I can't. It's got a puncture.
5 Students do the exercise in pairs, taking it in turns to make requests.
6 Reporting: Ask students to report the requests they made and the replies they gave:
    e.g. I asked him to lend me his bike, but he refused.
▶ W7 Ex 1 ◀ for making requests.
▶ W7 Ex 4 ◀ for reporting requests.

7.2 GETTING PEOPLE TO STOP   Presentation and practice

> **Language:** 'Negative' request structures:
> *Would you mind not...-ing...?*
> *Do you think you could stop ...-ing...?*
> Sequence of tenses after:
> *I thought...*
> *I didn't realise...*

1 Play the example on the tape. Establish that:
   i)   The verb *stop* is followed by a *gerund* (-ing form).
   ii) The expression *Would you mind...* is followed by a *gerund* or by *not + gerund*:

Would you mind	being quiet?
	not talking?

   iii) 'I thought', 'I didn't realise' are in the Past tense, so what follows must also be in the Past tense.
        (*Note:* There is no need to go into detail about sequence of tense rules at this stage.)
2 Look at the seven prompts with the class and explain any new vocabulary (e.g. tap, snore, hum).
3 Demonstrate the pairwork by doing (1) with the whole class.
4. Students have conversations in pairs, taking it in turns to make requests.
5 As a possible round-up, ask different pairs what they said.
▶ W7 Ex 3 ◀

7.3 REQUEST NOTES   Writing

> **Language:** Practice of language introduced in 7.1.
> Reporting a request that still applies to the
> present: 'X wants me to...'
> (*Note:* Another way to say this is 'X has asked
> me to...')

1 Read the two notes with the class. Check comprehension by asking questions:
e.g. Which of the notes was written first? How do you know?
Who is the regular teacher of the class?
What can you say about John? Rita? Mandy?
2 Divide the class into pairs. Working together, each pair writes *one* note.
Either tell each pair which note to write, or let them choose themselves.
3 When a pair finishes a note, take it and give it to another pair. On the same
piece of paper, they add a note to a third person. When they have finished,
give it to another pair.
4 Ask one student from each pair to read out the notes they have received.

7.4 ASKING FOR PERMISSION

> **Language:** Practice of language introduced in 7.1.
> Structures for making *requests for permission*
> (i.e. asking if you can do something you want
> to do).
> Formulae for giving and refusing permission.
> Structures for reporting requests for
> permission.
>
> *Note:* As in 7.1, the choice of structure used for making
> requests in this exercise depends on how much trouble you
> are causing the other person.

Presentation and practice

1 Look at the examples and present these structures on the board:

Neutral	*Careful*
<u>Do</u> you mind if I <u>Is</u> it all right if I + Present Tense	<u>Would</u> you mind if I <u>Would</u> it <u>be</u> all right if I + Past Tense

Point out that:
i)   The changes of tense (Do you → Would you, Is it → Would it be,

Present → Past) make the request sound less direct, and so more 'careful'.

ii) The 'neutral' forms presented here can be used even for very casual requests for permission:

e.g. to a friend: 'Do you mind if I use this pen for a moment?' (although for very casual requests like this, you can simply say 'Can I...?').

2 Elicit from the class *why* the hitchhiker asks more carefully about his shoes than his rucksack.

3 Students make other requests based on the prompts in (1):
e.g. (a) Do you mind if I open the window?

4 Ask students to make as many requests for permission as they can for the three situations in (2):
e.g. (a) Would it be all right if I gave you a definite answer in about a week?

Practice

1 🔊 Play the example on the tape. Point out the formulae for giving and politely refusing permission:
Yes, of course.
I'd rather you didn't.

2 Look at the four situations, and ask students to suggest what 'second' requests they might make:
e.g. (1) Would it be all right if they stayed for a few days?

3 Students have conversations in pairs. Make sure that in their second request, they also give a *reason*.

4 Reporting: Look at the example, and point out that:
i) 'He asked' is in the Past tense, so 'could' must also be in the Past tense (see 7.2).
ii) 'Let' is followed by infinitive without 'to'.

5 Ask students to make sentences reporting the requests they made and the answers they gave:
e.g. Student 1: I asked him if I could invite some friends over.
Student 2: I let him invite them over.

▶ W7 Ex 1 ◀ for making requests for permission.
▶ W7 Ex 4 ◀ for reporting requests for permission.

7.5 MAKING OFFERS

> **Language:** Structures for making:
>   i) offers ('I'll do X if you like').
>   ii) offers of permission ('You can do X if you like').
>
> *Note:* 'Appropriateness' is not important in making offers as it is in making requests (although there are special 'elaborate' ways of offering (e.g. 'I'd be delighted if...'), these are not taught here).
>   *Making* offers and offers of permission is dealt with here fairly briefly, but *reporting* offers is dealt with fully in the next exercise. This is because structures for making offers are fairly simple compared with those for requests; but the use of the verb *offer* for reporting offers is a major area of difficulty.

Presentation

Look at the pictures, and ask students to suggest appropriate offers.

Possible answers: *Picture 1*
                    Shall I give you a hand with the engine?/mend it for you?
                    Would you like a nice cup of tea to keep you warm?
                    Would you like to come and have some lunch?
                    Picture 2
                    Would you like a cigar?
                    Would you like me to get you a drink?
                    I'll ring your solicitor if you like.

If necessary, do some basic practice of these structures round the class.
► RP ◄

Practice

Either do the exercise round the class, or let students do it in groups and go through the answers afterwards. Point out that there may be more than one offer possible for each situation:

e.g. (1) He looks thirsty. Shall I get you a drink?
                       Would you like something to drink?
                       Would you like me to make you some tea?

► W7 Ex 2 ◄

7.6 REPORTING OFFERS

> **Language:** Use of the verb *offer* for reporting offers and
> offers of permission.

Presentation

This is a Listening Presentation. (See 'Dealing with listening' in Part 3.)

Henry: Cigarette?

Tony: Oh...er...thanks, Henry...Um, do you have a light?

Henry: Sorry. Here.

Tony: Thanks. (sigh) Lovely day. Pity I'm on duty.

Henry: I'll stand in for you if you like. I've got nothing else to do.

Tony: Oh no, I couldn't possibly...

Henry: Go on. Go off and have a good time. Here – you can have the Mini if you like.

Tony: But...are you sure, Henry?

Henry: Of course I am. Take Jill up the mountains, or something.

Tony: That's ever so good of you, Henry. Oh, you...er...won't tell anyone, will you...I mean, I am on duty.

Henry: Not a word. Bye, Tony – enjoy yourself.

Tony: Thanks Henry. I won't forget this...

Henry: Damned right you won't, you poor fool!

1 Play the tape. Students answer (1)–(6), which check general comprehension.

Answers: (1) Colleagues (possibly caretakers, porters, policemen) at their place of work.

(2) Because it's a lovely day, and he's on duty.

(3) He offers to stand in for him (i.e. be on duty instead of him).

(4) Accept his offer.

(5) Not tell anyone, keep quiet about it; because Tony will be in trouble if he is discovered.

(6) (Several possible answers) Something sinister, e.g. tell the boss, steal some money and blame it on Tony.

2 Play the tape again. Students complete (7), which you can use as a basis for your presentation of *offer*.

Answers: (a) He offers him a light (or the keys).

(b) He offers to stand in for him.

(c) He offers to let him take the car.

3 Write the three possible structures with *offer* on the board:

OFFER	+	SOMEONE	+	NOUN
He offered		him		a light.
OFFER	+	TO	+	INFINITIVE
He offered		to		stand in for him.
OFFER	+	TO LET SOMEONE	+	INFINITIVE
He offered		to let him		take the car.

If necessary, give other examples of your own.

Practice

Ask students to report the offers round the class. In some cases, there is more than one possible way to report the offer:
e.g. (1) She offered me a sandwich.
She offered to give / make / buy me a sandwich.

Writing

1 Play the tape again.
2 As a preparation for the writing, ask students to tell you the story of what happened orally, first from the point of view of Tony, then of Henry:
e.g. (Tony's story): I was in the office, and I felt very depressed because it was a lovely day and I was on duty. Then Henry came in. He was very friendly – he sat down and...
3 The writing can be done in class or for homework.
▶ W7 Ex 5 ◀

7.7 PROBLEMS   Free practice

> **Language:** Free practice of language for making requests and offers.

1 Introduce the activity by giving a few 'problems' yourself, and asking students to suggest (i) suitable requests (ii) suitable offers, as in the examples.
2 Divide the class into groups of three for the activity. They can take it in turns to be Student A, going round and round the group.
3 As a possible round-up, ask each group to tell you some of their 'problems'.

7.8 GREAT BORES OF TODAY

Reading

For procedure, see 'Dealing with reading' in Part 3.
Answers: (1) A drink, probably gin or whisky.
(2) That he used to drink a lot, but he realised how stupid it was and gave it up.
(3) (a) He has had too much alcohol and damaged his liver.
(b) He's drunk a lot of spirits.
(c) He suddenly realised what he was doing.
(d) It makes you realise how dangerous alcohol is.
(4) (Many possible answers) e.g. (a) Managing to give up smoking.
(b) Taking an umbrella if it looks like rain.
(5) He's accepting a drink after all. He's still pretending that he doesn't *really* want a drink.

(6) You leave a coin in a bottle of gin. After some time it has an effect on the coin (e.g. wears it down, polishes it) – it has the same effect on you!

(7) See dialogue in Writing section below.

(8) He talks non-stop about himself, and what he says isn't even true – he just likes hearing his own voice.

Writing

The writing can be done in class or for homework. A possible version:

'What would you like – a gin and tonic?'

'No, just a tonic for me.'

'Are you sure?'

'Yes, quite sure.'

'Why not have just a small one?'

'No, really, I'd rather not, if you don't mind. You see, the way I look at it is this: I've given my old liver a bit of a hard time these last thirty years, and I suddenly woke up one evening and asked myself, "Do I really need it?"'

'Do you mind if I have one?'

'No, I don't mind you having one. God knows how much of that stuff I've poured down my throat. If I had a penny for every Scotch I've drunk, I'd be a rich man today, I tell you.'

'Don't you miss it? You must have a lot of willpower.'

'No, I don't miss it at all. It's not so much willpower as common sense, isn't it? Have you ever seen that thing they do with a coin and a bottle of gin? It's a bit of an eye opener.'

'Are you sure you won't have just one?'

'Oh, all right, just to be sociable. But just a small one, if you insist...'

Note: This is a difficult exercise and it may be necessary to do some oral preparation in class.

Unit 8 Recent actions and activities

This is the second in the series of units concerned with relating *the past and the present*. It deals with language for talking about recent actions and activities.

The unit falls into two sections, followed by a general Free Practice exercise and a Listening Comprehension. The first section is concerned with recent past actions and their present results, and practises the use of the Present Perfect, Past, and Present tenses; the second section is concerned with recent activities and achievements, and practises the Present Perfect Continuous and Present Perfect Simple.

8.1 MAKING PREPARATIONS
Presentation of: Present Perfect versus Past tense. Practice

8.2 PREPARATIONS AND RESULTS
Practice

8.3 LEAVING NOTES
Writing

8.4 THE PRESENT PERFECT CONTINUOUS
Presentation of: Present Perfect Continuous versus Present Perfect Simple.

8.5 RECENT ACTIVITIES
Practice

8.6 RECENT ACTIVITIES AND ACHIEVEMENTS
Practice

8.7 A BUSY TIME
Writing

8.8 RECENT DEVELOPMENTS
Free practice

8.9 SUMMER JOBS
Listening

8.1 MAKING PREPARATIONS

> **Language:** Present Perfect Simple tense for talking about recent past actions (contrasted with Past Simple).

Presentation

1 Read the passage. Check general comprehension by asking questions round the class:
   e.g.   Who are Ronnie and Julia?
          What are they planning to do?
          Why is he talking to her on the telephone?
2 Ask students to say what important things he has done:
   e.g. He's hired a car.
3 Establish that:
   i)   The text tells a story, giving events in sequence – it tells us when, where and how Ronnie did things and in what order. So it uses the *Past Simple* tense (see Unit 5).
   ii) When we make a *list* of the seven things, we are not interested in when, where or how he did them, or in what order, but just in what he has done. So we use the *Present Perfect Simple* tense.
4 Make sure students can form Present Perfect sentences, questions and short answers.

Practice

1 ⊑ Play the example on the tape. Point out that:
   i)   Julia only wants to know whether Ronnie has done things or not, so she uses the *Present Perfect Simple* (see 3(ii) above).
   ii) In Ronnie's second reply, he gives details of when, where, and how he did things, so he uses the *Past Simple* (see 3(i) above).
2 Ask students to give Julia's other questions:
   e.g. (1) Have you made a copy of your birth certificate?
3 Students have conversations in pairs.
4 As a round-up, ask different students what their second reply was in each case.
5 Ask students to suggest what Julia's preparations were.
▶ W8 Ex 1 ◀

8.2 PREPARATIONS AND RESULTS   Practice

> **Language:** Practice of Present Perfect Simple for talking
> about recent past actions.
>
> *Note:* This exercise is concerned with the relationship
> between *recent past actions* and the *results* of those actions.

1 Establish the relationship between present results and recent actions by
  writing a list of results on the board. Beside it, build up a list of what *has
  happened*.

Present Results	Recent Actions
The students <u>are</u> in the room.	The students <u>have come</u> into the room.
He <u>is</u> awake.	He <u>has</u> wok<u>en</u> up.
The window <u>is</u> open.	Someone <u>has</u> open<u>ed</u> the window.

2 Ask students to say what Archibald *has done*:
  e.g. He's drawn the curtains.
3 Demonstrate the pairwork by taking the part of Archibald's mother and
  asking the first question:
     'Why have you drawn the curtains?'
  Students suggest possible excuses:
  e.g. 'Because there was someone staring at me from across the street.'
4 Divide the class into pairs. Some pairs are *both* A, others are *both* B.
  Working together, they prepare what they will say.
5 Students form new pairs, so that each pair has one A and one B. They
  improvise the conversation.

8.3 LEAVING NOTES   Writing

> **Language:** Practice of language introduced in 8.1 and 8.2
> Practice of request structures (introduced in
> Unit 7).

1 Read through the instructions to the whole exercise, and ask students to
  suggest ideas for each topic. Discuss what students might want to say,
  pointing out that they should use:
  i)   Present Perfect Simple (e.g. I've hoovered the carpet).
  ii) Present Tense (e.g. The key is under the mat).
  iii) Request structures (e.g. Do you think you could feed the cat?).
  In the *reply*, they should also use the *Past Simple* for talking about what
  happened at the party, because they are talking about a particular time in
  the past.

2 Divide the class into pairs. Working together, each pair writes *one* note.
3 When a pair has finished, give their note to another pair, who write a reply.
4 When they have finished, each pair reads out the note they received, and their reply.

8.4 THE PRESENT PERFECT CONTINUOUS   Presentation

> **Language:** Present Perfect Continuous and Simple, for describing recent activities and achievements.

This is a Listening Presentation. (See 'Dealing with listening' in Part 3.)

1 Play the tape. Students answer (1)–(4), which check comprehension and focus attention on the key structures.

2 Elicit answers to (5). Establish that:
   i) *Both* tenses are used for saying how you spent a recent period of time.
   ii) *Present Perfect Continuous*: for describing general *activities* you have been involved in. (They may have stopped now or still be going on.)
   iii) *Present Perfect Simple*: for describing the *individual things you have achieved* during that period.

Alan: Hello, Charles – I haven't seen you all day. What have you been doing?

Charles: Actually, I've been working on my first novel.

Alan: Oh yes? How far have you got with it?

Charles: Well, I've thought of a good title, and I've made a list of characters, and I've designed the front cover...

Alan: Have you started writing it yet?

Charles: Oh yes, I've written two pages already.

Alan: Only two?

Charles: Well yes – I haven't quite decided yet what happens next.

3 Illustrate the difference by writing these examples on the board:

Activities	Achievements
What <u>have</u> you <u>been</u> doing today?	What <u>have</u> you <u>done</u> today?
I<u>'ve been</u> writing letters.	I<u>'ve</u> hoover<u>ed</u> the carpet, but I
I<u>'ve been</u> cleaning my flat.	<u>haven't</u> dust<u>ed</u> the furniture yet.

4 Check that students can form Present Perfect Continuous sentences, questions and negatives.
5 Ask students to make sentences from the phrases. The purpose of this is to check that students understand the basic difference between the two forms.
   Answers: Have been doing: read, take photographs, visit museums.
   Have done: read two books, wash all the glasses, take several photographs, visit two museums and an art gallery.
   Either: read a book, do the washing-up.

8.5 RECENT ACTIVITIES   Practice

> **Language:** Practice of Present Perfect Continuous
> (positive and negative).

1 After going through the example, demonstrate the exercise by asking 'Why is your hair wet?', and getting as many explanations from the class as possible.
2 Divide the class into groups of four to do the exercise. They take it in turns to ask a question.
3 As a round-up, ask different groups what explanations they gave.
4 Either discuss the four situations with the whole class, or let students continue working in groups, and go through their answers afterwards.
▶ W8 Ex 3 ◀

8.6 RECENT ACTIVITIES AND   Practice
ACHIEVEMENTS

> **Language:** Practice of language introduced in 8.4.
> Questions about achievements:
> *How much have you done?*
> *How far have you got (with it)?*
> Use of *so far* and *not...yet.*

1 ▣ Play the example on the tape, and point out the two alternative questions.
2 Ask students to suggest what B might reply he has done as part of each activity:
   e.g. (1) I've hoovered the carpet, I've dusted the woodwork, I haven't cleaned the windows yet.
3 Students have conversations in pairs.
4 Introduce the group activity by telling the class what you have been doing and what you have done recently.
5 Divide the class into groups for the activity.
6 As a round-up, ask different students to tell you what they found out about others in their group.
▶ W8 Ex 2 ◀

8.7 A BUSY TIME   Writing

> **Language:** Practice of:
> i) Language introduced in 8.4.
> ii) Past Simple for giving details.

1 Read the letter, and quickly check comprehension by asking questions round the class:
   e.g. What were the floors / the walls like before?
        What are they like now?
        What's the difference between a second-hand shop and a sale?
   Explain any new vocabulary, e.g. lino, cork, wallpaper.
2 Point out the variety of tenses in the passage:
   i)   Present Perfect Continuous for describing *recent activities*.
   ii) Present Perfect Simple for describing *recent achievements*.
   iii) Past Simple for *giving details* of *when*, *where* or *how* you did things.
3 The writing can be done in class or for homework.

8.8   RECENT DEVELOPMENTS   Free practice

> **Language:** Free practice of language introduced in this
>   unit.

The topics for this discussion are deliberately left wide open. If you like you can limit it by choosing specific topics of relevance or interest to your class.
1 Introduce the activity by choosing one topic and briefly talking about it with the whole class.
2 Divide the class into groups for the activity.
3 As a round-up, ask each group to summarise what they talked about.
► W8 Ex 4 ◄

8.9   SUMMER JOBS   Listening

This is a Listening Comprehension Passage. For procedure, see 'Dealing with listening' in Part 3.

Interviewer: And Christine, what about you? What have you been doing this summer?
Christine: Working, mostly.
Interviewer: You mean you've been studying?
Christine: Oh no, I've been doing a job to earn money.
Interviewer: And have you made your fortune yet?
Christine: Hardly! But I haven't done too badly. I've been getting about £40 a week, plus my meals and my accommodation, so I've earned over £500 and I've managed to save most of it.
Interviewer: That sounds pretty good.

What kind of work have you been doing exactly?
Christine: I've been working in a hotel.
Interviewer: What, as a waitress?
Christine: No I've been helping in the kitchen most of the time – washing and peeling vegetables, preparing breakfast trays, washing up – that sort of thing.
Interviewer: And have you been enjoying it? Or has it been rather boring?
Christine: No, it hasn't been too bad. I've found it quite interesting here, in fact. Not so much the work itself, but the people I've got to know and the

friends I've made, and I've managed to do lots of things in my spare time too. It's a seaside town, so there's been quite a lot going on in the evenings – you know, dancing, bowling, cinemas and so on – and on my afternoons off I've been doing quite a bit of sunbathing and swimming.

Interviewer: Yes, I can see you've got quite brown. You've obviously been having some reasonable weather here. Now what about Kevin here? Kevin, you've managed to get a fantastic suntan. How have you been spending your time here? Have you been doing a holiday job?

Kevin: Yes, I've been working down on the beach. I like an outdoor job. I've been mostly hiring out deck chairs – you know, going round collecting the money, but I've also been selling papers.

Interviewer: And have you earned a lot of money?

Kevin: Not a lot. I came here for a cheap holiday more than anything else. My brother's the one who's been making money this summer.

Interviewer: Has he been working here in Brighton too?

Kevin: No, he's in Italy working as a courier for a travel firm. He's been taking Americans round Italy on coach tours and having a fantastic time. And one of them has invited him to go and work in America next summer.

Interviewer: Lucky him!

Answers: (1) (a) In a hotel. (b) On the beach. (c) In Italy.
(2) (a)
(3) (a) False. (b) True. (c) False. (d) True. (e) False. (f) True.
(4) (a) Hiring out deck chairs. (b) Selling newspapers.
(5) He wanted a cheap holiday.
(6) He's been invited to go and work in America next summer.
(7) See Listening Text.

Activities (following Unit 8)

FAVOURS

> **Language:** This activity draws on language from:
> Unit 2 (expressing intention)
> Unit 7 (requests and offers).

This game works best if students are free to move around the class. If possible, move desks aside to make space before you begin.
1 Explain the game carefully, reading through the instructions with the class. If necessary, show students how to fill in the table by writing an example entry on the board.
2 Give time for students to fill in the table, working individually.
3 Demonstrate the game by making one or two requests yourself. Point out that students can only agree to do things:
– that are not on their own list
– that do not interfere with their other plans.
If a student is free to do something, he *must* agree to do it.
4 Students move freely round the class, asking each other for help.
5 The winner is the first person to find other people to help him with all five things on his list.

COMPOSITION

> **Language:** The compositions draw on language from Units
> 2, 6 and 7.

The writing can be done in class or for homework.

SITUATIONS

> **Language:** The situations draw on language from Units
> 5, 6, 7 and 8.

For procedure, see Activities following Unit 4.

Unit 9 Comparison

This is the first of a series of units concerned with *comparison* and evaluation. It deals with language used for comparing things, people, and the things people do.

The unit falls into two sections, followed by a Reading Comprehension and Free Practice. The first section is concerned with significant differences between things or people and comparing advantages and disadvantages, and practises comparison of adjectives; the second section is concerned with comparing things people do, and practises comparison of adverbs and comparisons involving two verbs.

9.1 COMPARISON OF ADJECTIVES
Presentation of: ...-er than; more ... than; not as ... as.
Practice

9.2 SIGNIFICANT DIFFERENCES
Practice

9.3 WHICH WOULD YOU RATHER?
Free practice
Writing

9.4 COMPARISON OF ADVERBS
Presentation of: ...-er / more ...-ly than; not as ... (-ly) as.
Practice

9.5 COMPARISONS INVOLVING VERBS
Presentation and practice

9.6 SALARY SCALES
Free practice

9.7 SUN AND SKIN
Reading

9.8 ADVERTISE-MENTS
Free practice
Writing

9.1   COMPARISON OF ADJECTIVES

> **Language:** Comparison of adjectives:
> adjective + *-er* + *than*
> *more* + adjective + *than*
> *not as* + adjective + *as*.
> 'Adjective + infinitive' structures (e.g.
> 'expensive to run').
> *I'd rather...*
>
> *Note:* Students should already know the basic rules for
> *forming* comparative adjectives (if not, these should be
> presented and practised before starting the exercise)
> ▶ RP ◀. This exercise concentrates on the *use* of
> comparative adjectives for discussing advantages and
> disadvantages, and practises comparisons involving adjectives
> with nouns and infinitives.

Presentation

1 Read the examples, and present *comparative adjective structures* by writing this table on the board (comparing two people):

A is	friendlier more interesting	than B.

B isn't as	friendly interesting	as A.

Students make similar sentences using the adjectives in (1):
e.g. Supermarkets are cheaper than corner shops.
       Corner shops aren't as cheap as supermarkets.

2 Show how comparative structures can include *nouns* and *infinitives*, by adding these examples on the board:

A is	a friendlier person more interesting to talk to	than B.

Students make similar sentences using the expressions in (2):
e.g. Supermarkets have a wider range of goods than corner shops.

3 Introduce the expression:
   I'd rather + *infinitive* (without 'to'!).
Ask students to say briefly which type of shop they'd rather shop at and why.

Practice

1 Look at the sets of cars and fires, and the adjectives and phrases beside them. Explain any new vocabulary.
2 Divide the class into pairs or groups to make comparisons about each set.
3 As a round-up, ask different students to tell you which car and which fire they would rather have, and why.
▶ W9 Ex 1 ◀

9.2 SIGNIFICANT DIFFERENCES   Practice

> **Language:** Practice of language introduced in 9.1.
> Use of *much* with comparative adjectives.
> Superlative adjective structures.

1 Look at the examples with the class, and ask which country is being described in each sentence.
  Answers: (1) Saudi Arabia.
            (2) India.
            (3) Saudi Arabia.
2 Write this table on the board to show how *much* is used in comparisons:

A is <u>much</u>	friendli<u>er</u> <u>more</u> interesting	than B.

3 To demonstrate the exercise, choose one of the cities from (1), and make two comparisons. Students guess which city it is:
  e.g. It's smaller than Hong Kong and it's further east than Athens.
      (**Answer:** Beirut)
4 Students do the exercise in groups, taking it in turns to make comparisons.
5 Make sure students know how to form superlative adjectives. If necessary, present the forms and do some basic practice. ▶ RP ◀
  Present *superlative adjective structures* by writing this table on the board:

A is the	friendli<u>est</u> <u>most</u> interesting	person <u>in</u> this class. <u>of</u> all (of them).

6 Ask the four questions about the countries.
  Answers: (1) India.
            (2) Saudi Arabia.
            (3) Turkey (although India has the highest mountain).
            (4) Japan.
7 In groups, students ask and answer questions about the other sets. Point out that it is enough to say: India has the largest population ('of the five countries' is understood).
▶ W9 Ex 2 ◀

9.3 WHICH WOULD YOU RATHER?

> **Language:** Free practice of language introduced in 9.1.

Free practice

1 Introduce the exercise by referring back to the discussion of cars and fires in 9.1. Tell students that they should make the same kind of comparisons here.
2 Students discuss the questions in groups.
3 As a round-up, ask each group what conclusions they came to.

Writing

The writing can be done in class or for homework.
Note: If you like, you can add other topics which are of local interest to your class, e.g. two restaurants, two parts of a town.

9.4 COMPARISON OF ADVERBS

> **Language:** Comparison of adverbs:
>   adverb + *-er* + *than*
>   *more* + adverb + *than*
>   *(not) as* + adverb + *as*.
> 'Short' forms of verbs in comparative structures.
> *Much* and *a bit* in comparative structures.
>
> *Note:* Students should already know how to form adverbs from adjectives.

Presentation

1 Look at the examples with the class and elicit rules for *comparative adverb* formation:
  i) Adverbs that are the same as adjectives (mostly one-syllable): comparative formed with *-er*, e.g. hard*er*, fast*er*.
  ii) Adverbs that are formed from *adjective* + *-ly*: comparative formed with *more*, e.g. *more* beautifully, *more* neatly, *more* quickly.
  iii) Irregular forms: well – better; badly – worse; far – further.
2 If necessary, do some basic practice of these forms. ▶ RP ◀
3 Present *comparative adverb structures* by writing this table on the board:

A types	faster more quickly	than B does.

B doesn't type as	fast quickly	as A does.

Practice

1 🔲 Play the example on the tape. Then go through the exercise, asking students to tell you the comparative forms of the adverbs:
   e.g. earlier, more heavily, better.
2 Ask the class to give B's answer for (1), (3) and (4).
   Point out the short forms: 'than he *does*', 'than he *did*', 'than he *can*'.
3 Students do the exercise in pairs, taking it in turns to be A.
4 🔲 Play the example for the second exercise. Point out the use of *a bit*, which has the opposite meaning to *much*.
5 Look at the prompts, and ask students to give the adverb forms (the prompts are adjectives) and their comparatives:
   e.g. (1) quietly – more quietly (2) carefully – more carefully (3) fast – faster
   (4) well – better.
6 Demonstrate the exercise by doing (1) with the whole class.
7 Students do the exercise in pairs.
▶ W9 Ex 3 ◀

9.5 COMPARISONS INVOLVING VERBS   Presentation and practice

> **Language:** Comparisons involving a change of verb.

1 Ask students to complete the sentences orally and then to write them down. Write them on the board if you like.
   Answers: (1) (a) He spends more than he earns.
   (b) He doesn't earn as much as he spends.
   (2) (a) That cheese tastes much better than it smells.
   (b) That cheese doesn't taste as bad as it smells.
2 Either ask students to change the sentences round the class, or let them do the exercise in groups and go through the answers afterwards.
▶ W9 Ex 4 ◀

9.6 SALARY SCALES   Free practice

> **Language:** Free practice of language introduced in this unit.
> Superlative adverb forms.

1 Before beginning the exercise, make sure students know how to form *superlative adverbs*. Write this table on the board:

| A types | the fast*est*
the <u>most</u> quickly | (of all). |

2 Read the instructions, and prepare for the discussion by establishing what each of the five factors in the list involves:
   e.g. Training – How long? How difficult? What qualifications at the end?
3 Divide the class into groups for the discussion.
4 As a round-up, ask each group what conclusions they came to.
   ▶ W9 Ex 5 ◀

9.7 SUN AND SKIN

Reading

For procedure, see 'Dealing with reading' in Part 3.

Answers: (1) If he doesn't protect his skin, he burns. If he uses a protective oil, he tans much more slowly.
  (2) (a) It protects your skin *and* lets you tan fast.
     (b) It protects your skin from the ageing effect of the sun.
  (3) (a) You tan more slowly. (b) You tan faster.
  (4) Suggested answers:
     (a)...produce more melanin / produce melanin more quickly.
     (b)...tan faster / more quickly...
     (c)...less than Bergasol.
     (d)...looks older than it is / ages more quickly.
     (e)...more slowly / more safely...
     (f)...will stay younger longer.
  (5) As you get a better tan (= you look more attractive) you realise that it was worth paying the extra money for Bergasol (= the price looks more attractive).

9.8 ADVERTISEMENTS

> **Language:** Free practice of language introduced in this unit.

Free practice

1 As a preparation for the groupwork, briefly discuss with the class what the products are and what might be 'special' about them:
   e.g. Sea-fresh Deodorant – probably a deodorant spray, may have a new 'formula', new perfume, special long-lasting effect, etc.
2 Divide the class into groups, and either assign one product to each group, or let them choose their own. They should discuss particular 'selling points' of their products.

Writing

The best way to do the writing is in groups, as a continuation of the discussion: i.e. all the students in the group work together to produce the advertisement, with one person acting as 'secretary' and actually writing it down.

It can of course also be done individually in class or for homework.

Unit 10   The past and the present

This forms part of two series of units – those concerned with relating *the past and the present*, and those concerned with *comparison*. It deals with language for remembering past events and states, comparing the past and the present, and saying how things have changed.

The unit falls into two sections, followed by a general Free Practice exercise and a Reading Comprehension. The first section is concerned with past events and states and remembering the past, and practises *used to*, the Past Simple, structures with *remember*, and the past use of *would*. The second section is concerned with recent changes and comparing the past and the present, and practises the Present Perfect Simple active and passive, and time comparison structures.

As this unit involves talking about past events, present situations, recent changes, and differences, it brings together language from Units 5, 6, 8 and 9.

10.1   USED TO
Presentation of: used to.
Practice

10.2   LIFE IN THE PAST
Practice
Writing

10.3   REMEMBERING THE PAST
Presentation of: remember; used to; would.
Free practice

10.4   THINGS HAVE CHANGED
Presentation and practice of: Present Perfect; not ... any more / longer.

10.5   THE PRESENT PERFECT PASSIVE
Presentation of: Present Perfect Passive.
Practice

10.6   CHANGES OF HABIT
Practice

10.7   MODERN DEVELOPMENTS
Free practice
Writing

10.8   HALLOWE'EN
Reading
Writing

10.1   USED TO

> **Language:**   Forms of *used to* + *infinitive*, for talking about
> past habitual actions and states.
> Time phrases indicating a period in the past:
> *at one / that time, in those days.*

Presentation

1   Present *used to* by writing the positive and negative forms on the board:

> Eskimos used to live in igloos.

They	didn't use to used not to	live in houses.

Establish that:
i)   There are two negative forms.
ii)   *Used to* is used for talking about past states or past habitual actions
which have now stopped (but *not* single events):
e.g.   I used to live in the country.
   I used to get up at seven every morning.
   but *not*: I used to get up at seven on my tenth birthday.
2   Read the passage, and ask students to make sentences about it using forms
of *used to*:
e.g.   They didn't use to live in houses. They used to live in igloos.

Practice

This section checks that students can use these forms of *used to*:
   positive, negative, questions, there..., passive, 'have' passive.
1   Point out the use of time phrases indicating a period in the past:
      at one time
      at that time
      in those days.
2   Students change the sentences:
   e.g.   (1) He used to live in France (as a boy).
3   If necessary, do further practice of forms students have difficulty with,
using examples of your own.

10.2 LIFE IN THE PAST

> **Language:** Practice of language introduced in 10.1.
> Practice of Past Simple for talking about
> periods in the past (see Unit 5).

Practice

1 Look at the pictures, and teach any new vocabulary that might be needed for the exercise.
2 Demonstrate the exercise by asking for sentences about one picture from the whole class:
   e.g. The cities used to be very dirty.
         There used not to be any motor traffic.
         The men wore hats.
3 Students discuss the other pictures in groups.
4 As a round-up, ask each group to tell you some of the things they said.

Writing

The writing can be done in class or for homework.

10.3 REMEMBERING THE PAST

> **Language:** Practice of language introduced in 10.1.
> Use of *would* for describing habitual actions in
> the past.
> *I remember* + *-ing* or clause.

Presentation 🔲

This exercise begins with a Listening Model. (See 'Dealing with listening' in Part 3.)

I remember sailing on a pond that used to be by my grandfather's sawmill – we had a boat, and we used to go sailing on this. Also, we used to do a lot of climbing trees. We used to climb these trees for apples, which we then ate and made ourselves very sick. And my mother would come along and complain very strongly, but I don't think that stopped us at all. And of course in those days I had a bike, too, and I remember I used to push it up this very long hill near our house and then I'd get on and ride down as fast as I could go. My mother used to complain about that, too.

1 Play the tape. Students answer (1), which checks general comprehension, and (2), which focusses on the main structures.

Unit 10: The past and the present

2 Point out that *I remember* can be followed by *-ing* or a *clause*:

> I remember (that) we used to sail on the pond.
> I remember sailing on the pond.

3 Point out that *would* can be used instead of *used to* to describe habitual events in the past (but not for past states):
e.g. I used to / would get up at 7 every morning.
I used to (*not* would) live in the country.

Free practice

1 Introduce the activity by telling the class a few things that you used to do when you were a child. Use the same range of structures as in the Listening Model.
2 Divide the class into groups for the activity.
3 As a round-up, ask each group to tell you some of the things they talked about.
▶ W10 Ex 1 ◀ for *used to* and *would*.
▶ W10 Ex 2 ◀ for '*remember + -ing*'.

10.4 THINGS HAVE CHANGED Presentation and practice

> **Language:** *Not...any more / longer.*
> Present Perfect Simple for talking about recent changes (see Unit 8).
> Past Simple for giving details of recent events (see Unit 8).

1 🔊 Play the example on the tape.
Write these sentences on the board to show the relationship between the different structures:

Before:	I used to live in Newcastle.
Now:	I don't live in Newcastle any more / longer.
Change:	I've moved from Newcastle.
Details of event:	I moved from Newcastle a few months ago.

2 Look at the exercise with the class and ask students to make sentences with:
i) not...any more / longer
ii) Present Perfect Simple.
e.g. (1) He's not at college any longer.
He's left (college).

95

3 Students have conversations in pairs, taking it in turns to be A. Student B should give further details each time, using the Past Simple.
4 The sentences can be written in class or for homework.
▶ W10 Ex 3 ◀

10.5 THE PRESENT PERFECT PASSIVE

> **Language:** Present Perfect Passive for talking about recent changes (where the agent is unknown or unimportant).
> Vocabulary: verbs of 'change'.

Presentation

1 Read the passage with the class, and check comprehension by asking questions:
e.g. What was there before by the harbour? in the square?
What is there now?
Why is the café 'awful'?
Why is the sign ridiculous?
2 Point out that all the verbs in the passage express *changes* that people have made. Explain the meaning of any new ones.
3 Check that students know how to form the Present Perfect Passive. If necessary, present it by referring to passive forms already taught (Units 3, 5, 6):

Passive: BE + Past Participle	Example: be paid
Present Simple IS / ARE + p.p.	The workers <u>are</u> pai<u>d</u> every Friday.
Past Simple WAS / WERE + p.p.	The workers <u>were</u> paid last Friday.
Present Perfect Simple HAS / HAVE BEEN + p.p.	The workers <u>have been</u> pai<u>d</u>.

4 Students make Passive sentences from the passage, beginning with the words given.
e.g. The atmosphere of the village has been completely destroyed.

Practice

1 Before you begin, it may be useful to write these 'verbs of change' on the board for students to refer to:

destroy	build	turn...into...
cut down	widen	put
pull down	resurface	

2 Students ask and answer questions in pairs.
3 As a check, go through the changes with the whole class.
▶ W10 Ex 4 ◀

10.6 CHANGES OF HABIT   Practice

> **Language:** Time comparison structures:
> *more (often) than...used to*
> *not as much / often as...used to.*
>
> *Note:* These structures combine language introduced in this
> unit (*used to*) and language introduced in Unit 9 (*more...than,*
> *not as...as...*).

1 🔊 Play the example on the tape.
Present time comparison structures by referring to structures practised in
9.5:

> He spends <u>more than</u> he earns.
> He spends <u>more than</u> he <u>used to</u>.

> He does<u>n't</u> earn <u>as</u> much <u>as</u> he spends.
> He does<u>n't</u> earn <u>as</u> much <u>as</u> he <u>used to</u>.

2 Demonstrate the exercise by asking different students, 'Do you go to parties
as often as you used to?'. They should give one of the three replies in the example.
3 Students interview each other in pairs. Make sure they make a note of their
partner's answers.
4 *Either:* Students form new pairs by turning round to someone else, and talk
about their previous partner as in the example.
Or: Simply ask individual students to tell the class about their partners.
5 Introduce the groupwork by telling the class some of the ways in which
you've changed over the last few years. Use language from the whole unit.
6 Divide the class into groups for the activity.
7 As a possible round-up, ask different students what they found out about
other people in their group.

10.7 MODERN DEVELOPMENTS

> **Language:** Free practice of language introduced in this unit.

Free practice

1 Introduce the activity by discussing some of the effects of television with the whole class.
2 Students discuss the other topics in groups.
3 As a round-up, ask different groups what conclusions they came to.

Writing

The writing can be done in class or for homework.
► W10 Ex 5 ◄

10.8 HALLOWE'EN

Reading

For procedure, see 'Dealing with reading' in Part 3.
Answers: (1) (a) It was a religious festival / a time when people fought the influence of evil spirits.
      (b) It's a traditional social occasion / a time to have parties.
  (2) (i) Farmers used to light fires. (ii) They would sing songs and hymns. (iii) They would walk around the fields. (iv) They would lock up their animals. (v) The priests would say prayers to the good spirits. (vi) They would hang rowan leaves over the doors.
  (3) (a) An apple is put in a bucket of water. One person is blindfolded; he puts his head in the water and tries to pick up the apple in his mouth.
      (b) The owner of the house must give the children a 'treat' (e.g. sweets); if he doesn't, the children will play a trick on him.
  (4) (This is a discussion question.)

Writing

The writing can be done in class or for homework. As an alternative to the topic given, you could ask students to write about a similar traditional custom in their own country, and how it has changed.

Activities (following Unit 10)

BALLOON DEBATE

> **Language:** This activity draws on language from:
> Unit 2 (intentions and plans)
> Unit 8 (recent achievements)
> Unit 9 (comparison).

1 Choose four people to make the speeches. Help them choose suitable roles, and give them time to prepare their speeches (ideally, tell them a day or more in advance).
2 The four balloonists give speeches in turn. When they have finished, organise questions from the class.
3 After their closing speeches, the balloonists leave the room. The class then votes on who should be thrown out of the balloon *first*. The person voted out is called back into the room, and can then vote with the others. The voting continues until only one person is left in the balloon – he is the winner.

COMPOSITION

> **Language:** The compositions draw on language from Units 8 and 9.

The writing can be done in class or for homework.

Unit 11   Likes and dislikes

This is the second in the series of units concerned with giving *personal information*. It deals with language for describing your own and other people's likes, dislikes and preferences.

The unit falls into three sections, followed by a Listening Comprehension. The first section is concerned with saying what you like and dislike doing and how much, and what you prefer doing and why; the second section is concerned with saying what you like and dislike other people doing to you. Both these sections practise 'like' and 'dislike' verbs used with nouns and with active and passive gerund forms. The third section is concerned with describing preferred or 'ideal' life-styles, and practises *like to* and the Present Simple.

11.1 DEGREES OF ENJOYMENT
Presentation of: like and dislike verbs + ing or noun.

11.2 RESPONDING TO SUGGESTIONS
Practice

11.3 PREFERENCES
Presentation of: prefer ... -ing / noun to ... -ing / noun.
Practice

11.4 YOUR OWN LIKES AND DISLIKES
Free practice

11.5 THINGS THAT HAPPEN TO YOU
Presentation of: like and dislike verbs with active and passive gerund forms.
Practice

11.6 TYPES OF PEOPLE
Free practice
Writing

11.7 PREFERRED LIFE STYLES: LIKE TO
Presentation and practice of: like to.
Writing

11.8 FOND OF FLYING
Listening
Writing
Discussion

11.1 DEGREES OF ENJOYMENT Presentation

> **Language:** 'Like and dislike' verbs.
> Use of noun or gerund after these verbs.

1 Read the text, and check general comprehension by asking questions round the class:
  e.g. Who are Cilla, Alice and Sidney?
       What is strange about Alice and Sidney?
       Who do you think Cilla likes better, Alice or Sidney?
2 Working individually or in groups, students complete the table. The purpose of this is to check their comprehension of the like / dislike verbs in the passage. They should write *gerunds* or *nouns*, as in the examples.
3 By asking questions (e.g. How does Alice feel about sunbathing? Answer: She *loves* sunbathing.), build up this table of verbs on the board:

No!	No	—	Yes	Yes!
I hate I loathe I can't stand	I don't like I'm not very fond of	I don't mind	I like I enjoy I'm fond of	I love I adore I'm crazy about

▶ W11 Ex 1 ◀ (Students copy the table into the space provided.)
Point out that all the verbs follow the same pattern as 'like', i.e. they are followed by a *noun* or a *gerund*:

I like	parties dancing going to parties

4 Without looking at the text, students make sentences about the three people's likes and dislikes:
  e.g. Alice is crazy about sunbathing.
▶ W11 Ex 1 ◀

11.2 RESPONDING TO SUGGESTIONS Practice

> **Language:** Practice of language introduced in 11.1.

1 🔲 Play the examples on the tape. Demonstrate the exercise by making a few appropriate suggestions to individual students:
  e.g. You: Why don't we go to Switzerland this winter?
       Student: No thanks – I'm not very fond of skiing.
2 Students have conversations in pairs, taking it in turns to make suggestions. They should use the full range of like / dislike verbs.

11.3   PREFERENCES

> **Language:** Practice of language introduced in 11.1.
> Structures with *prefer*.

Presentation

This exercise begins with a Listening Model. (See 'Dealing with listening' in Part 3.)

Woman: Which do you prefer: driving a car yourself or being a passenger?
Man: Well – that depends. I enjoy driving, especially on long empty roads where I can go nice and fast. But I'm not very fond of sitting in traffic jams waiting for lights to change, and things like that. I suppose I don't mind being a passenger, but only if I'm sure that the other person really can drive properly.
Woman: So you don't really like being in other people's cars, then?
Man: Well, as I say, it's all right with a good driver. Then I can relax, sit back and enjoy the scenery. But yes, you're right – on the whole I certainly prefer driving to being a passenger.

1   Play the tape. Students answer the questions.
    Possible answer to (4): On the whole he prefers driving to being a passenger because he doesn't have much confidence in other drivers.
2   Make sure students understand these structures with 'prefer':

> Which do you prefer, driving or being a passenger?
> I prefer driving.
> I prefer driving to being a passenger.
> I prefer tea to coffee.

Point out that 'to' in 'prefer...to...' is a preposition (not infinitive 'to'), and must be followed by a noun or gerund.

Practice

1   Students interview each other in pairs. They conduct two interviews each.
2   As a check, ask individual students to read out their sentences.
▶ W11 Ex 2 ◀

11.4 YOUR OWN LIKES AND DISLIKES   Free practice

> **Language:** Free practice of language introduced so far in this unit.

1 Introduce the activity by interviewing a student about one of the topics or by getting a student to interview you.
2 Divide the class into groups for the activity.
3 As a possible round-up, ask different students to report on the favourite activities of other people in their group.

11.5 THINGS THAT HAPPEN TO YOU

> **Language:** Like / dislike verbs used for talking about what other people do to you, with:
> i) gerund with change of subject (*I like people ...-ing ...*)
> ii) passive gerund (*I like being ...-ed*)
> iii) gerund form of *have something done* (*I like having my ... -ed*).
>
> *Note:* 'Have something done' is used in this exercise to talk about *things that happen to you* (as opposed to *services*, as in Unit 1). Compare:
> I often have my windows cleaned. (= I get someone to do it for me.)
> I often have my windows broken. (= It often happens to me.)

Presentation

1 Read the text, and ask the class:
   i) what people do to the actress herself (e.g. they ask her for her autograph, they push her about at airports).
   ii) what people do to her work (e.g. they criticise her films, they praise her work).
2 Write on the board:

> People ask her for her autograph.
> She is asked for her autograph.

Point out the connection between these structures and structures in Unit 3: 'They pay Ron Glib a huge salary' and 'he is paid a huge salary'.

Write on the board:

> People criticise her films.
> She has her films criticised.

Point out the connection between these structures and structures in Unit 1: 'They wash my hair' and 'I have my hair washed'.

3 Get students to make sentences using *loves* and *hates*, and write them on the board:

People ask her for her autograph.	She loves people asking her for her autograph.
She is asked for her autograph.	She loves being asked for her autograph.
People criticise her films.	She hates people criticising her films.
She has her films criticised.	She hates having her films criticised.

4 Ask students to change the seven sentences, choosing *being* or *having*:
e.g. (1) I hate being telephoned early in the morning.
     (2) I love having my photograph taken.

Practice

1 🔊 Play the examples on the tape. Look through the exercise, and explain any new vocabulary (e.g. twist, compliment).
2 Divide the class into groups of three to do the exercise.
3 As a round-up, ask individual students what answers they gave.
► W11 Ex 3 ◄

11.6 TYPES OF PEOPLE

> **Language:** Free practice of language introduced in the unit so far.

Free practice

1 If necessary, introduce the activity by discussing one of the four people with the whole class.
2 Students discuss the people in groups.

Writing

The writing can be done in class or for homework.
► W11 Ex 5 ◄

11.7   PREFERRED LIFE STYLES: LIKE TO

> **Language:** Use of *like to* + *infinitive*.
>
> *Note:* There is a slight difference in meaning between *like doing* and *like to do*:
> > *Like doing* refers to things you enjoy doing, that give you pleasure.
> > *Like to do* refers to preferred life styles, things you think are the right thing to do. (See the examples below.)
>
> This distinction only applies to British English; in American English 'like to' is used for both meanings.

Presentation and practice

1 Show the difference between *like doing* and *like to do* by giving examples:
   e.g. I like getting up early = I enjoy it, I feel pleasure when I do it.
   > I like to get up early = I think it's a good idea, I think it's the right thing for me to do (although I may not actually enjoy it).
2 Read the example with the class, and point out that the second sentence makes a *general* statement.
3 Either do the exercise with the whole class, or let them do it in groups and go through the answers afterwards.
   Possible answers: (1) she likes to keep fit, get plenty of exercise.
   > (2) he likes to be sociable, have a good social life, enjoy himself.
   > (3) she likes to keep in touch with her friends / her family / her home.
   > (4) he likes to keep his class under control / in order, likes to keep control of his class.
   > (5) they like to keep their house clean / tidy / looking nice.
4 Read the text, which shows how *like to* is used for a series of actions. Ask students to suggest how it might continue.
5 In groups, students discuss what they like to do in the three situations.
6 As a round-up, ask different groups what they like to do.

Writing

1 Prepare for the writing by discussing with the class how (1) might develop as a paragraph.
2 The writing can be done in class or for homework.
▶ W11 Ex 4 ◀

11.8 FOND OF FLYING

Listening 🔊

This is a Listening Comprehension Passage. For procedure, see 'Dealing with listening' in Part 3.

Section 1

You travel a great deal. Do you enjoy it?

Oh yes, I absolutely love travelling. I love going from place to place, and however much I travel I never get sick of it. I'm always excited, particularly when I get on a plane, because I very much like flying. I don't know why, because people nowadays say that it's a very mundane way to travel, but I don't find it so. I think flying is very exciting indeed. You get on the plane, there's the noises at the airport, and I'm crazy about the whole thing, when it...the engines start, and it starts to go down the runway, and there's a great thrill as it goes down the runway – this is the only real thrill about flying – the sense of speed as you go down a runway. And I enjoy all that enormously.

Mind you, I don't like everything about flying. I like it once you're in the aircraft but I don't like sitting around airports, particularly if the plane's delayed. I absolutely hate it then, because the airport's crowded with people, nobody knows what's happening, and I hate people not telling me what's happening – so I don't know whether I'm going to wait for an hour, I don't know whether I'm going to wait for about four hours.

Section 2

The trouble is today that many aircraft have got so fast that short flights are very short and you don't really have time to even get a drink, or a meal, and all the things they do. So I much prefer going on long flights to short flights. Perhaps not too long, but long enough to enjoy it. When you get to really long flights, say 24 hours, I'm not so fond of those, because it's very tiring, and it's difficult to get to sleep, and you get very disorientated because of the difference in time and I don't like that very much at all. But there are things you can do to make a long flight easier to deal with, and what I like to do is, if possible, it's easier if you can fly wherever you're going when it's mostly dark, because then there's a fair chance of getting to sleep. What I like to do for my ideal long-distance flight is to have a long enough spell that you could go to sleep.

What I don't like is the habit they have on long-distance flights of constantly waking you up, because they think that you may be bored, when of course really all you want to do is sleep. And I'm not at all fond of – I hate it when they come along and say to me 'Oh it's time for your meal now.' or it's 'Would you like another drink?' – I just can't stand that because all I want to do is to go to sleep.

Answers: (1) Yes. (The interviewer says so, and she obviously knows a lot about flying.)
(2) The excitement of it, particularly the take-off.
(3) That it's 'mundane' – it's so ordinary now that it isn't exciting any more.
(4) She doesn't like waiting around at airports when planes are delayed.

Because the airports are crowded, and she doesn't know how long she'll have to wait.

(5) She prefers long flights – because on short flights you don't have time to enjoy the flight, have a meal, etc.

(6) They're tiring, it's difficult to get to sleep, and the change in time zones makes you disorientated.

(7) Travel in darkness, so she can get to sleep.

(8) Because they think the passengers are bored, or because it's time for another meal.

Writing

This section gives practice in summary writing; there are similar exercises, of increasing difficulty, after Listening and Reading Passages in later units. This summary can be done very simply by joining answers to the questions, but you should encourage students to fill it out slightly with other information from the tape.

The writing can be done immediately after answering the comprehension questions, or can be left for homework.

Discussion

Either conduct the discussion with the whole class, or let students discuss the questions in groups and ask them to tell you afterwards what conclusions they came to.

Unit 12 Events and circumstances

This is the second in the series of units concerned with *narration* of past events. It incorporates language covered in Unit 5, and deals with ways of relating past events to their circumstances and consequences, and saying what you saw, heard, or felt.

The unit falls into two sections, followed by a general Writing exercise and a Listening Comprehension. The first section is concerned with giving the circumstances in which an event took place and talking about its consequences, and practises the Past Continuous and Past Simple tenses and the use of *when* and *while*. The second section is concerned with describing what you saw, heard or felt, and practises structures with verbs of perception.

12.1 EVENTS AND CIRCUMSTANCES
Presentation of: Past Continuous versus Past Simple; 'when' and 'while'.
Practice

12.2 CIRCUMSTANCES AND CONSEQUENCES
Practice

12.3 HEADLINE NEWS
Practice
Writing

12.4 EXPERIENCES
Free practice
Writing

12.5 EVIDENCE OF THE SENSES
Presentation of: verbs of perception; (see) someone do versus (see) someone doing.

12.6 WITNESSES
Practice

12.7 RUPERT AND THE SPACE PIRATES
Writing

12.8 THE GHOST OF FERNIE CASTLE
Listening
Discussion

12.1 EVENTS AND CIRCUMSTANCES

> **Language:** Use of Past Simple and Past Continuous
> tenses to talk about past events and the
> circumstances in which they took place.
> Use of *when* and *while* to link events and
> circumstances.

Presentation

1 Read the passages in turn, and for each one:
   i) check general comprehension by asking briefly what it is about.
   ii) ask students to tell you the *events* and the *circumstances* mentioned in
   the passage. (The point of this is to focus attention on the Past Simple and
   Continuous tenses.)
2 Ask students how *when* and *while* are used, and write this table on the
   board:

> CIRCUMSTANCE + WHEN + EVENT
> I was having lunch when he walked in.

> EVENT + WHILE + CIRCUMSTANCE
> He walked in while I was having lunch.

3 Check that students know how to form the Past Continuous tense.

Practice

1 Look at the example, and go through the lists of events and circumstances,
   explaining any new vocabulary (e.g. blank, lose consciousness, run out).
2 Either do the exercise round the class, or let students do it in pairs and go
   through the answers afterwards.
▶ W12 Ex 1, Ex 2 ◀

12.2 CIRCUMSTANCES AND   Practice
CONSEQUENCES

> **Language:** Practice of language introduced in 12.1.
> Use of *so* to link two events, one the
> consequence of the other.

1 🎧 Play the example on the tape. Establish the difference between the two questions:

What *were* you do*ing* when you saw the accident? (asking about the circumstances)

and What *did* you *do* when you saw the accident? (asking about the consequence or reaction)

2 Demonstrate the exercise by doing (1) with the whole class.

3 Divide the class into groups of three to do the exercise. They take it in turns to be Student A.

4 Ask students from different groups to report their answers, joining them with *when* and *so*.

12.3 HEADLINE NEWS

> **Language:** Further practice of language introduced in 12.1.

Practice

Ask students to show what the headlines mean by expanding them as in the example. They should make the following additions:

i)   full Past Simple Passive (e.g. *was* derailed)

ii) articles (e.g. *an* express)

iii) Past Continuous verb after *while* (e.g. *while it was travelling*).

Possible answers: A Boeing 747 was hijacked while it was flying over the Atlantic.

An Ambassador's son was kidnapped while he was walking to school.

Tomatoes were thrown at the education minister while he was making a speech.

150 people were arrested while they were taking part in an anti-nuclear demonstration.

A man who was carrying a bomb was arrested while he was trying to go through the customs at Heathrow Airport.

A man was struck by lightning while he was playing golf.

Writing

The writing can be done individually or in groups, or set for homework.

12.4 EXPERIENCES

> **Language:** Free practice of language introduced so far in this unit.
> **Present Perfect Simple** for talking about experiences.

Free practice 🔊

This exercise begins with a Listening Model. (See 'Dealing with listening' in Part 3.)

A: Have you ever been chased by a dog, Keith?
B: No I haven't, but I have been chased by a bull.
A: Really?
B: Yes, it was a couple of weekends ago – I was, er, I was going for a walk out in the country following this foot-path and it went through a field, and I was so busy looking out for the footpath that I didn't notice that the field was full of young bullocks. And the trouble was I was wearing this bright red anorak, and suddenly the bulls started bucking and jumping up and down and started chasing me.

C: What did you do?
B: Well I was pretty scared – I just ran for the nearest fence and jumped over it.
C: Actually I do know somebody who once got bitten by a dog while he was jogging.
A: Was he? How did that happen?
C: Well he was running past a farm when suddenly this sheepdog came out and started barking at him, so he tried to kick it out of the way but then suddenly the dog jumped up and bit him in the leg. I think he had to go to the doctor to make sure it wasn't infected.

1 Play the tape. Students answer the questions.
2 Ask students how the Present Perfect Simple, the Past Simple and Past Continuous are used in the model and establish that the speakers use:
   i)   Present Perfect Simple for saying whether they have experienced something or not.
   ii) Past Simple for giving details of the experience, i.e. telling the story of what happened.
   iii) Past Continuous for giving the circumstances in which the events happened.
3 Divide the class into groups to talk about their own experiences, using the ideas given. Point out that if they haven't had any of the four experiences, they should talk about the most similar experiences they have had (e.g. (1) Being chased by another animal or another kind of experience with a dog).

Writing

The writing can be done in class or for homework.

12.5 EVIDENCE OF THE SENSES Presentation

> **Language:** Use of:
> i) *saw / heard / felt* someone *do* something
> ii) *saw / heard / felt* someone *doing* something.

1 Read the examples with the class, and establish that:
   i) saw / heard / felt something *happen* (i.e. + infinitive) is used about a complete event, (something that *happened*): you saw / heard / felt the whole of it.

ii) saw / heard / felt something *happening* (i.e. + *-ing* form) is used about an incomplete or extended event (something that *was happening*): you saw / heard / felt part of it only.

2 Students either write the correct forms, or work through the exercise in pairs. The purpose of this section is to check that students understand the two forms.

3 Go through the answers.

> Answers: (1) sitting reading get go
> (2) slithering
> (3) coming brake
> (4) break
> (5) explode shake
> (6) talking shout

12.6 WITNESSES Practice

> **Language:** Practice of language introduced in 12.5.
> Use of *could* with *see / hear / feel / smell* + *-ing*.

1 Point out the use of *could see*, *could hear*, etc. with *-ing* forms instead of *saw*, *heard*, etc.

2 Divide the class into pairs. Some pairs are *both* A, others are *both* B. Working together, they read their story and practise retelling it to each other, using *saw / heard / felt* and *could see / hear / feel*:
e.g. I could hear some children playing in the street...

3 Students form new pairs, so that each pair consists of one A and one B. *Without looking* at their story, they compare what they saw, heard, etc.

4 As a round-up, ask the class to try and tell you the complete story of what happened, in the right order.
▶ W12 Ex 3 ◀

12.7 RUPERT AND THE SPACE PIRATES Writing

> **Language:** Free practice of language introduced in this unit.

1 As a preparation for the writing, look at the pictures with the class, and ask students to tell the story orally.
Note: The pictures give the *outline* of the story only. You should encourage students to expand it with details of their own (e.g. Why couldn't the aliens stand mice? How exactly did Rupert get hold of the mice?).

2 The writing can be done in class or for homework.
▶ W12 Ex 4 ◀

12.8 THE GHOST OF FERNIE CASTLE

Listening 🔲

This is a Listening Comprehension Passage. For procedure see 'Dealing with listening' in Part 3.

I was on holiday in Scotland, and I was staying at Fernie Castle Hotel, which used to be just Fernie Castle when it was built about 600 years ago. And I was staying in a small room up in the West Tower, and I went to bed after a good meal, and I think I was probably just falling asleep when I heard someone knocking at the door. So I got up, put the light on and went to the door, but there was no-one there. So I went back to bed and decided it must have been a dream or my imagination. And I was just falling asleep again when I heard someone knocking again – a very light tapping, not a loud knock – and I thought 'There must be somebody there, maybe somebody's playing a trick or...', so I got up, put the light on, went to the door, and there was nobody there. And I wasn't scared, but it's a bit worrying when you're staying by yourself in a very old castle in a place where you haven't been before. So I locked the door and went back to bed but I left the light on, and nothing else happened; I slept until morning.

When I went down to breakfast I didn't say anything, and all the other guests in the dining room looked quite normal and nobody looked like the kind of person who would knock on your door in the middle of the night, so I pretty well forgot about it.

Well the next night I went to bed and there was no knocking at the door, but in the middle of the night I woke up for some reason and I saw a woman standing in the room, and I got a bit of a fright because – well you would if you woke up and found someone you didn't know standing in the room. She was wearing a green dress with a high neck and she was looking at me, and I thought perhaps she'd come to give me a message, but when I switched on the light she disappeared, she wasn't there. And by this time I was really very worried and I stayed awake for the rest of the night, but nothing else happened.

So next morning when I went down to breakfast I said to the owner of the hotel that I'd seen a woman in my room the night before, and he said 'Was she wearing a high-necked green dress?', and I said 'Yes she was – why, was it one of your staff?' and he said 'No, but many people have seen this woman, although I haven't myself. She's supposed to be the wife of a man who was running away with her to get married, and her father didn't want her to marry this man, and they escaped to Fernie Castle and hid in a tiny room at the top of the West Tower, and her father's men eventually tracked them down and found this room where they were hiding and there was a terrible struggle, and somehow while she was trying to escape she fell out of the window and fell three floors to her death on the stone courtyard below. And now her ghost haunts the West Tower and occasionally appears in people's bedrooms with a sad expression, never says anything, and sometimes knocks at doors, and that's probably what you saw,' he said. 'Either that or you had too much champagne the night before!'

Answers: (1) (a) She heard someone knocking at the door.
          (b) She was just falling asleep.

        (c) She got up, put the light on, and went to the door.
(2) (a) That it was a dream or her imagination.
      (b) That someone was playing a trick on her.
(3) (a) A bit worried. (b) She forgot about it.
(4) (a) She went to bed, woke up in the middle of the night, saw a woman in a green dress, switched on the light, the woman disappeared, she stayed awake.
      (b) She couldn't explain what was happening.
(5) See Listening Text.
(6) (a) Knocking at door, woman in high-necked green dress, bedroom in the West Tower, woman silent.
      (b) It was a ghost, or she'd had too much champagne the night before.

Discussion

1 Students discuss the questions in groups.
2 Ask students from each group to tell you what conclusions they came to, and to tell you any interesting experiences.

Activities (following Unit 12)

FOR BETTER, FOR WORSE

> **Language:** This activity draws on language from:
> Unit 8 (recent changes)
> Unit 9 (comparison)
> Unit 10 (comparing the past and
> the present).

1 Read through the list of topics, and make sure students understand what they mean.
2 Preparation stage. Divide the class into pairs. Students in each pair are either *both* A or *both* B. Working together, they prepare what they will say.
3 Students form new pairs, so that each pair consists of one A and one B. They discuss the topics.
4 As a round-up, ask different pairs what conclusions they came to.

COMPOSITION

> **Language:** This is an extension of the previous activity, and draws on the same language areas.

The writing can be done in class or for homework.

SITUATIONS

> **Language:** The situations draw on language from Units 6, 7, 8, 9, 10, 11 and 12.

For procedure, see Activities following Unit 4.

Unit 13 Leisure activities and skills

This is the third in the series of units concerned with giving *personal information*, and it further develops areas covered in Units 3 and 11. It deals with ways of talking about leisure activities, quantity and skill.

The unit falls into two sections, followed by a general Free Practice exercise and a Reading Comprehension. The first section is concerned with saying how much you do of particular activities, and practises expressions for talking about leisure activities and expressions of quantity; the second section is concerned with saying how good you are at particular activities, and practises expressions for talking about degree of skill.

13.1 LEISURE ACTIVITIES: ADVERBS
Presentation of: vocabulary; go + -ing; (quite) a lot, not (very) much, (not) at all.
Practice

13.2 THINGS YOU CAN 'DO'
Presentation and practice of: vocabulary; do + (quite) a lot of / not very much / (not) any + noun.

13.3 HOW MUCH?
Practice

13.4 KINDS OF PEOPLE
Free practice

13.5 SKILLS
Presentation of: 'skill' adjectives; (good) at ...-ing / noun; a (good) ...-er.

13.6 ASKING FAVOURS
Practice

13.7 JOBS
Practice
Writing

13.8 YOUR OWN LEISURE ACTIVITIES AND SKILLS
Free practice
Writing

13.9 CHIPS WITH EVERYTHING
Reading
Discussion

13.1 LEISURE ACTIVITIES: ADVERBS

> **Language:** Use of *go + -ing* for talking about activities.
> Quantity expressions used as *adverbs* (i.e.
> after a verb or phrase).

Presentation

Look at the pictures with the class, and ask students to name the leisure activities and say which can be used with *go + -ing*.

Answers: (those marked * can be used in the form *go + -ing*)
(1) Sunbathing, listening to the radio. (2) Dancing*, going to parties.
(3) Mountaineering* / mountain climbing* / climbing mountains.
(4) Cycling*. (5) Running* / jogging*. (6) Birdwatching* / watching birds.
(7) (Playing) tennis. (8) Knitting, watching TV. (10) Playing cards.

Practice

1 Read the examples and, if necessary, show how the structures are formed by writing these tables on the board:

Do you	ski go skiing play chess	at all?

I	ski go skiing play chess	a lot. quite a lot.

I don't	ski go skiing play chess	(very) much. at all.

Point out that these quantity expressions are *adverbs*, i.e. they come after a verb or verb phrase.
2 Demonstrate the exercise by asking a few questions round the class.
3 Students ask each other questions in groups.

117

13.2 THINGS YOU CAN 'DO'   Presentation and practice

> **Language:** Use of the verb *do* with names of
> leisure activities.
> Quantity expressions used as
> *determiners* (i.e. before a noun or
> verbal noun).
> Practice of language introduced in 13.1.
> Vocabulary: leisure activities.

1 Look at the example, and point out the use of *do* and quantity expressions before nouns. If necessary, write a list of these on the board, to show how they are different from the adverbs in 13.1:

		Adverbs
		...at all?
	VERB	...a lot
not...		...much
not...		at all

Before Nouns
...any +NOUN?
...a lot of + NOUN
not...much + NOUN
not...any + NOUN

2 Go through the list of leisure activities and present any new items.
3 Students make sentences about each activity:
   e.g. I don't do much fishing.
4 The point of the questions is to link this exercise with 13.1, and to show how there are different ways of talking about the same leisure activities.
   Possible answers: (1) I swim a lot, don't swim much / at all, etc.
         I go swimming a lot, etc.
         I do a lot of swimming, etc.
   (2) I do a lot of yoga, don't do much / any yoga, etc.
         I go to yoga classes a lot, etc.
   (3) I read a lot, etc.
         I do a lot of reading, etc.

Note: If you like, point out to the class that *play* + names of games and sports can be used in the same way as *do*:
e.g. I play quite a lot of football.
   I don't play much chess.
However, in question and negative forms, it is more natural to leave out the word 'any':
e.g. I don't play backgammon (at all).
   Do you play tennis (at all)?

13.3 HOW MUCH? Practice

> **Language:** Practice of language introduced in 13.1 and 13.2.

This exercise begins with a Listening Model. (See 'Dealing with listening' in Part 3.)

1 Play the tape. Students answer the questions.

2 Point out that:
   i) This exercise, like the Model, is a *game*, i.e. they are not answering questions about themselves in 'real life', but according to what they have written down.
   ii) The point of the game is to find out what their partner has written in his table.
   iii) They find this out by asking and answering questions as in the Model.

A: Do you ski at all?
B: No I don't.
A: Do you play tennis?
B: Yes, I do.
A: How much?
B: Oh I play tennis quite a lot.
A: What about gardening? Do you do any gardening?
B: Yes.
A: Do you do a lot of gardening?
B: No I don't do very much.

3 Each student secretly writes nine activities from 13.1 or 13.2 in his own table.
4 Divide the class into pairs to play the game.

13.4 KINDS OF PEOPLE Free practice

> **Language:** Free practice of language introduced in the unit so far.
> Other expressions for describing how people spend their leisure time:
> frequency adverbs (see Unit 3)
> *spend...(time)...-ing...*

This exercise begins with a Listening Model. (See 'Dealing with listening' in Part 3.)

He's quite a solitary type of person, really. You know, he spends most of his time at home, reading, listening to the radio, things like that. He goes out to the pub occasionally, and he does quite a lot of singing, too – he belongs to the local choir, I believe – but you never see him at weekends. He's always off somewhere in the country, walking or fishing. He does a lot of fishing, actually – but always on his own. Funny sort of bloke.

1 Play the tape. Students answer the questions.
   Possible answers to (4): He's always off walking in the country.
   He goes walking or fishing in the country.
   He spends the weekend walking or fishing, etc.

2 Working in groups, students discuss the people in the pictures.
3 Each group chooses one picture. Working together, they write a paragraph about the person in it.
4 Ask one person from each group to read out their paragraph.
▶ W13 Ex 1 ◀

13.5 SKILLS   Presentation

> **Language:** Expressions for talking about degree of skill:
> e.g. *He's good at gardening.*
> *He's a good gardener.*
> Range of 'skill' adjectives.

1 Read the text, and check general comprehension by asking questions round the class:
 e.g. Where are the two people?
  What is the relationship between them?
  What kind of person is the man? the woman?
  How does the woman feel? Why?
2 Working individually or in groups, students complete the table. The purpose of this is to check comprehension of the 'skill' expressions in the passage. They should write the names of *activities* (gerunds or nouns), as in the example.
3 Build up these tables on the board, to show the full range of expressions:

He's	brilliant / terrific / fantastic (very) good quite good not bad not very good hopeless / useless	AT	gardening. (playing) chess. looking after children.

He's	a brilliant / terrific / fantastic a (very) good quite a good not a bad not a very good a hopeless / useless	gardener. chess player.

▶ W13 Ex 2 ◀ (Students copy the expressions into the table.)
Point out: i) the use of *at* + noun / gerund
   ii) the position of the article in 'quite *a* good', 'not *a* bad', 'not *a* very good'.
4 Without looking at the text, students make sentences about the three people, as in the example.
▶ W13 Ex 2 ◀

13.6 ASKING FAVOURS   Practice

> **Language:** Practice of language introduced in 13.5.

1 ▄ Play the example on the tape. Look at the other situations, and ask students to suggest what skills might be needed for each one:
e.g. (1) You might need someone who is good at decorating, carpentry, plumbing, gardening, etc.
2 Divide the class into groups. Students take one situation each, and ask favours of all the other people in their group.

13.7 JOBS

> **Language:** Further practice of language introduced in 13.5.

Practice

Either discuss each job with the whole class, or let them discuss them in groups and then ask each group what they decided.

Writing

The writing can be done in class or for homework.
Note: This is a good opportunity to deal with formal letter-writing skills:
e.g. position of address and date, use of 'Dear Sir / Dear Mr X', use of 'Yours faithfully / Yours sincerely', etc.

13.8 YOUR OWN LEISURE ACTIVITIES AND SKILLS

> **Language:** Free practice of language introduced in this unit.

Free practice

1 Introduce the pairwork by telling the class about one of your own leisure activities, how much you do and how good you are at it.
2 Divide the class into pairs. Students take it in turns to interview each other. Make sure that they *both* take notes.

Writing

The writing can be done in class or for homework.
▶ W13 Ex 3, Ex 4 ◀

13.9   CHIPS WITH EVERYTHING

Reading

For procedure, see 'Dealing with reading' in Part 3.
Answers: (1)   In a pub.
        (2)   The old man at the next table.
        (3)   (i)   They're too old to play 'real' basketball.
             (ii)   You can't play real golf at night.
             (iii) The man says 'It beats me' (the computer).
        (4)   'I suddenly understood.'
        (5)   (i)   People will have more leisure time.
             (ii)   They'll spend a lot of their time playing electronic games.
        (6)   (i)   Where they get the money from.
             (ii)   How they find enough time to practise and become so skilful.
        (7)   (i)   Games involving 'physical' skill (e.g. football, space invaders).
             (ii)   'Intellectual' games (e.g. chess) played against a computer.
        (8)   People may not do so much real sport; they may play games less with each other; some could become addicted, and steal money to play the machines.
        (9)   (a) Not very good. (b) Very good.
     (10)   He probably doesn't approve – see (8) – although he does play space invaders himself.

Discussion

Either conduct the discussion with the whole class, or let students discuss the questions in groups and ask them afterwards what conclusions they came to.

Unit 14 Advice

This is the third in the series of units concerned with taking, initiating and commenting on *action*. It deals with language for making suggestions and giving specific and general advice.

The unit falls into two sections, followed by a Listening Comprehension. The first section is concerned with suggesting solutions to problems and reporting suggestions: the second section is concerned with advising people to take precautions, warning people what might happen and giving general advice.

The unit practises a range of advice / suggestion structures, some of which students should have come across before; it also practises the sentence connectives *otherwise*, *in case* and *so that*, and the use of *might* in giving reasons for advice.

14.1 SUGGESTIONS AND ADVICE
Presentation of: advice / suggestion structures; reporting advice.
Practice

14.2 ALTERNATIVE SOLUTIONS
Practice

14.3 PROBLEMS
Free practice

14.4 TAKING PRECAUTIONS
Presentation and practice of: general advice structures; might; otherwise; in case; so that.

14.5 JUST IN CASE
Practice

14.6 ROAD SIGNS: WARNINGS
Practice

14.7 GENERAL ADVICE
Free practice
Writing

14.8 VISITING BRITAIN
Listening
Writing

123

14.1   SUGGESTIONS AND ADVICE:

> **Language:**   Basic expressions for giving advice and making
> suggestions.
> Structures for reporting advice and suggestions.

Presentation

1   Read the situation, and ask students to complete the remarks in the bubbles.
If necessary, write examples on the board to show how the expressions
continue:

> You should(n't) tell Don.
> You'd better(not)tell Don.
> You ought (not) to tell Don.
> Why don't you tell Don?
> If I were you, I'd (I wouldn't) tell Don.

2   Point out that:
   i)   *You should(n't)* and *you'd better (not)* are followed by infinitive without
   'to'; *you ought (not)* is followed by *to* + infinitive.
   ii)   All the expressions can be used for the situations in this exercise, but
   there are slight differences between them, e.g. 'Why don't you...?' is
   used for helpful suggestions, 'If I were you' is used for more serious
   advice.
3   If necessary, do some quick basic practice of these structures. ▶ RP ◀

Practice

1   In groups, students make as many suggestions as they can for each situation.
They should imagine they are actually talking to the person:
e.g. (1) You should go and look for him.
2   Look at the examples with the class. (*Note:* You *cannot* say: 'I suggested
her to...')
3   Ask each group to tell you what advice they gave, using *advised* and
suggested:
e.g. We suggested that she should go and look for him.

14.2 ALTERNATIVE SOLUTIONS   Practice

> **Language:** *Try + -ing*, used for suggesting ways to solve a
> problem.

1 [▣] Play the example on the tape. Ask students to make more suggestions:
   e.g. Have you tried putting more petrol in the tank?
   Why don't you try kicking it?
2 Beginning with the ideas given students have conversations in pairs, taking
   it in turns to make suggestions.
3 As a round-up, ask different students what suggestions they made.
4 If you like, point out the difference between *try to do* and *try doing* by
   giving a few contrastive examples:
   e.g. He tried *to* get to sleep = He found it difficult to get to sleep.
   He tried count*ing* sheep (as a way of getting to sleep). (He didn't find it
   difficult to count sheep!).
▶ W14 Ex 1, Ex 2 ◀

14.3 PROBLEMS   Free practice [▣]

> **Language:** Free practice of language introduced so far in
> this unit.

This exercise begins with a Listening Model. (See 'Dealing with listening' in
Part 3.)

1 Play the tape. Students answer
   the questions.
2 Divide the class into groups to
   think of a problem.
3 Students form new groups. Each
   new group should contain at
   least one person from each of the
   original groups. In turn, each
   student tells the others his
   problem, and they give suitable
   advice.
4 As a round-up, ask one student
   from each group to tell you what
   problems others in his group had,
   and what advice they gave.

My problem is with my mother, who is
now well over 70 and a widow and
becoming very fragile, and she really
needs my help. But where she lives, in
the country, there's no work
available for me – I'm a designer –
and she can't come and live with me
because she says she doesn't like the
climate because it's too bad for her
rheumatism, which is actually true –
it's very cold here. And if I go and
work there as something else where
she lives, perhaps as a secretary, it
means we have to take a drastic drop
in salary. So I don't really know what
to do.

14.4 TAKING PRECAUTIONS   Presentation and practice

> **Language:** Use of *should* and *It's a good idea to...*
> for giving general advice.
> Giving reasons for taking precautions
> by predicting what might happen, using:
> *might*
> *otherwise, if you don't*
> *in case* + Present Simple
> *so that* + Present Simple negative.

1 Giving other examples if necessary, establish the difference between the two example sentences. In the exercise there are two kinds of reason why you should do things:
   i) because of what might happen anyway:
     because...might...
   ii) because of what might happen if you don't take precautions:
     because... $\genfrac{}{}{0pt}{}{\textit{if you don't}}{\textit{otherwise}}$ *might...*

2 In groups, students ask the questions and give two answers each time.
3 Go through the answers with the class.
   Possible answers: (1) It might be full. / Otherwise you might not get a seat.
                 (2) You might need a filling. / Otherwise your teeth might fall out.
                 (3) Someone might try to steal it. / Otherwise it might get stolen.
                 (4) There might be ice on the road. / Otherwise you might skid.
                 (5) You might touch a live wire. / Otherwise you might get an electric shock.
                 (6) You might fall off. / Otherwise you might damage your head.
                 (7) You might lose yours. / Otherwise you might not be able to get back in.
4 Go through the examples of *in case* and *so that*. Point out that:
   i) *In case* and *so that* are followed by the Present Simple, although they refer to the future (cf. *if* and *when*).
   ii) 'In case it *happens*' and 'so that it *doesn't* happen' both mean 'because (otherwise) it *might* happen'.
5 Students can either give the sentences orally round the class, or write them down.
▶ W14 Ex 3 ◀

14.5 JUST IN CASE   Practice

> **Language:** Use of *you'd better* and *I think you should* for
> giving advice in a particular situation.
> Practice of language introduced in 14.4.

1 🔲 Play the example on the tape. Ask students to suggest possible reasons for the advice in the other situations:

e.g. (1) They might run out of petrol; there might not be another garage.
2 Demonstrate the exercise by doing (1) with the whole class.
3 Students have conversations in pairs, taking it in turns to be A.
▶ W14 Ex 4 ◀

14.6 ROAD SIGNS: WARNINGS   Practice

> **Language:** Practice of language introduced in 14.4 and
> 14.5, for giving advice in a particular situation.
> Vocabulary: driving 'hazards'.

1 Look at the road signs, and ask students to say what each one indicates.
   Answers: *Left diagram*, Row 1: level crossing, road narrows, school. Row 2: cross-
      roads, danger of skidding (water or ice on road), double bend. Row 3: steep
      hill, traffic lights, danger of farm animals on the road.
      Right diagram, Row 1: danger of rocks falling, bend, danger of wild
      animals on the road. Row 2: road works (people mending the road),
      quay or riverbank, steep hill. Row 3: bridge, main road, airport (low
      flying aircraft).
      Note: The usual way to talk about the meaning of these signs is *There's* a
      level crossing *ahead*, etc.
2 Before you begin the game, give some language preparation by asking
   students to suggest suitable warnings for a few of the signs:
   e.g. You'd better drive slowly in case you skid.
3 Demonstrate the game by playing it on the board (using a simple diagram)
   with the whole class.
4 Divide the class into groups of three to play the game.
Note: If you don't want to do the exercise as a game, you can simply ask
students to make warnings for each sign round the class.

14.7 GENERAL ADVICE

> **Language:** Free practice of language introduced in 14.4.
> 'General advice' structures.

Free practice

1 Read the notice and explain any new vocabulary (e.g. weather forecast,
   compass, anorak=waterproof jacket).
2 Introduce the groupwork by discussing the first piece of advice with the
   whole class.
3 Divide the class into groups to discuss why the other precautions are necessary.
4 Discuss the answers with the whole class.

5 For the second part of the exercise, either assign one activity to each group, or let them choose their own.
6 One student from each group gives advice about their activity to the rest of the class.
7 Students discuss their activity in groups.

Writing

The writing can be done in class or for homework.
► W14 Ex 5 ◄

14.8   VISITING BRITAIN

Listening

This is a Listening Comprehension Passage. For procedure, see 'Dealing with listening' in Part 3.

Expert: Well, I think the first important thing is to choose the course that you're going to join very carefully. There are a variety of courses from advanced right down to elementary, and perhaps one of the best ways of finding out about them is first of all to go to your local British Council office. They keep a list, a register of the various colleges, schools, universities in Britain that offer courses to overseas students.

Interviewer: It must be very difficult trying to choose the right course for yourself when there are so many courses offered. Would they be able to advise on the right course?

Expert: To a certain extent, yes, but basically I think the foreign student has to work out for himself by writing to various addresses that he might get from the British Council. He's got to write to various schools – these may be private language schools or further education colleges or universities that offer courses in English for foreign students. I think the important thing is to write to all these and get as much information as possible and then make a selection. Or an alternative is of course to find other people in one's own country who've been to Britain and quite

simply to collect information from them.

Interviewer: Once the student has been accepted for a course in Britain, what are the other things that he should plan carefully for before he arrives? For example, what about accommodation?

Expert: Well yes, accommodation is very important. And I think as far as accommodation is concerned, it's a good idea to stay if possible in an English family. However much you learn at classes in Britain, you still need the experience of practising English in a real life situation, and staying with an English family is far and away the best way of acquiring that kind of practice. But you should be just as careful in choosing your family as you are in choosing your school, otherwise you might find yourself with a family who hardly speak to you at all or you might find yourself with a family that you don't get on with. And I think as with choosing a school, it's important to get a personal recommendation – try and find a family that one of your friends has already stayed with or that you've heard about or that somebody has met.

Interviewer: And how about other

things? Everybody talks about the British weather being very bad. What kind of advice would you give on clothing?

Expert: Ah yes, that's very important. I think it's a good idea to come prepared for the English weather. Even in summer the weather can change and so I think it's a good idea to bring a raincoat in case it rains and to bring one or two pullovers in case the weather suddenly turns cold.

Interviewer: What about money? Is it better to bring traveller's cheques or to bring cash?

Expert: Oh I think traveller's cheques

every time, just in case one's money gets stolen.

Interviewer: If you run out of money when you're on a course in Britain, is it possible to get a job?

Expert: Well no, you shouldn't really work when you're an overseas student in Britain. You should really come to Britain with enough money for the whole of your stay, because if you do take on a job while you're in Britain there's a risk that you'll get into trouble with the immigration authorities, and you might get thrown out.

Answers: (1) (a)
  (2) (i) Write to schools.
    (ii) Ask people who've been on a course.
  (3) (i) Private language schools.
    (ii) Further education colleges.
    (iii) Universities.
  (4) (a) It's the best way to practise English.
    (b) Otherwise you might find yourself with a family who don't speak to you or who you don't get on with.
  (5) (a) In case it rains.
    (b) In case the weather turns cold.
    (c) In case one's money gets stolen.
  (6) They aren't allowed to take jobs.

Writing

This gives practice in summary writing. Students should use their answers to the comprehension questions and add any other information from the tape they think is important. Point out that as the leaflet is not more than 150 words long, they should not go into too much detail.

The writing can be done immediately after answering the comprehension questions, or can be left for homework.

Activities (following Unit 14)

ROUND EUROPE

Language: This activity draws on language from: Unit 9 (comparison) Unit 11 (preferences) Unit 14 (general advice).

1 Choose four students to be the 'travellers'. Divide the rest of the class into four groups, each group representing a group of consultants. The travellers prepare individually, the consultants prepare in their groups.
2 Each of the travellers 'visits' each of the groups of consultants in turn and asks their advice.
3 As a round-up, ask each of the travellers to say how he has decided to travel, and why.

COMPOSITION

Language: The compositions allow for a wide range of possible language, but especially draw on language from Units 5, 6, 7, 8 and 14.

The writing can be done in class or for homework.

Unit 15 Origin and duration

This is the fourth in the series of units concerned with relating *the past and the present*. It deals with language for talking about the origin and duration of present situations.

The unit falls into two sections, followed by a Reading Comprehension and a Free Practice. The first section is concerned with saying how long ago a present situation or activity started and how long it has been going on for, and practises the Present Perfect Continuous (and Simple) with *since* and *for* and the Past Simple with *in* and *ago*. The second section is concerned with saying how long it is since you last did something, and practises 'negative' duration structures with the Present Perfect and Past Simple.

15.1 ORIGIN AND DURATION

> **Language:** Structures for talking about the origin and
> duration of present situations:
> i) Present Perfect Continuous + *for / since*
> ii) Past Simple + *ago / in*.

Presentation 🔲

This is a Listening Presentation. (See 'Dealing with listening' in Part 3.)

1 Play the tape. Students write
down the questions and answers
from the three dialogues.
Quickly go through the answers.
Note: The point of this is to focus
attention on the key structures of
the unit, and to establish how
familiar they are with them
already.

2 Use (1) to establish that:
   (a) The Present Perfect Continuous is used to talk about *how
   long* a present situation has
   been going on (i.e. its duration).
   (b) *For* refers to a period of time
   (e.g. for a week), *since* refers
   to a point of time (e.g. since
   March).

3 Use (2) to establish that:
   (a) The Past Simple is used to
   talk about *when* a present
   situation started (i.e. its
   origin).
   (b) *Ago* refers to a period of time
   (e.g. a week ago), *in* refers to
   a point of time (e.g. in
   March).
   Note: Instead of *in*, we can
   use phrases with *on, at* or no
   preposition (e.g. on Saturday,
   last Tuesday) – see Unit 5.

4 Build up this table on the board
to show the relationship between
the structures:

Dialogue 1
A: Hmm. You're a good squash player.
How long have you been playing?
B: Oh, I've been playing since the
beginning of last term. What about
you?
A: Me? Oh, I've been playing for about
two years now – but I'm still not
very good.

Dialogue 2
A: I suppose you know how to waltz,
do you?
B: Yes, but not very well, I'm afraid. I
only learnt a few weeks ago. When
did you learn?
A: Oh, I learnt to waltz in about 1970
– just after I left school. Er – shall
we dance, then?

Dialogue 3
A: And this is my cousin, Sue.
B: Ah yes – we already know each
other actually.
A: Do you? How long have you known
each other, then?
B: Oh, we've known each other for
about six months now, I think,
haven't we?
C: Oh no much longer than that. We
met about a year ago, at that
Christmas party – remember?

Present situation	He plays tennis.	
Duration 'up to now'	He <u>has been</u> playing tennis	<u>for</u> 3 years. <u>since</u> 1979.
Past event (origin)	He started to play	3 years <u>ago</u>. <u>in</u> 1979.

5 Use (3) to establish that certain verbs, e.g. be, own, know, believe and have (meaning 'possess'), have *no continuous form*. With these verbs the Present Perfect Simple is used instead of the Present Perfect Continuous: e.g. He *has known* how to play tennis for three years.

Practice

Either ask students to give questions and answers round the class, or let them ask and answer in pairs or groups. The purpose of this section is to check that students can form 'origin' and 'duration' structures correctly.
▶ W15 Ex 1 ◀

15.2 ASKING QUESTIONS   Practice

> **Language:** Practice of questions about origin and duration:
> i) *How long?* + Present Perfect Continuous (or Simple)
> ii) *When? / How long ago?* + Past Simple.

1 Go through the example, and establish the difference between *How long...?* and *How long ago...?*
2 Students make both kinds of questions.
   Note: In this exercise, there are two different meanings of the verb *to have*:
   i) 'to possess' (he's got a dog)
   ii) 'to do something' (he has piano lessons).
   This second use of *have* appears in many common phrases (e.g. 'have a bath', 'have lunch'), and has a continuous form like any other verb ('He's having lunch', 'How long have you been having piano lessons?').
▶ W15 Ex 2 ◀

15.3 POINTS AND PERIODS   Practice

> **Language:** Practice of language introduced in 15.1,
> especially the use of *for*, *since*, *ago*, and past
> time phrases with *in* and *at*.

1 🔊 Play the examples on the tape.
2 Demonstrate the exercise by doing (1) with the whole class.
3 Students have conversations in groups, taking it in turns to begin.
4 As a check, go through the answers with the whole class.

15.4 'SINCE' WITH   Presentation and practice
CLAUSES

> **Language:** Use of *since* followed by a clause.

1 🔊 Play the example on the tape. Establish that:
  i)   In each sentence, *since* is followed by a clause representing a past event.
  ii) *Ever since* means the same as *since*, but emphasises that the person has
       been doing something continuously.
2 If you like, show the connection between clauses and time phrases by
  writing this table on the board:

He's been driving a Volvo (ever) since	last April. his promotion. he was promoted.

3 Demonstrate the groupwork by doing the first item with the whole class,
  asking for as many explanations as possible:
  e.g. (1) ...ever since my wife left me.
       ...since I lost my job.
       ...ever since I gave up smoking, etc.
4 Students do the exercise in groups, taking it in turns to be A.
5 As a round-up, ask different groups what explanations they gave.
▶ W15 Ex 3 ◀

15.5 TALKING ABOUT YOURSELVES   Free practice

> **Language:** Free practice of language introduced so far in
> this unit.

1 Demonstrate the activity by telling the class about where you live, how long
   you've been living there, etc., and asking individual students to tell you the
   same about themselves.
2 Divide the class into groups for the activity.
3 As a round-up, ask different students to tell you about the others in their
   group.

15.6 THE LAST TIME   Presentation

> **Language:** 'Negative' duration structures, for measuring
> the time since you *stopped* doing something:
> *I last ... + ago.*
> *It's ... since I last...*
> *I haven't ... for / since...*

1 Read the passage, and check comprehension by asking questions round the
   class:
   e.g. Where is the speaker?
        What is his philosophy of life?
        How does he save money on food? transport? cigarettes? washing?
        phone bills?
2 Students write the four sentences. Go through the answers.
   Answers: (1) I haven't bought any food for over a week.
             (2) It's ages since I paid a taxi fare.
             (3) I last bought a packet of cigarettes about two years ago.
             (4) I haven't been to a launderette since last September.
3 Show the relationship between the structures by writing this table on the
   board:

I haven't bought any food	for a week. / since last week.
I last bought some food a week ago.	
It's a week since I last bought some food.	

   Point out that in the negative, the Present Perfect *Simple* is used to express
   duration (i.e. I *haven't bought*, not 'I haven't been buying').
4 Students give two more forms of the other sentences.

15.7   WHEN DID YOU LAST...?   Practice

> **Language:**   Practice of language introduced in 15.6.
> Questions about 'negative' duration:
> *When did you last...?*
> *How long is it since you last ...?*

1 Ask students to give the questions for each topic:
   e.g. When did you last go swimming?
   How long is it since you last went swimming?
2 Demonstrate the activity by telling students when you last went swimming and asking individual students when they last went swimming.
3 Students ask each other questions in groups. They should try to practise all the structures.
▶ W15 Ex 4 ◀

15.8   LAZY DAYS   Reading

For procedure, see 'Dealing with reading' in Part 3.
Answers: (1) They make you do things that you are too lazy to do otherwise.
　　　　(2) (a) He doesn't do all the housework, doesn't bother much about his appearance, doesn't keep up with culture or fashion.
　　　　　　(b) He works fairly hard, keeps his flat fairly clean.
　　　　(3) (a) False.
　　　　　　(b) True.
　　　　　　(c) True.
　　　　　　(d) True.
　　　　　　(e) False.
　　　　　　(f) False.
　　　　(4) (a) Pleased and excited.
　　　　　　(b) First performances of plays, operas, etc.
　　　　　　(c) A play by Agatha Christie (famous for being the longest running play in London).
　　　　　　(d) From memory.
　　　　　　(e) When you play them they make a noise.
　　　　　　(f) Make contact with.
　　　　(5) (a) Someone gave him a ticket for his birthday.
　　　　　　(b) To get out of the rain while waiting for a bus.
　　　　　　　　In neither case did he go because he was keen on seeing it.
　　　　(6) (a) Everything has changed, but he has stayed the same.
　　　　　　(b) Fashions keep changing, and so eventually what was in fashion in the sixties will be in fashion again.
　　　　(7) (a) His friends arrived.
　　　　　　(b) Because the quiz would show that he is very lazy.
　　　　(8) (This is a discussion question.)
　　　　(9) Students should write questions that: (i) are of an 'objective test' type, like those found in real personality quizzes (e.g. in magazines); (ii) use the language of the unit as far as possible.

15.9 PERSONALITY QUIZ

> **Language:** Free practice of language introduced in this
> unit.

Free practice

1 Prepare for the pairwork by discussing briefly with the class what kind of
   questions they might ask, i.e. what kind of questions might show how
   careful or fashionable a person is. As in the previous exercise, encourage
   students to think of questions that use the language of the unit.
2 Divide the class into pairs. Give each pair a letter, A or B. Working together,
   they think what questions they will ask. They can either write the questions
   or simply make brief notes.
3 Students form groups of four, so that each group has one pair A and one
   pair B. They take it in turns to ask the others their questions.
4 Ask each pair to comment on the personalities of the pair they tested.

Writing

The writing can be done in class or for homework.
▶ W15 Ex 5 ◀

Unit 16   Location

This is the third in the series of units concerned with *physical description*. It incorporates language covered in Unit 1, and deals with ways of expressing precise location.

The unit falls into two sections, followed by a Listening Comprehension. The first section is concerned with describing the position of things, both in relation to other things and as part of a whole, and practises location prepositions and phrases. The second section is concerned with geographical location and describing features of countries, and practises a range of location expressions.

16.1   IN, ON & AT
Presentation of: the location prepositions 'in', 'on' and 'at'.
Practice

16.2   WHOLE AND PARTS
Presentation and practice of: location prepositions (e.g. behind) and prepositional phrases (e.g. at the back of).

16.3   PRECISE LOCATION
Practice

16.4   LOCATION QUIZ
Practice

16.5   DESCRIBING PLACES AND THINGS
Free practice

16.6   GEOGRAPHICAL LOCATION
Presentation and practice of: expressions of geographical location.
Practice

16.7   DESCRIBING COUNTRIES
Free practice
Writing

16.8   SKIING IN SCOTLAND
Listening

16.1 IN, ON & AT

> **Language:** Uses of the prepositions *in*, *on* and *at*, for
> expressing location.
>
> *Note:* Students should already be aware of the basic uses
> of these prepositions. Concentrate on areas of confusion,
> which may be connected with certain groups of nouns
> (where English differs from the student's own language).

Presentation

Read the examples, and discuss uses of *in*, *on* and *at*.
Establish the five basic uses as shown in the examples, using diagrams if you
find them useful:

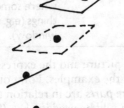

IN   completely *inside* something, e.g. a
       box, a cupboard.

IN   in an *area with boundaries*, e.g. a
       field, a street.

ON   on a *surface*, e.g. a table, a wall.

ON   on a *line*, e.g. a river, a road.

AT   at or near a *point*, e.g. a bus stop,
       or a 'point on the map', e.g. an
       airport.

Note: In the examples, the lake is seen as: a volume of water; an area; a
surface; a line (the edge of the lake); a point on the map.

Practice

1   Ask students to suggest as many possibilities as they can. The purpose of
this section is to establish major meaning differences between *in*, *on* and *at*.
Possible answers: (1) In: water, people swimming, islands.
                                On: boats, ice, towns.
                           (2) In: water, wine, a cork.
                                On: a label, dust.
                           (3) In: someone asleep, insects.
                                On: blankets, someone having a rest.
                           (4) On: a knocker, a message, a number.
                                At: a visitor.
                           (5) In: insects, a snake (= long grass).
                                On: people sitting (= short grass).
                           (6) In: people swimmming.
                                At: people changing, watching, drinking tea.

(7) In: a lamp, a wastepaper basket (= indoors).
At: someone waiting, a letter box (= of a street).
2 Gap-filling: students can either write the answers or work through the
exercise in pairs.

Answers: (1) on in   (6) on
       (2) at   (7) on
       (3) on   (8) at
       (4) on   (9) on
       (5) at   (10) at

16.2 WHOLE AND PARTS   Presentation and practice

> **Language:** This exercise deals with two sets of
> prepositions:
> i) (introduced here) Prepositional phrases
> indicating the position of something *as
> part of a whole* (e.g. a room in relation
> to a house).
> ii) (taught in Unit 1) Prepositions indicating
> where something is in relation to other
> things (e.g. a door in relation to a
> window).

1 Look at the picture and the expressions with the class.
2 Go through the examples. Point out that the phrases given are used for
saying where *parts* are in relation to a *whole* (the study *is part of* the house)
and these should be used in (1) – (9).
3 Point out that in the second part of the exercise, students should use the
prepositions they learnt in Unit 1. Here students are saying where things are
in relation to *other things* (the study is not part of the sitting room, nor part
of the bedrooms).
4 Divide the class into groups to do the exercise.
5 As a round-up, ask different groups what answers they gave.
▶ W16 Ex 2 ◀

16.3 PRECISE LOCATION   Practice

> **Language:** Prepositional phrases similar to those in 16.2,
> but using:
> i) *in* and *on* as well as *at*, to indicate precise
> location
> ii) a variety of nouns indicating parts or
> features (e.g. roof, handle).

1 Go through the examples, and point out that *in*, *on* and *at* are used in the same
way as in 16.1.

2 Students make as many sentences as they can about each picture.
  Possible answers: Restaurant at the top of the tower; hole in the bottom of the
        bucket; initials on the lid, padlock at / on the front of the box; pub at one
        end, café at the other end of the street; café or pub at / on the corner of
        the street; engine at the front, buffet car at the back of the train; roof-rack
        on the roof, flag on the bonnet / front of the car; address at the top / in
        the corner, signature at the bottom of the letter; 'No Vacancies' sign in
        the window of the hotel; craters on / in the surface of the moon.
▶ W16 Ex 3 ◀

16.4 LOCATION QUIZ   Practice

> **Language:** Practice of language introduced so far in
>   this unit.

Either ask the questions round the class, or let students work through them in
groups and go through the answers afterwards.

Answers: (1) (a) It's got a single horn in the middle of its head.
              (b) It's a man at the front and a horse at the back.
         (2) The moon comes between the earth and the sun, so that the earth is in
              the shadow of the moon.
         (3) (a) A white flag with a solid red circle in the middle.
              (b) It has red and white stripes running across it; in the top left-hand
                   corner there is a blue square with white stars.
         (4) (a) At the front of a Mercedes.
              (b) At the top / on the front of a pair of Levi's® jeans.
              (c) On the side of a London underground train or bus, at the entrance
                   to an underground station, on a bus stop (it's the London Transport
                   symbol).
              (d) In the window of a restaurant.
         (5) (a) At the back or side of a theatre.
              (b) At the front and back of a car.
              (c) At the end of a cigarette.
              (d) In the roof of a house.
              (e) At the end of a sentence.
         (6) (a) A sausage between two halves of a roll.
              (b) Coffee with Irish whisky in it, and cream on top.
         (7) Back row: the two castles in each corner, the knights next to them, the
              bishops next to the knights, the king and queen on the middle two
              squares (the king always goes on his own colour). The eight pawns go in
              the second row, in front of the other pieces.

Note: The importance of this quiz, like others in the book, is not in getting the
correct answer, but in the language practised while answering the questions.

16.5   DESCRIBING PLACES AND THINGS   Free practice

> **Language:**   Free practice of language introduced so far in
> this unit.

1   Demonstrate the activity by describing the arrangement of rooms in your own house or flat.
2   Divide the class into groups for the activity.
3   As a round-up, ask individual students to tell you what they said about the topics.

16.6   GEOGRAPHICAL LOCATION

> **Language:**   Geographical expressions using *in*, *on* and *at*.
> Expressions showing relative geographical
> position.
> Vocabulary: geographical features.

Presentation and practice

1   Look at Map 1 with the class and read the examples. Ask questions (e.g. Which river is Khartoum on?) to elicit the following expressions:

on the Equator, Nile on the ...Ocean / Sea on the north coast of... on the northern shore of... at the mouth / source of...	north / south / east / west of... northeast, southwest, etc., of...

2   Ask students to describe the six other places in as many ways as they can:
e.g. Lake Victoria is at the source of the River Nile.
    It is on the Equator.
    It's south of Khartoum.
3   Look at Map 2 and read the examples. Point out these expressions:

on the way to ...(from...) on the A470 on the southern edge of...	35 miles north of... 20 miles southwest of...

4   Ask students to describe the four other places in as many ways as they can:
e.g. Brecon is on the northern edge of the Brecon Beacons.
    It's on the way to Abergavenny from Llandeilo.
    It's about 20 miles northwest of Abergavenny.

Practice

1 Demonstrate the groupwork by thinking of a place yourself and asking students to tell you where it is.
2 Students write down the names of three places.
3 Divide the class into groups for the activity.
▶ W16 Ex 1 ◀

16.7 DESCRIBING COUNTRIES

> **Language:** Free practice of language introduced in this unit.
> Vocabulary: names of continents, seas, etc., and
> geographical features.

Free practice

1 Go through the checklist with the class, and present any new items.
2 Divide the class into groups. Using the list, they build up a description of their own country. If most students come from the same country, go through the description with the whole class afterwards.

Writing

The writing can be done in class or for homework.
▶ W16 Ex 4 ◀

16.8 SKIING IN SCOTLAND   Listening

This is a Listening Comprehension Passage. For procedure, see 'Dealing with listening' in Part 3.

Susan: What are you doing over half-term, Steve? Are you staying in London?
Stephen: No actually I'm going skiing.
Susan: Skiing? You must be joking. What, in the Alps?
Stephen: Oh no, I can't afford that – it's too far anyway. No, I'm going to Scotland.
Susan: Oh yes of course – that's a clever idea. I'd forgotten you could ski in Scotland.

Stephen: Oh yes – it's not quite the same as going to Austria or Switzerland, mind you – I mean it's no good if you want to sit in the sun and get brown all day, but it's OK if you're really going there for the skiing. Anyway, there's supposed to be quite a bit of snow on the hills at the moment, so I decided to go up on the spur of the moment.
Susan: Whereabouts are you going?
Stephen: Aviemore – have you heard of

it? It's a little place in the Eastern Highlands just south of Inverness. It's on the River Spey, it's a really lovely valley. Of course I've been there before but that was in the summer, so it'll be nice to see what it's like in the winter.

Susan: Spey Valley – that's where all the whisky distilleries are, isn't it?

Stephen: Yes they're in the Spey Valley too, but down the river more towards the sea. The ski slopes are across the valley from Aviemore right up in the Cairngorms – they're some of the highest mountains in Scotland.

Susan: Mm, sounds lovely. How are you getting there? You're not driving at this time of the year.

Stephen: Oh no, I'm going by train. I picked up this leaflet at Euston Station a few weeks ago, and I found there's a special five-day return fare by overnight sleeper. You leave London on Thursday night and you get back on Tuesday morning. It couldn't be easier. There's a station at Aviemore on the main line to Inverness, too, so you don't even have to change trains. And I've booked to stay at a bed and breakfast.

Susan: But will the weather be good enough for skiing?

Stephen: Ah well, that's the trouble. It might be too cold up on the slopes. But if it is I'll go walking along the valley, which'd be quite nice too – there are lakes and lots of forests with deer in them and...

Susan: Stop, you're making me envious. It sounds a lot more fun than staying in London.

Stephen: Well, why don't you come?

Answers: (1) They're students or teachers.
(2) (a) She doesn't believe him.
(b) Envious.
(3) It's too far and too expensive.
(4) –
(5) Four.
(6) It might be too cold to ski.
(7) Go walking along the valley or in the lower hills.
(8) He invites Susan to come with him.
(9) (a) False.
(b) True.
(c) False.
(d) True.
(e) True.
(f) False.

Activities (following Unit 16)

HOLIDAY PICTURES

> **Language:** This activity draws on language from:
> Unit 1 (describing towns and amenities)
> Unit 5 (relating past events, giving the
> history of a place)
> Unit 6 (describing a scene)
> Unit 16 (geographical location).

1 Before the lesson, ask students to bring postcards or holiday photos to class.
  Bring some of your own to supplement those that students bring.
2 Divide the class into groups, and give pictures to those that don't have any.
  Demonstrate the activity by showing a picture yourself and talking about it.
3 Students take it in turns to talk about their picture.
4 The writing can be done in class or for homework. Students can prepare for
  it by making brief notes in class about the place they have chosen to write
  about.

COMPOSITION

> **Language:** The compositions draw on language from Units
> 5 and 12.

SITUATIONS

> **Language:** The situations draw on language from Units 4,
> 11, 13, 14, 15 and 16.

For procedure, see Activities following Unit 4.

Unit 17   Similarities and differences

This is the third in the series of units concerned with *comparison* and evaluation. It deals with language for talking about similarities and differences between people and things, and classifying.

The unit falls into three sections, followed by a Reading Comprehension. The first two sections are mainly concerned with saying what you have in common with other people and how you are different from them. The first section practises structures with *so, too, nor / neither* and *not...either*; the second section practises structures with pronouns. The third section is concerned with classifying things according to similarities and differences, and practises linking sentences with *both ... and ... , neither ... nor ... ,* and *whereas*.

17.1 DISCOVERING SIMILARITIES
Presentation and practice of:
so (do I); (I do) too;
nor / neither (do I);
(I don't) either.

17.2 SIMILARITIES AND DIFFERENCES
Practice

17.3 THE SAME THING IN A DIFFERENT WAY
Practice

17.4 BOTH & NEITHER
Presentation and practice of:
both(of); neither(of);
all, none, a few, most (of).

17.5 IDENTIFYING FEATURES
Presentation and practice of:
questions with 'either (of)'.

17.6 TASTES IN COMMON
Free practice

17.7 CLASSIFYING
Presentation and practice of:
both... and...; neither... nor...; whereas.

17.8 SIMILAR BUT DIFFERENT
Free practice
Writing

17.9 COLLOQUIAL AND WRITTEN ARABIC
Reading
Discussion

17.1 DISCOVERING   Presentation and practice
SIMILARITIES

> **Language:** Structures for 'agreeing' with people, in the
> sense of finding things in common with them:
> i) *So* and *nor / neither*, with inversion
> ii) *too* and *not...either*, involving use of
>   pronouns.

1 🔊 Play the examples on the tape. Present the main structures by building up
   this table on the board:

I've been to France.	<u>So</u> have I. I've been there <u>too</u>.
I haven't been to France.	<u>Nor</u> / <u>Neither</u> have I. I have<u>n't</u> been there <u>either</u>.

2 Point out that with *so* and *nor / neither* structures, only the subject and the
   first auxiliary (form of *have, be, do*, or modal) are repeated, and they
   change places:
   e.g. *I have ...   So have I.*
   If necessary, do some basic practice of these forms. ▶ **RP** ◀
3 Point out that with *too* and *not...either* structures, you can choose how
   much of the sentence to repeat, using nouns or pronouns. Write this
   example on the board:

I've been to France.	I've been to France too. I've been there too. I have too.

Make sure students can use pronouns correctly with these structures:
   e.g. I've read that book.   I've read *it* too.
         I've got a book.   I've got *one* too.
         I've lost my keys.   I've lost *mine* too.
   If necessary, do some basic practice of these forms. ▶ **RP** ◀
4 Students give two responses to each of the remarks in the bubbles.
5 Introduce the groupwork by giving a range of remarks using 'breakfast',
   and asking for responses:
   e.g. I enjoy breakfast in the morning.
         I was late for breakfast today.
6 Students do the exercise in groups of three.
   ▶ **W17 Ex 1** ◀

17.2 SIMILARITIES AND DIFFERENCES   Practice

> **Language:** Practice of language introduced in 17.1.
> Structures for 'disagreeing', using short forms.

1 🔲 Play the example on the tape. Build up this table on the board to show how 'disagreement' structures are formed:

I've been to France.	Oh, I haven't.
I haven't been to France.	Oh, I have.

Point out that the auxiliary is repeated, as in *so* and *nor / neither* structures.

2 Demonstrate the exercise by doing (1) with the whole class.

3 Students do the exercise in groups of three. Make sure they add an explanation each time.

17.3 THE SAME THING IN A   Practice
DIFFERENT WAY

> **Language:** Ways of agreeing with people by repeating
> the *sense* of their remark but not necessarily
> the precise *words*.
> Use of *myself.*

1 🔲 Play the example on the tape. Point out the use of *myself* (not reflexive), and its position at the end of the remark.

2 Do the exercise round the class, or let students do it in groups and go through their answers afterwards.

17.4 BOTH & NEITHER   Presentation and practice

> **Language:** Classifying, using 'quantifier' pronouns:
> *both, all, neither, none, some, most, a few.*
>
> *Note:* Students should already be familiar with most of
> these pronouns. You should concentrate on any
> particular difficulties in structure or meaning.

1 Working in pairs, students complete the table by asking each other the questions. Make sure every student completes the columns for himself *and* his partner.

2 Build up this table on the board, to show the range of structures:

| We've <u>both</u>
Both of us have been abroad. | <u>Neither</u> of us has been abroad.
<u>None</u> of us has / have been abroad. |
| We've <u>all</u>
All of us have been abroad. | <u>Most</u>
<u>Some</u> of us have been abroad.
<u>A few</u> |

Point out that *neither* is usually followed by a singular verb, and *none* can be followed by singular or plural.
3 Students form new pairs. Using the table, each student tells his new partner only what he has *in common* with his old partner:
   e.g. Neither of us does much skiing.
       We both know how to drive.
4 Discuss with the whole class what all of them do, none of them do, etc., by going through the items in the table.
▶ W17 Ex 2 ◀

17.5 IDENTIFYING   Presentation and practice
FEATURES

> **Language:** Questions with *either (of)*.
>   Practice of *both* and *neither*.

1 Look at the examples and the pictures with the class. Make sure students realise that *either*, like *neither*, is followed by *of* and a *singular* verb.
2 Demonstrate the game by choosing two houses yourself and asking students to guess which they are. Point out that they can only ask and answer about *two* houses together.
3 Divide the class into pairs to play the game.

17.6 TASTES IN COMMON   Free practice

> **Language:** Free practice of language introduced so far
>   in this unit.
>   Like / dislike verbs (see Unit 11).

This exercise begins with a Listening Model. (See 'Dealing with listening' in Part 3.)

Woman A: I can't stand places like Majorca or the Costa Brava.
Man: No, nor can I.
Woman A: You know, where you have to share the beach with thousands of other people and everyone speaks English.
Woman B: Oh I don't mind that.
Man: Oh I do. I never go to places like that. I like to get right away

from all the tourists, go somewhere that's really quiet and peaceful, like an island or something..
Woman A: Yes, so do I – where no-one speaks English.
Woman B: What's wrong with people speaking English? I like meeting people when I'm on holiday. I like places with a good night life, and plenty of men around, and...well you know, where you can have a good time...

1 Play the tape. Students answer the questions.
   Answer to (1): The first woman and the man.
2 Divide the class into groups to have similar conversations. They should try to use structures for agreeing and disagreeing where appropriate, as well as 'like / dislike' expressions. Allow them to work through the topics at their own speed.
3 As a round-up, ask students in each group who they have most and least in common with, and why.

17.7 CLASSIFYING   Presentation and practice

> **Language:** Linking devices expressing:
>   i) similarity: *both...and...*
>   *neither...nor...*
>   ii) contrast: *...whereas...*

1 Show how *both...and...*, *neither...nor...*, and *...whereas...* are used to link sentences by writing these examples on the board:

YES – YES	Ants are insects. Butterflies are insects. <u>Both</u> ants <u>and</u> butterflies are insects.
NO – NO	Spiders don't live in colonies. Butterflies don't live in colonies. <u>Neither</u> spiders <u>nor</u> butterflies live in colonies.
YES – NO	Ants are insects. Spiders aren't insects. Ants are insects, <u>whereas</u> spiders aren't.

Point out that *neither...nor...* is followed by a *positive* verb form.
2 The exercise can be done as a class discussion, or in groups.
   Note: The sets are designed so that it should be possible to find a reason for *each* member being the odd man out, as in the example.
▶ W17 Ex 3, Ex 4 ◀

17.8 SIMILAR BUT DIFFERENT

Language: Free practice of 'classifying' language.

Free practice

1 Read the passage with the class, and discuss the questions.
2 Divide the class into groups for the discussion.
3 As a round-up, ask a student from each group what conclusions they came to.

Writing

The writing can be done in class or for homework.

17.9 COLLOQUIAL AND WRITTEN ARABIC

Reading

For procedure, see 'Dealing with reading' in Part 3.
Answers: (1) That Arabic is just one language that all Arabs understand, speak and write.
(2) Written Arabic and pan-Arabic mean roughly the same. Classical Arabic and Modern Arabic are two different kinds of written Arabic. Colloquial Arabic is the everyday spoken language, which varies from country to country.
(3) Educated people who speak different languages can use it to communicate with each other.
(4) (a), (c), and (d): pan-Arabic; (b): colloquial Arabic.
(5) Colloquial English is recognised as 'real English'; it is written and taught in schools. This is not true of colloquial Arabic.

Discussion

Either conduct the discussion with the whole class, or let them discuss the questions in groups, and ask them afterwards what conclusions they came to.

Part 4: Teaching notes

Unit 18   Obligation

This is the fourth in the series of units concerned with taking, initiating and commenting on *action*. It deals with language for talking about obligation and lack of obligation.

The unit falls into two sections, followed by a general Free Practice exercise and a Listening Comprehension. The first section is concerned with expressing and talking about obligation and permission, and practises a range of modal verbs and related structures; the second section practises a range of structures for giving complete freedom of choice.

18.1 OBLIGATION AND PERMISSION
Presentation of: must, have to; mustn't, can't, not allowed to; needn't, don't have to; can, allowed to.

18.2 DOCTOR'S ORDERS
Practice

18.3 NOTICES
Practice

18.4 MAKE & LET
Presentation of: make; let; don't make; don't let.
Practice

18.5 PAST OBLIGATIONS
Free practice

18.6 FREEDOM OF CHOICE
Presentation of: you can do (whatever / anything) you like; I don't mind (what) you do; you can do it as (often) as you like.

18.7 IT'S UP TO YOU
Practice

18.8 AWAY FROM HOME
Free practice
Writing

18.9 COAL MINES
Listening
Writing

152

18.1 OBLIGATION AND PERMISSION Presentation

> **Language:** Verbs used to express:
> i) obligation to do things – *must, have to*
> ii) obligation not to do things – *mustn't, can't, aren't allowed to*
> iii) permission to do things – *can, are allowed to*
> iv) permission not to do things – *needn't, don't have to.*

1 Read the two paragraphs and check comprehension by asking a few questions round the class:
  e.g. Who is the speaker in Paragraph A?
       Who is he talking to and what about?
       Who is the speaker in Paragraph B?
       What kind of place is he describing?
2 Students complete the sentences. The purpose of this is to establish the four groups of verbs, and to provide a 'checklist' for the student.
3 Show the difference between the four groups by writing this table on the board:

	Obligation	*Permission*
TO DO THINGS	have to must	can are allowed to
NOT TO DO THINGS	mustn't can't aren't allowed to	needn't don't have to

4 Establish that the verbs are different in the two paragraphs because:
  i) In Paragraph A, the doctor is *giving* orders and permission (he is making the rules himself).
  ii) In Paragraph B, the student is *talking about* obligation and permission (he is not making the rules himself, but merely explaining what they are).
    Note: You should point this distinction out, but do not make too much of it: it is not as important as the basic distinction between the four groups of verbs.
5 Point out that *must, mustn't, can, can't* and *needn't* are modal verbs, and are followed by infinitive without 'to'.
6 If necessary, make any differences between the meaning of particular verbs clear (e.g. mustn't, needn't) by giving further examples of your own.

18.2 DOCTOR'S ORDERS Practice

> **Language:** Practice of language introduced in 18.1.

1 🔊 Play the examples on the tape. Demonstrate the groupwork by making a few of the remarks to individual students and getting other students to comment.
2 Divide the class into groups of four to do the exercise.
▶ W18 Ex 1 ◀

18.3 NOTICES Practice

> **Language:** Further practice of language introduced in 18.1.

Either discuss the notices with the whole class, or let them discuss them in groups and go through the answers afterwards.

Possible answers: (1) At a military base, airport, etc. You aren't allowed to take photographs.
  (2) Outside a historic building, museum, etc. Adults have to pay 20p to get in; children don't have to pay anything.
  (3) In a shop or restaurant window. You can pay with a credit card.
  (4) On the door of a waiting room, office, etc. You don't have to knock before you go in.
  (5) On a ticket. You can only use it on the day you bought it, and no-one else is allowed to use it.
  (6) On an invitation to a party. You needn't wear evening dress, but you can if you like.
  (7) In a library, waiting room, etc. You mustn't make any noise.
  (8) In the window of a souvenir shop for example. You can come in and look at the goods, but you needn't buy anything.
  (9) On a bus. You must have the correct money.
  (10) Above a door in a public building. You aren't allowed to go out that way except in an emergency.
  (11) On an envelope. You don't have to put a stamp on it, because the postage has been paid already.
▶ W18 Ex 4 ◀

18.4   MAKE & LET

> **Language:** Use of *make* and *let* for talking about
> obligation and permission.

Presentation

1 Read the passage, and from the questions establish the connection
  between *make* and *let* and the verbs introduced in 18.1. Build up this
  table on the board:

	Obligation	*Permission*
TO DO THINGS	she has to... they make her...	she is allowed to... they let her...
NOT TO DO THINGS	she isn't allowed to... they don't let her...	she doesn't have to... they don't make her...

2 Point out that *make* and *let* are followed by infinitive without 'to'.
3 Students make sentences with *make* and *let* about the student hostel.
  e.g. They let them have guests in their rooms.
       They make them leave by nine o'clock.

Practice

1 In groups, students discuss the three topics.
2 As a round-up, ask each group to tell you some of the things they said.
▶ W18 Ex 2 ◀

18.5   PAST OBLIGATIONS   Free practice

> **Language:** Past tense forms of verbs for talking about
> obligation and permission.

1 Demonstrate the activity by telling the class about a few of your own
  obligations as a child.
2 Divide the class into groups for the activity.
3 As a round-up, ask one student from each group to tell you about the
  past obligations of the others in his group.

18.6 FREEDOM OF CHOICE   Presentation

> **Language:** Structures for giving complete freedom of choice:
>
> e.g. You can do *whatever you like.*
>   You can do *anything you like.*
>   *I don't mind what* you do.

This is a Listening Presentation. (See 'Dealing with listening' in Part 3.)

When parents make a lot of rules about their children's behaviour, they make trouble – for themselves. I used to spend half my time making sure my rules were obeyed, and the other half answering questions like 'Jack can get up whenever he likes, so why can't I?' or 'Why can't I play with Angela? Jack's mum doesn't mind who *he* plays with' or 'Jack can drink anything he likes. Why can't I drink wine too?' Jack's mum, I decided, was a wise woman. I started saying things like 'Of course, dear. You can drink as much wine as you like' and 'No, I don't mind how late you get up' and 'Yes, dear, you can play with Angela as often as you like.' The results have been marvellous. They don't want to get up late any more, they've decided they don't like wine, and, most important, they've stopped playing with Angela. I've now realised (as Jack's mum realised a long time ago) that they only wanted to do all these nasty things because they weren't allowed to.'

1 Play the tape, and establish who is talking and what in general she is talking about.
2 Students answer the questions.
   Answers: (1) They have to make sure their rules are obeyed, and they have to answer a lot of questions.
   (2) Get up late, play with Angela, drink wine.
   (3) Get up whenever he likes, play with whoever he likes, drink whatever he likes.
   (4) Let her children do whatever they liked.
   (5) Because they were allowed to do the things they wanted, they didn't want to do them any more.
3 Look at sentences (1), (2) and (3), and point out that they are three different structures that mean the same. Elicit the other two forms of each:
   (1) You can get up *any time* you like.
     I don't mind *when* you get up.
   (2) You can play with *whoever* you like.
     You can play with *anyone* you like.
   (3) You can drink *whatever* you like.
     I don't mind *what* you drink.

Get the class to help you build up these three lists of pronouns on the board:

when	whenever	any time
who	whoever	anyone
what	whatever	anything
where	wherever	anywhere
how	however	any way

4 Look at sentences (1), (2) and (3) (the speaker's remarks to her children), and point out that they use *adverbs* and *much / many*. Elicit the other forms of each:
(1) I don't mind *how* much wine you drink.
(2) You can get up *as* late *as* you like.
(3) I don't mind *how* often you play with Angela.

18.7   IT'S UP TO YOU   Practice

> **Language:** Practice of language introduced in 18.6.

1 🔲 Play the example on the tape. Demonstrate the exercise by asking some of the questions yourself and getting answers from the class.
2 Divide the class into groups of four to do the exercise.
3 As a check, ask some of the questions round the class.
▶ W18 Ex 3 ◀

18.8   AWAY FROM HOME

> **Language:** Free practice of language introduced in this unit.

Free practice

1 After introducing the situation, divide the class into pairs. Students in each pair are either *both* A or *both* B. Working together, they prepare what they will say.
2 Students form new pairs, so that each pair has one A and one B. They act out the conversation.
3 As a round-up, ask individual students whether they are satisfied with their landlords/landladies, and vice versa.

Writing

The writing can be done in class or for homework.

18.9 COAL MINES

Listening

This is a Listening Comprehension Passage. For procedure, see 'Dealing with listening' in Part 3.

Interviewer: Were conditions in coal mines in the nineteenth century really as bad as people imagine?

Woman: Well, up to the middle of the nineteenth century at least, miners did work in terrible conditions, even worse than most people imagine probably. And of course it wasn't only the men who had to work in the mines – most mining families were so poor, you see, that the women and children had to go down the mine as well. Now the men had the job of actually digging the coal out, which meant that sometimes they had to crouch doubled up in tiny tunnels and dig away at the coal face. And the women had the job of carrying the coal away, and in the very early days they actually had to carry the coal in sacks on their backs from the coal face all the way up to the surface, up steep ladders. Later on of course they introduced steam engines which they used to pull the coal up, and that made things much easier, and they started using horses to pull the coal along in trucks.

Interviewer: What about the children?

Woman: Well they could only use horses in the widest tunnels, and when the tunnels were too low for the horses then they used the children instead, and these children had to pull trucks of coal weighing ooh sometimes as much as half a ton or a ton along passages that were only a few feet high. And the owners sometimes made the children work for 12 hours or more at a time, and they made them stay down the mine underground all that time, and they didn't let them have breaks for food or anything like that. They just had to work. And this was really the worst part of it, that the mine owners had complete power, you see, they could do more or less whatever they liked. If they wanted to they could reduce the miners' wages or they could make them work longer hours and there wasn't really anything the miners could do about it. And this went on for quite a long time, partly because mining communities were so isolated that people didn't realise that mine owners were making children do these terrible jobs, and later when the public did find out about it people began to raise objections.

Interviewer: So then laws were introduced were they to make it illegal to use children?

Woman: Yes that's right, in the 1840s. But the interesting thing was that even when they did know what was happening people weren't so worried about children having to work in mines, the main thing they objected to was women and young girls working in the mines with men, which they thought was immoral. You see it was very hot down the mines and so the miners wore very few clothes, and people found this very shocking. And that was why after the first law was passed in 1842 women weren't allowed to work in mines but children were still allowed to work underground for several more years. And even after it was made illegal for children to work in mines, it was very difficult to enforce the law, and so probably children continued to work in mines for a long time after that.

Interviewer: Of course at that time I suppose there were no unions or anything like that – the miners had no power at all?

Woman: No, none at all, at first. In fact at the beginning of the nineteenth century there were actually laws called Combination Laws. Now according to these laws, workers weren't allowed to join together in any way to fight for more pay or shorter hours or better working conditions, and if they did then those responsible would be arrested and put into prison. And it was only later that the miners were actually allowed to form unions, and of course this made an enormous difference, because then the owners had to start improving conditions and introduce safety measures – but it all happened very slowly and things didn't really start to improve until very late in the nineteenth century.

Answers: (1) (a) They had to dig the coal out.
        (b) They had to carry the coal up to the surface.
        (c) They had to pull trucks of coal.
        Men: they had to crouch in tiny tunnels and dig away at the coal face.
        Women: they had to carry sacks of coal up steep ladders.
        Children: the trucks were very heavy, the passages were low.
    (2) (a) Work for 12 hours or more at a time, and stay down the mine all day.
        (b) Have breaks for food.
    (3) They could reduce miners' wages, or make them work longer hours.
    (4) Because mining communities were isolated, so people didn't know what was happening.
    (5) They thought it was immoral for women to work in mines with men.
    (6) (a) Workers weren't allowed to join together to fight for better conditions.
        (b) Owners had to improve conditions and introduce safety measures.

Writing

This gives practice in summary writing.
Students should use their answers to the comprehension questions, and add any other information from the tape they think is important. Point out that the paragraph should not be longer than 150 words, so they should not go into too much detail.

The writing can be done immediately after answering the comprehension questions, or can be left for homework.

Activities (following Unit 18)

THE NEW MOTORWAY

> **Language:** This activity draws on language from:
> Unit 2 (making decisions and expressing intention)
> Unit 4 (direction)
> Unit 9 (advantages and disadvantages)
> Unit 14 (advice)
> Unit 16 (geographical location).

1 Look at the map and the notes with the class, and explain what they have to do. Divide the class into four groups for the preparation stage.
2 Students form new groups, so that each new group contains at least one person from each original group. They discuss the problem and try to reach agreement.
3 As a round-up, ask each group what solution they reached, if any.

COMPOSITION

> **Language:** The compositions are an extension of the previous activity, and draw on the same language areas.

The writing can be done in class or for homework.

Unit 19   Prediction

This is the first of a series of units concerned with *explanation* and speculation about the past, present and future. It deals with language for predicting future actions, events and situations, and for estimating the probability of future events.

The unit falls into two sections, followed by a general Free Practice exercise and a Reading Comprehension. The first section is especially concerned with degree of probability in making predictions, and practises a range of prediction structures, including the use of adverbs and modals. The second section is concerned with making predictions about the immediate future, using *going to*, and about specific times in the future, using *will be doing* and *will have done*.

19.1 DEGREES OF PROBABILITY
Presentation of:
certainly, definitely, probably; may, might, could; I should think, I expect, I doubt if.
Practice

19.2 REASSURING PREDICTIONS
Practice

19.3 IF & UNLESS
Practice

19.4 WHAT WILL IT BE LIKE?
Free practice
Writing

19.5 GOING TO
Presentation of: 'going to' versus 'will'.
Practice

19.6 WILL BE DOING & WILL HAVE DONE
Presentation and practice of:
'will be doing' and 'will have done'.
Practice

19.7 FUTURE DEVELOPMENTS
Free practice
Writing

19.8 POSTCRIPT TO THE FUTURE
Reading
Writing

19.1 DEGREES OF PROBABILITY

> **Language:** Structures for expressing probability in
> predictions:
> i)   adverbs and modals: *certainly / definitely/*
>   *probably; may / might / could*
> ii) *I should think / I expect / I doubt if*
> iii) questions with *do you think?*

Presentation

This is a Listening Presentation. (See 'Dealing with listening' in Part 3.)

A: No luck then, John?

B: Afraid not sir. Not yet, anyhow.
We're still checking on stolen cars.

A: Mm.

B: Where do you think he'll head for,
sir?

A: Well, he definitely won't try to
leave the country yet. He may try
to get a passport, and he'll certainly
need clothes and money. He'll
probably get in touch with Cornfield
for those, so I expect he'll make for
Birmingham.

B: Right. I'll put some men on the
house.

A: Yes, do that. Mind you, I doubt if
he'll show up there in person.
Hammond's no fool, you know. I
should think he'll probably telephone.

B: What about his wife?

A: Mm. I shouldn't think he'll go
anywhere near her – though he
might get her to join him after he's
left the country. And when he does
leave, he probably won't use a
major airport, either. So you'd
better alert the coastguard, and
keep an eye on the private airfields.

B: Right, sir. I'd better get his description circulated.

A: Yes. He may change his appearance,
of course, but I don't expect he'll
be able to do much about the tat-
toos... And John – be careful. He
could be armed. And if I know
Hammond, he certainly won't give
himself up without a fight.

1 Play the tape. Students answer (1) and (2), which check general comprehension.
Answers: (1) A man has just escaped from prison, and the police are organising
a search for him.
(2) Hammond is the escaped prisoner; Cornfield is his contact, or an
accomplice.
If you like, ask more questions of your own at this point:
e.g. What do we know about Hammond?
Tell me some of the things he might do.
What are the police going to do?

2 Play the tape again. Students answer (3) by noting down each prediction
in the correct space in the table, so that it means the same as what they
hear. The purpose of this is to check comprehension of prediction
structures, and to provide a basis for the pairwork stage.

3 Go through the answers.
   Answers:

He will certainly do this:	need clothes and money.
He will probably do this:	get in touch with Cornfield; make for Birmingham; telephone.
Perhaps he will do this:	try to get a passport; get his wife to join him abroad; change his appearance.
He probably won't do this:	go to the house himself; go near his wife; use a major airport; disguise his tattoos.
He certainly won't do this:	try to leave the country yet; give himself up without a fight.

4 Look at (4). Ask students to give some of the other prediction expressions
   the Chief uses. From their answers, build up these tables on the board,
   showing the range of expressions:

Adverbs and
Modals:

	He	will certainly / definitely will probably may / might / could probably won't certainly / definitely won't	go there.

Think / expect /
doubt:

I should think I expect	he'll go there.	= he'll probably go there

I shouldn't think I don't expect I doubt if	he'll go there.	= he probably won't go there

▶ W19 Ex 1 ◀ (Students can write the expressions in the table.)
5 Point out that:
   i)   The adverbs in the table come after *will* but before *won't*.
   ii)   *May, might,* and *could* all mean the same (=perhaps).
   iii) *Doubt* has a negative meaning, so *I doubt if he will* means 'he probably
         won't'.
   iv)   We say 'I *don't* expect he *will*', not 'I expect he won't'.

Practice

1 Point out the way questions are formed with '*do you think?*'
2 Students ask and answer questions in pairs. They should try to use the
   whole range of structures in their replies.
   ▶ W19 Ex 1 ◀

19.2 REASSURING PREDICTIONS   Practice

> **Language:** Practice of language introduced in 19.1,
> concentrating on:
> i)   predictions using *think / expect / doubt*
> ii) predictions using *modals*.

1 🔊 Play the examples on the tape. Ask students to suggest other things Don might be wondering about, and other predictions his friends might make.
2 If necessary, demonstrate the groupwork by doing (1) with the whole class, being the 'worried' person yourself.
3 Students do the exercise in groups, taking it in turns to be the 'worried' person.
4 As a round-up, ask individual students to tell you what they were worried about, and what predictions their friends made.

19.3 IF & UNLESS   Practice

> **Language:** Practice of language introduced in 19.1.
> Use of *if* and *unless* + Past Simple for making
> conditional predictions.

1 Go through the examples. Point out that:
   i)   *If* and *unless* are followed by the Present Simple tense, although they refer to the future (see Unit 14).
   ii) *Unless* = if...not...
2 Either do the exercise as a class discussion, introducing other topics of your own, or let students discuss the topics in groups and ask them afterwards what conclusions they came to.
   ▶ W19 Ex 2 ◀

19.4 WHAT WILL IT BE LIKE?

> **Language:** Free practice of language introduced in the
> unit so far.
> Practice of Future tense of *have to* and *be
> able to*(see Unit 18).

Free practice

1 Imagine you are Cordelia, and ask students to tell you what to expect. Ask them a few specific questions in addition to the three general ones given:

e.g. Will I have to have it vaccinated?
      Will I be able to take it abroad?
2 Divide the class into pairs. Give a few minutes for students to choose an
   activity and think of questions to ask. Make sure each student in a pair
   chooses a different activity.
3 Students take it in turns to ask each other about their activity.

Writing

The writing can be done in class or for homework.

19.5 GOING TO

Language: Use of *going to* in making predictions.

Presentation

Read the examples, and elicit from the class when *going to* is used for making
predictions. Establish that it is used when there are already signs that something
will happen, it is already 'on the way', e.g. in (1b) the speaker can already see
the rain clouds approaching, in (2b) the woman is already pregnant.

Practice

1 Ask for suggestions round the class. The purpose of this section is to give
   more examples of predictions with *going to* and show students how it is
   used. There may be several possible answers in each case:
   e.g. (1) He can smell them frying, he's just seen someone coming in with some
           sausages, he's seen a plate of sausages in the fridge, etc.
2 Pictures – either ask for predictions round the class, or let students
   discuss them in groups and go through the answers afterwards. They
   should make more than one prediction about each picture.
   Possible answers: (1) The bridge is going to collapse, the train's going to crash
                   into the water, and it's probably going to hit the boat.
               (2) The locusts are going to land in the field, they're going to eat all
                   the corn, the harvest is going to be ruined.
               (3) The man's going to fall asleep, he's going to drop the cigarette, it's
                   going to set light to the bed.

19.6 WILL BE DOING & WILL HAVE DONE

> **Language:** Future tense structures – *will do, will be doing, will have done.*
> Use of *by* in future time expressions.

Presentation and practice

1 Look at the situation and the table. Ask students to tell you what *will happen* on the dates shown in the table:
   e.g. In 1988 he will invent a 'speed of light' spaceship.
      In 1990 he will go to Venus.

2 Write this table on the board to show the three Future tense structures:

In 1995, he <u>will</u>	marry a Venusian. <u>be</u> living on Venus. <u>have left</u> Earth.

3 Establish that:
   i)   *Will do* is used for talking about single events in the future.
   ii) *Will be doing* is used for talking about activities which will be *in progress* at a specific time in the future. Give examples to show the connection between *will be doing* and the Present Continuous:
      e.g. At the moment I *am* living in London.
          This time next year I *will be* living in London.
   iii) *Will have done* is used for talking about events that will be *completed* by a specific time in the future.
      Give examples to show the connection between *will have done* and the Present Perfect:
      e.g. He *has* left university (now).
          By the end of this year he *will have* left university.

4 Point out that *by* means 'at or before' a particular time, and is especially used with *will have done.*

5 Look at the example, and ask students to make sentences about the other dates:
   e.g. In 1991 he will be living on Venus.
      By 1991 he will have left Earth.
      In 1997 he will be living on Venus.
      By 1997 he will have married a Venusian.

Practice

1 Demonstrate the groupwork by telling the class what you think you will be doing this time next week and what you will have done by then.
2 Divide the class into groups to discuss the questions.
3 As a round-up, ask each group to tell you some of the answers they gave.
▶ W19 Ex 3 ◀

19.7 FUTURE DEVELOPMENTS

> **Language:** Free practice of language introduced in this
> unit.

Free practice

1 Introduce the groupwork by discussing the first picture with the whole class.
2 Divide the class into groups for the activity.
3 As a round-up, ask each group what conclusions they came to.

Writing

The writing can be done in class or for homework.
▶ W19 Ex 4 ◀

19.8 POSTSCRIPT TO THE FUTURE

Reading

For procedure, see 'Dealing with reading' in Part 3.
Answers: (1) A book of predictions about what life may be like in 50 years' time,
of a 'popular scientific' kind.
(2) (b)
(3) The face of life will be very different because of scientific and technologi-
cal developments, but people will keep the same values and still be
able to live as they like.
(4) (a) Plenty available, new sources (nuclear fusion, the sea).
(b) More leisure time, more automation, more labour-saving devices,
longer education.
(c) Longer life.
(5) Possible answers: most people will have cars and radios; people will be
able to watch world events on screens in their homes; man will reach the
moon, and will see the other side of it; man will learn how to split the
atom and cause terrible explosions; it will be quite normal to fly across
the Atlantic.
(6) (a) Technology was less advanced.
(b) The general pattern of life was similar.
(7) (a) The human mind and human values will remain the same.
(b) Life will change on the surface, but the basic pattern of life will stay
the same.
(8), (9) (These are discussion questions.)

Writing

This section gives practice in summary writing. As this is the first time in the course that students have to write a summary from a reading passage, it may be useful to give the following general guidelines:
- the purpose of summarising the passage is to give the *main* information in a shortened form;
- the summary should convey the same 'message' as the original; but because it is shorter it will also be more *general* and details will be omitted;
- a good technique of summary writing is to take brief notes from the passage, and then to write the summary from the notes (*not* to try to write the summary directly from the passage).

The writing can be done directly after answering the questions, or left for homework.

Unit 20   Objects

This is the fourth in the series of units concerned with physical *description* of places, things and people. It deals with language used for describing, classifying and defining objects.

The unit falls into two sections, followed by a Listening Comprehension. The first section is concerned with describing different types of objects and identifying them by their features; the second section is concerned with classifying objects according to their purpose, and giving definitions of objects.

The unit practises formation of compound nouns, the use of *with* for describing features, subject and object relative clauses, and the structure *use... for + -ing*.

20.1   IDENTIFYING TYPES AND FEATURES

Presentation and practice

> **Language:** Compound noun phrases for identifying
> particular types of objects:
> i)   Adjective + Noun
> ii) Noun + Noun.
> Use of *the one(s) with* ... and *the one(s) that...*
> for identifying features of objects.
>
> *Note:* The main point of this exercise is to show what
> structures are used to identify objects rather than to teach
> specific vocabulary.

1 Look at the example, and ask students to name the other objects. Build
   up a list on the board.
   Answers: (1) Alarm / grandfather clock.
   (2) Riding / football boots.
   (3) Electric / gas fire.
   (4) Pen (or pocket) / bread (or carving) knife.
   (5) Feeding (or baby's) / wine bottle.
2 Point out that some of these phrases are formed from Adjective + Noun,
   some are formed from Noun + Noun.
3 Ask students to identify the features in the list under the pictures, and
   explain any new words.
4 Point out the use of *the one* (plural *the ones*, e.g. the riding boots are the
   ones ...) and *with*. Make sure students understand the difference between:
   Describing an object: The bread knife *has* (got) a serrated edge.
   Identifying an object: The bread knife *is the one with* a serrated edge.
5 Students ask and answer questions in pairs.

20.2   THE LOST PROPERTY OFFICE   Practice

> **Language:** Practice of language introduced in 20.1.
> Vocabulary: features of coats and bags.

This exercise begins with a Listening Model. (See 'Dealing with listening' in
Part 3.)

Assistant: Good morning, sir.
Man: Good morning. I wonder if you
can help. I've lost my coat.
Assistant: Where did you lose it, sir?
Man: Er...I left it on the...um...under-
ground yesterday morning.
Assistant: Can you describe it?
Man: Well, it's a full-length brown

overcoat with a check pattern on it.
It's got a wide belt, and one of
those thick furry collars that keep
your ears warm. It's a very nice
coat, actually.
Assistant: Hmm. I'm afraid we haven't
got anything like that, sir. Sorry.
Man: Well, to tell you the truth, I lost

another coat last week. On the bus. It's a three-quarter length coat – it's grey, with big black buttons and a black belt.
Assistant: Sorry, sir. Nothing like that.
Man: Hmm. And then only this morn-ing I left my white raincoat in a park. It's got a silk lining...
Assistant: Look, sir. I'm a busy woman. If you really need a coat so badly, there's a very good second-hand clothes shop just round the corner...

1. Students complete the table.
2. Go through the answers.
   Teach any new words for types of coat (overcoat, raincoat, fur coat), lengths (full-length, three-quarter-length, half-length) and features (e.g. belt, collar, buttons, lining).
3. Ask students to describe the three coats in the pictures.
   Note: This involves *extended description* of objects. So as well as using *compound nouns* and *with*, students should add sentences beginning with *It's got...*, as in the Listening Model.
4. Teach any new words for types of bag (shoulder bag, suitcase, handbag), features (e.g. strap, handle, zip, pockets) and patterns (e.g. stripe, check).
5. Ask students to describe the three bags.
6. Divide the class into pairs. They improvise a conversation like the one in the Listening Model.

20.3 WHAT DO THEY DO? RELATIVE CLAUSES

> **Language:** Defining Relative Clauses:
> i) Subject Relative Clauses, for describing what things do
> ii) Object Relative Clauses, for describing what you can do with things.

Presentation and practice

1. Read the text.
   Check general comprehension by asking questions round the class, e.g. What is an Ideal Home Exhibition?
   Why did the writer go there?
   What was the problem?
   Teach any new vocabulary (e.g. done (=ready), microwave, plug into, peel).
2. Students write two lists of relative clauses. The point of this is to establish the difference between *subject* relative clauses (first list) and *object* relative clauses (second list).
3. If necessary, show the difference between the two types by writing these sentences on the board:

This cooker lights itself. (Cooker:Subject)

This is a cooker that / which lights itself.

SUBJECT RELATIVE CLAUSE

You can light this cooker with a match. (Cooker: Object)

This is a cooker (that) / (which) you can light with a match.

OBJECT RELATIVE CLAUSE

Point out that, in Object Relative Clauses:
i)   the object pronoun ('it') is omitted.
ii) the relative pronoun (*which* or *that*) can be omitted.
4 Students make sentences about the other things in the exhibition, using the ideas given.

Practice

1 Divide the class into groups to imagine things in a future Ideal Home Exhibition.
2 Ask each group what things they thought of.
▶ W20 Ex 2 ◀

20.4 ONEUPMANSHIP   Practice

> **Language:** Practice of:
> i)   *with* + noun
> ii)   subject and object relative clauses
> iii) pronoun *one*.

1 🔊 Play the example on the tape. Demonstrate the exercise by asking for responses to (1) from the whole class. Point out that Student B has to invent a better type of object each time.
2 Students have conversations in pairs.
3 As a round-up, ask individual students to tell you what objects they thought of.
▶ W20 Ex 1 ◀

20.5 WEDDING PRESENTS

> **Language:**   Free practice of language introduced so far in the unit.

Free practice

1 Demonstrate the groupwork by thinking of a wedding present yourself and describing to the class exactly what you want.
2 Give a few minutes for students to think of three presents they want, making notes if they like.
3 Divide the class into groups of four for the activity. Students take it in turns to be Student A.
4 As a possible round-up stage, ask each group what presents they are giving.

Writing

The writing can be done in class or for homework.

20.6 OBJECTS WITH A PURPOSE   Presentation and practice

> **Language:** Classifying objects by their purpose, using three types of compound noun phrase:
> List A: Adjective (-*ing*) + Noun
> List B: Noun + Noun (-*er*)
> List C: Noun + Noun.
> Practice of subject and object relative clauses.
>
> *Note:* In the noun phrases in List A, the *adjective* indicates the purpose of the object (e.g. a sewing machine = a machine for sewing).
> In those in List B, the *whole phrase* indicates the purpose of the object (e.g. a dishwasher = a machine for washing dishes).
> In those in List C, the *first noun* indicates the purpose of the object (e.g. nail varnish = varnish for your nails).

1 Look at the three lists with the class, and discuss the differences between them. Establish the three basic forms and how they indicate the purpose of the objects.
2 Students explain what each object is for, using relative clauses, as in the example. They should try to give *precise* explanations:
e.g. 'pills that help you get to sleep' is a better explanation than simply 'pills you use for sleeping'.
3 Look at the six items (brush, opener, glasses, paper, basket, cards). Ask students to suggest as many kinds as they can. Help them by asking questions:
e.g. What do you use for cleaning your teeth?
If you like, write new words on the board in three lists.
(*Note:* Kinds of opener will belong to List B, all the other objects to Lists A and C.)

Possible answers:

brush	*opener*	*glasses*	*paper*	*basket*	*cards*
shaving	bottle	reading	writing	bread	playing
tooth	can / tin	sun	wrapping	waste paper	visiting
hair		opera	toilet	shopping	post
paint		wine	news	picnic	birthday
			note		credit

▶ W20 Ex 3 ◀ (Students can write these words in the table.)

20.7 ASKING FOR THINGS YOU NEED   Practice

> **Language:** Saying what the purpose of an object is, with
> *for* + *-ing* and the verb *use*.

1 Go through the examples and point out the use of *for* + *-ing* and the
verb *use* (active and passive). Establish what the person is asking for.
Answers: (1) Correcting fluid.
(2) A corkscrew.
(3) A mousetrap.

2 Either get students to ask questions round the class, or let students work
in pairs or groups and go through the answers afterwards.
Note: The main point of this exercise is not the actual names of the
objects, but how to describe them if you *don't* know what they're called.
The names of the objects are:

(1) Hairdrier.
(2) Shoe polish / Shoe brush.
(3) Lemon squeezer.

(4) Pencil sharpener.
(5) Stain remover.
(6) Coffee grinder.
(7) Vacuum (or thermos) flask.

▶ W20 Ex 3 ◀

20.8 DEFINITIONS QUIZ   Free practice

> **Language:** Free practice of language introduced in this
> unit.

1 If necessary, demonstrate the groupwork by asking five questions yourself.
2 Give time for students to write down five words (secretly!) and to think
about how to define them. Point out that the words may be noun phrases
or single nouns (e.g. refrigerator).
3 Divide the class into groups. Students take it in turns to ask questions.
4 As a possible extension to the exercise, ask each group to choose their
five 'best' definitions, and ask them to the rest of the class.
▶ W20 Ex 4 ◀

20.9   A DIFFICULT CHOICE

Listening 📼

This is a Listening Comprehension Passage. For procedure, see 'Dealing with listening' in Part 3.

It was my little niece's birthday last week, and I found myself faced with the problem of thinking of something to give her. I have to confess that I am the kind of uncle who has no idea what sort of things seven-year-old girls play with, so I took the easy way out and actually asked her what she would like as a present. The answer was a very simple one – a doll. But when I went off to the biggest toy shop in town, I soon found that it wasn't so simple after all.

I wonder if *you* have realised how many different kinds of dolls there are. I was shown big dolls and little dolls, black ones and white ones. The majority were plastic dolls, but there were also wooden dolls and cloth dolls that you could make yourself. And there were baby dolls and teenage dolls, as well as boy dolls and girl dolls. I saw dolls with blonde hair and with dark hair, and some cheaper ones with no hair at all. Some had no clothes, others had just one set of clothes, and there were some with a vast wardrobe of clothes to wear on every conceivable occasion. And on top of all that, I discovered that there are dolls which do different things and which you can do different things with: dolls that close their eyes when you lay them in their beds, dolls whose hairstyle you can change, dolls that say 'Mama' (and all sorts of other astonishing things) when you pick them up, and dolls that you feed with a bottle and which then wet the bed.

I spent a fascinating and bewildering half-hour making my choice, and eventually walked out of the shop carrying under my arm the most expensive one of all. It must be the best-dressed, the most talkative, the thirstiest – and as a result the most troublesome – doll in town.

Answers: (1) (a) His niece.
　　　　　　　(b) It was her birthday.
　　　　　(2) (d)
　　　　　(3) (a) Plastic, wooden, cloth.
　　　　　　　(b) Plastic.
　　　　　(4) Baby dolls, teenage dolls.
　　　　　(5) He saw dolls with blond hair and with dark hair, and some with no hair at all.
　　　　　(6) Some had no clothes, some had one set of clothes, some had a vast wardrobe of clothes.
　　　　　(7) See Listening Text.
　　　　　(8) Half an hour.
　　　　　(9) (a)

Writing

Students should listen to the tape again, and make notes. The writing can be done immediately, or left for homework.
▶ W20 Ex 5 ◀

Activities (following Unit 20)

CALL MY BLUFF

> **Language:** This activity draws on language from Unit 20.

This is an adaptation of a TV panel game of the same name. It begins with a Listening Model. You will need to give each group one of the definitions; before the lesson, photocopy them and cut them up.

Voice 1: Well, hunk is a verb. And it means to carry something, particularly something that's heavy and difficult to move. So you can say something like 'When I saw the men they were hunking the piano down the stairs.'

Voice 2: Actually, hunk is the cry made by an elephant, especially when it's angry, or it's trying to contact other elephants. The word sounds like the noise they make –

'hunk, hunk'. So you can say, for example, 'The elephants are hunking a lot tonight'.

Voice 3: No, no, the truth is, hunk is a noun. And it means a piece of something, a big thick piece. So if you cut a thin piece of bread, that's not a hunk. When you tear off a thick piece of bread, that's a hunk. Today, for example, I had a big hunk of bread and cheese for my lunch.

1 Explain briefly how the game works. Then write the word 'hunk' on the board, and play the Listening Model. Ask the class to vote on which they think is the correct definition, and then tell them the correct answer ('hunk' = a thick piece of something).

2 Divide the class into groups of three. Give each group one piece of paper with a definition on it. Each group secretly works out two other possible definitions of their word; they should prepare to define the word and add an example of usage, as in the Listening Model.

3 Play the game by asking one group to come to the front of the class, and write their word on the board. In turn, they give the three definitions, *without using notes*. When they have finished, summarise the three definitions yourself, and ask the class to vote on which is the correct definition.

4 Repeat the procedure with the other groups.

Words for Call My Bluff

Any word that the students don't know is suitable for 'Call My Bluff'. The best word, however, is one whose definition a student could easily have made up as a 'bluff'. The list below gives some suggestions, as they could be given to students on pieces of paper:

Galoshes: they're like rubber boots that you can wear over your shoes in the rain.

Quod: a slang word meaning 'prison'.

Scrunch: like 'crunch', the noise you make when you walk on snow or on loose earth or stones.

Haughty: very proud, having a very high opinion of yourself.

Doily: this is a small round piece of cloth which is placed under dishes, vases, etc. to protect the table or shelf they're standing on.

Weal: long, red mark on the skin made by a whip or a stick.

Dank: damp and nasty, as in a wet, dark cave or underground prison.

Dirge: a slow, sad song – is sung at funerals, etc.

Toady: a person who is nice to you because he wants to get something from you. A flatterer. Also verb, to flatter.

Scut: a short tail, like a rabbit's or a deer's.

Barmy: a slang word meaning wrong in the head, crazy, stupid.

Botch: to do something badly, to spoil something by poor and clumsy work.

(All words in *Oxford Advanced Learner's Dictionary of Current English.*)

COMPOSITION

Language: The compositions draw on language from Units 8, 10 and 19.

The writing can be done in class or for homework.

SITUATIONS

Language: The situations draw on language from Units 7, 11, 12, 17, 18, 19 and 20.

For procedure, see Activities following Unit 4.

Unit 21   Degree

This is the fourth in the series of units concerned with *comparison* and evaluation. It deals with various aspects of degree.

The unit falls into two sections, followed by a Reading Comprehension. The first section is concerned with talking about excess and inadequacy, and practises structures with *too* and *not enough*; the second section is concerned with expressing degree by talking about results, and practises structures with *so* and *such*.

21.1 TOO & ENOUGH
Presentation of: 'too' and 'not enough' with adjectives and nouns.

21.2 THE WRONG MAN FOR THE JOB
Practice

21.3 LINKING SENTENCES
Presentation and practice of:
too and not enough (+ for me) + to + infinitive.

21.4 USELESS POSSESSIONS
Practice

21.5 FAULTS AND REMEDIES
Free practice
Writing

21.6 SO & SUCH
Presentation of:
so...that..., such...that...

21.7 READING GAME: SO & SUCH
Practice

21.8 HOLIDAYS
Practice
Free practice

21.9 THE UGLY NATURE OF EARTH'S TWIN SISTER
Reading
Writing

21.1 TOO & ENOUGH   Presentation

> **Language:** *Too much / many* + Noun and *not enough*
> + Noun
> *Too* + Adjective and *not* + Adjective +
> *enough*.

1 Read the letter, and check comprehension by asking questions round the
class:
e.g. How many meals do the prisoners have each day?
  Do you think it's summer or winter?
  How do you think the last sentence might continue?
Explain any new vocabulary (e.g. cell, mailbag, watery).
2 Look at the examples, and establish that:
  i) *Too* is used on its own before adjectives, with *much / many* before
    nouns.
  ii) *Enough* comes after adjectives, but before nouns (or adjective +
    noun).
3 Students make sentences with *too* and *not enough* based on the letter, as
in the examples.
▶ W21 Ex 1 ◀

21.2 THE WRONG MAN FOR THE JOB   Practice

> **Language:** Practice of *not enough* with adjectives and
> nouns, followed by *to* + infinitive.
> Vocabulary: adjectives and nouns describing
> characteristics of people.

1 Go through the list and explain any new words.
2 Ask students to give the noun forms.

  Answers: patience, ambition, strength, tact, imagination, courage, intelligence,
    dedication.

3 🔊 Read the example or play it on the tape. Go through the different
professions, and discuss with the class what qualities are most important
for each.
4 Divide the class into groups of three to do the exercise. They should
continue by thinking of other jobs.

21.3 LINKING SENTENCES   Presentation and practice

> **Language:** *Too* and *not enough* with:
> i)   'subject' infinitive structures, e.g. I'm
>   *too* busy *to* see you
> ii) 'object' infinitive structures, e.g. The tea
>   is *too* hot *to* drink
> iii) 'object' infinitive structures with *for*, e.g.
>   The tea is *too* hot *for* grandmother *to*
>   drink.

1 Go through the examples and point out that:
  i)   The first example is about the subject of the sentence:
        He can't climb the stairs.
     The second and third examples are about the object of the sentence:
        You couldn't read *that book*.
        The piano wouldn't go through *the doorway*.
  ii) With both types of structure, *too* and *not enough* are followed by *to
     + infinitive*:
     e.g. He's too weak *to climb* the stairs.
           That book is too long *to read*. (not 'to be read')
  iii) With 'object' infinitive structures, there is no 'it':
     e.g. That book is too long *to read*. (not 'to read it')
2 If necessary, do some basic practice of each of the three types of structure.
  ▶ RP ◀
3 The exercise can be done orally round the class or in writing.
  ▶ W21 Ex 2 ◀

21.4 USELESS POSSESSIONS   Practice

> **Language:** Practice of language introduced in 21.3.
> Use of *much too...* and *not nearly...enough*.

1 🔲 Go through the situation, and play the example on the tape. Ask
  students to suggest replies to the other questions:
  e.g. They're much too thick to wear for driving.
      They aren't nearly warm enough to wear in the winter.
2 Divide the class into groups for the exercise. They take it in turns to be
  the 'owner' of the objects.
3 As a round-up, ask different groups to tell you what they decided not to
  do with each object, and why.

21.5 FAULTS AND REMEDIES

> **Language:** Free practice of language introduced so far in this unit.
> *Should* and *ought to* + Passive Infinitive.
>
> *Note:* Structures with *should* and *shouldn't* are practised more fully in Unit 23.

Free practice

This exercise begins with a Listening Model. (See 'Dealing with listening' in Part 3.)

Woman: The trouble with education in Britain, I think, lies with the teachers. I don't think teachers get nearly enough training in actually how to teach rather than the subject. I think they're too serious, too academic, they're not imaginative enough. And that means that there's not enough excitement in the classroom for children to get interested in the subject.

Man: Yes, I agree. I think there's too much theoretical teaching given and not enough practical education, with the result that pupils are far too busy studying for exams to have time to learn about life itself and how to, how to live in the world.

Woman: Mm. I think all teachers should be at least 25 before they start teaching. I think they should be forced to live in the outside world, rather than go from the classroom to the university and back to the classroom again.

1 Play the tape. Students answer the questions.
2 Show how the Active and Passive Infinitive are formed by writing this table on the board:

> ACTIVE: They $\frac{\text{should}}{\text{ought to}}$ <u>train</u> teachers better.

> PASSIVE: Teachers $\frac{\text{should}}{\text{ought to}}$ <u>be trained</u> better.

3 Either choose one topic for all the groups, or assign a different topic to each group, or let them choose their own.
4 Students discuss their topic(s) in groups.
5 As a round-up, ask each group what conclusions they came to.

Writing

The writing can be done in class or for homework.

21.6   SO & SUCH   Presentation

> **Language:** Structures with *so...that...* and *such (a)... that...*

1 Read the examples with the class, and establish that:
   i) *So* is used before an isolated adjective or adverb:
       e.g. so tired, so fast.
   ii) *Such* is used before a *noun* or *adjective + noun*:
       e.g. such a mess, such a lovely day.
   iii) *So* is used before *much, many, little, few*, even if they are followed
       by nouns:
       e.g. so much, so much money, so little time, so few people.
2 Point out that *such* doesn't affect how articles are used:
   e.g. *a* nice day – such *a* nice day
       nice weather – such nice weather
3 Students add *so* or *such (a)* to the words and phrases. The purpose of
   this is to check that they understand the basic rules for *so* and *such*. If
   you like, ask students to expand the phrases into complete sentences,
   using *that*:
   e.g. Mary is *so* lovely *that* I can't stop looking at her.

21.7   READING GAME: SO & SUCH   Practice

> **Language:** Joining sentences using *so...that...* and *such...*
>   *that.*

1 Divide the class into groups of three, and give each student a letter: A, B
   or C.
2 Demonstrate the game by reading out Student A's sentence (1), changing
   it to: 'He worked so hard for his exams...'. Ask all Students B and C to
   look in their own section for a suitable continuation, and read it out,
   beginning with *that*: '...that he almost had a nervous breakdown'. Do the
   same thing again, reading out Student B's and C's sentence (1).
3 Give a few minutes for students to read through their own section
   silently. Answer any vocabulary questions.
4 Students play the game.
5 When most groups have finished, go through the answers with the class.
   Answers: (A) (1) (As in example.)
             (2) She looks so different wearing a wig that I didn't recognise her
                 at first.
             (3) He treated his wife so badly that in the end she poisoned him.
             (4) It was such a boring film that we left half way through.
             (5) I've got so few possessions that I only need one suitcase when I
                 move.
          (B) (1) The sea was so cold while we were there that we didn't go
                 bathing once.

     (2) I've heard such terrible stories about that restaurant that I'm not going to eat there again.

     (3) Such a lot of (or so many) people complained about the city bus services that they appointed a new transport manager.

     (4) Some parts of New York are so dangerous that taxi drivers refuse to take you there.

     (5) He spoke so fast that nobody understood him.

(C) (1) There was such a long queue at the bus stop that I decided to walk instead.

     (2) I'd drunk such a lot of (or so much) coffee that my hands were shaking.

     (3) The problem was so simple that even a child could have solved it.

     (4) I have such enormous feet that I have to have my shoes made specially.

     (5) He drank such a lot of (or so much) whisky that he collapsed on the floor.

▶ W21 Ex 3 ◀

21.8 HOLIDAYS

> **Language:** Practice of language introduced in 21.6.
> Free practice of language introduced in the
> whole unit.

Practice

1 ▭ Play the example on the tape. Look at the prompts with the class and establish what the questions should be:
e.g. Was the food good? *or* Did you have good food?
2 Demonstrate the pairwork by asking the first question yourself and getting responses from the class:
e.g. Yes, it was. In fact, we had such good food that I put on two kilos.
3 Students ask and answer about the other topics in pairs.

Free practice

1 Demonstrate the groupwork by telling the class about a holiday you had recently. Include *too, enough, so* and *such* expressions in your description.
2 Divide the class into groups for the activity.
3 As a possible round-up, ask individual students to tell you about their holidays.
▶ W21 Ex 4 ◀

21.9 THE UGLY NATURE OF EARTH'S TWIN SISTER

Reading

For procedure, see 'Dealing with reading' in Part 3.

Answers:
(1) (a) Although it's close to the Sun, it's covered in cloud which reflects the sunlight.
  (b) The day is so long that the heat has time to build up.
(2) The air is so thick that you would have to 'swim', and the slightest breeze would knock you down.
(3) (a) Because it's close to the Sun.
  (b) Because it's covered in dense clouds that absorb the Sun's light.
  (c) In the light coming from lightning flashes.
(4) It revolves clockwise, so the Sun rises in the west.
(5) (a) Hold or keep.
  (b) Thick.
  (c) Arm movement used for swimming.
  (d) Take in.
  (e) Half-darkness.
  (f) Unfriendly, not welcoming.
(6) Venus is mysterious, we don't know much about it because it's covered in cloud, it's traditionally compared to a woman (or goddess).
(7) (This is a discussion question.)

Writing

This section gives practice in summary writing.

The writing can be done immediately after answering the comprehension questions, or can be left for homework.

Unit 22   Setting a scene

This is the third in the series of units concerned with *narration* of past events. It incorporates language covered in Units 5 and 12, and deals with ways of setting a scene and filling in background details of a story.

The unit falls into two sections, followed by a general Free Practice exercise and a Reading Comprehension. Both sections are concerned with describing scenes in the past. The first section is especially concerned with describing background activities and features of a scene, and practises particular structures with the Past Continuous and Past Simple; the second section is especially concerned with events that had taken place previously, and practises the Past Perfect Simple active and passive.

185

22.1 SETTING A SCENE Presentation

> **Language:** Past continuous for describing a scene in the
> past.
> Past Simple for describing permanent
> characteristics of the scene.
>
> *Note:* This use of the Past Continuous is an extension of
> that introduced in Unit 12.

This is a Listening Presentation. (See 'Dealing with listening' in Part 3.)

Extract 1

It was early afternoon, and the beach was almost empty. It was getting hot now. Most of the tourists were still finishing their lunch back at the hotel, or taking their afternoon siesta in the air-conditioned comfort of their rooms. One or two Englishmen were still lying stretched out on the sand, determined to go home with a good suntan, and a few local children were splashing around in the clear shallow water. There was a large yacht moving slowly across the bay. The girl was on board. She was standing at the back of the boat, getting ready to dive. Jason put on his sunglasses and casually wandered down towards the sandy beach...

Extract 2

Jacqueline got out of the bus and looked around her. It was typical of the small villages of that part of the country. The houses stood in two long lines on either side of the dusty road which led to the capital. In the square, the paint was peeling off the Town Hall, and some small children were running up and down its steps, laughing. On the other side, there were a few old men sitting outside a café playing backgammon and smoking their pipes. A lonely donkey was quietly munching the long dry grass at the foot of the statue that stood in the centre of the square. Jacqueline sighed...

1 Play the tape and check general comprehension by asking students to tell you briefly what each passage is about.

2 Play the tape again. Students answer the questions, which focus on a range of structures used for describing scenes in the past. Point these out as you go through the answers, and write examples on the board if necessary:

i) Past Continuous structures for describing *background activities*:

e.g.
> The tourists <u>were</u> finish<u>ing</u> their lunch.
> There <u>was</u> a yacht mov<u>ing</u> slowly across the bay.
> She <u>was</u> stand<u>ing</u>, gett<u>ing</u> ready to dive.

Note: This language is dealt with more fully in 22.3.

ii) Past Simple for describing *permanent characteristics* of a scene:

e.g.
> The houses <u>stood</u> in two long lines
> The road <u>led</u> to the capital.

Note: This language is dealt with more fully in 22.2.

iii) Past Simple for telling events of a story (see Unit 12):
   e.g. Jason *put* on his sunglasses.
      Jacqueline *got* out of the bus.

22.2 TEMPORARY ACTIVITIES AND PERMANENT FEATURES   Practice

> **Language:** Practice of contrast between:
>   i) Past Continuous for describing temporary activities.
>   ii) Past Simple for describing permanent characteristics.

1 Go through the example with the class.
2 The exercise can be done orally round the class or in writing.
Answers: (1)   was crossing
        (2)   lay
        (3)   flowed
        (4)   was standing
        (5)   crossed
        (6)   stood
        (7)   were lying
        (8)   faced
        (9)   was flowing
        (10) was facing

22.3 SCENES FROM THE PAST   Practice

> **Language:** Practice of Past Continuous structures introduced in 22.1.
> Participle forms describing postures and positions e.g. bending, kneeling, lying.

1 Look at the pictures, and ask students to describe the people in them *in the past*, as in the example.
2 Look at the more extended examples, and point out:
   i) the use of *there* + Past Continuous:
      e.g. *There was* a man lean*ing* on a stick.
      (See Unit 6.3 for *there* + Present Continuous structures.)
   ii) the use of a *series* of participle forms:
      e.g. There was a woman, dressed..., stand*ing*...
      There was a man, lean*ing*..., watch*ing*...
3 Students give full descriptions of the photographs in the same way.
► W22 Ex 1, Ex 2 ◄

22.4 STRIKING SCENES   Free practice

> **Language:** Free practice of language introduced so far
> in this unit.

1 Demonstrate the groupwork by describing a scene you saw recently yourself.
2 Divide the class into groups for the activity.
3 As a possible round-up, ask each group to choose the scene they thought was most interesting and describe it to the rest of the class.

22.5 THE PAST PERFECT TENSE

> **Language:** Past and Past Perfect tenses (including the
> Past Perfect Passive) for relating past states to
> the previous events that led to them.
>
> *Note:* This is the same relationship as that between the
> Present and Present Perfect tenses in Unit 8.2.

Presentation

1 Read the passage, and establish that:
   i) It contains a mixture of Past and Past Perfect tenses.
   ii) The Past Perfect is used to talk about *previous events* (i.e. before the time described in the passage).
2 Show the connection between the Past Perfect and the Present Perfect by writing this table on the board:

Result	*Previous Event*
Present: The curtains <u>are</u> drawn.	Someone <u>has</u> draw<u>n</u> the curtains. The curtains <u>have been</u> draw<u>n</u>.
Past: The curtains <u>were</u> drawn.	Someone <u>had</u> draw<u>n</u> the curtains. The curtains <u>had been</u> draw<u>n</u>.

3 Students make sentences about the passage:
   e.g. (2) (a) The room had been cleaned. (*or* He had cleaned the room.)
              (b) The carpet had been rolled up. (*or* He had rolled up the carpet.)

Practice

Either do this section round the class, or let students do it in groups and go through the answers afterwards.

Possible answers: The windows had been broken / smashed.
The host had fainted / passed out / lost consciousness / been knocked out.
The building had caught fire / been set on fire; someone had set the building on fire.
The fire brigade had arrived / been called.
Most of the guests had gone home / left.
The stereo equipment had disappeared / been stolen.
The lift had broken down / stopped working.
A man had climbed onto the roof.

► W22 Ex 3 ◄

22.6 PREVIOUS EVENTS

> **Language:** Practice of language introduced in 22.5.

Practice

1 Introduce the groupwork by looking at (1) with the whole class, and asking students to suggest things that had happened:
e.g. They'd redecorated the kitchen.
They'd built a garage.
2 In groups, students think of continuations for the other sentences.
3 Ask different groups what continuations they thought of.

Writing

The writing can be done in class or for homework.
► W22 Ex 4 ◄

22.7 MEMORIES   Free practice

> **Language:** Free practice of language introduced in this unit.
>
> *Note:* In this exercise the Past Perfect and Past Continuous tenses are combined to give a complete 'background' to an important event.

This exercise begins with a Listening Model. See 'Dealing with listening' in Part 3.

Well, we met at a party in London.
You see I'd just moved to London because of my job and I didn't really know anybody, and one of the people at work had invited me

to this party and so there I was. But it was one of those boring parties, you know everybody was just sitting in small groups talking to people they knew already, and I was feeling really bored with the whole thing. And then I noticed this rather attractive girl sitting at the edge of one of the groups, and she was looking bored too, just about as bored as I was. And so we started, um, we started looking at each other, and then I went across and we started talking. And as it turned out she'd only just arrived in London herself so we had quite a bit in common – and well that's how it all started really.

1 Play the tape. Students answer the questions.
2 Divide the class into groups for the activity.
3 As a possible round-up, ask different groups what they told each other.

22.8 MORNING CALL

Reading

For procedure, see 'Dealing with reading' in Part 3.

Answers:
(1) (a) It had rained in the night and the water was dripping...; ...at that early hour; ...milkman doing his rounds...
(b) Low grey clouds were drifting...; ...there was a cold damp wind blowing off the sea...; ...nearly threw me off my feet...
(c) ...bare trees...; ...wearing a thick coat.
(d) ...badly needed a coat of paint; ...dirty glass...
(2) The Automobile Association. They would come and repair her car, or take it to a garage.
(3) The street ran parallel to the sea; it was joined to it by a number of side streets; bare trees lined it.
(4) (a) To see if there was any fish left in them.
(b) Because there almost certainly wasn't any.
(c) The town was empty, so she hadn't expected to find anyone in the call box.
(d) So that she wouldn't disturb the man.
(e) When liquid drips, it falls in separate drops; when it trickles, it flows in a thin stream.
(5) (a) Because he was dead.
(b) Because the man had his back to her.

Free practice

This can be done in pairs after the students have finished the reading and you have gone through the answers.

Activities (following Unit 22)

ESKIMOS 🔲

> **Language:** This activity draws on language from:
> Unit 4 (direction)
> Unit 16 (precise location)
> Unit 20 (describing features of objects).

This activity begins with a Listening Model.

A: Well it's got two big wheels one behind the other, and there's a kind of metal frame between the wheels that holds them together. And there's a little seat above the back wheel that you can sit on, and above the front wheel there's a sort of metal bar that sticks out on both sides. And you sit on the seat you see, and you put your hands on this metal bar thing – and the whole thing moves forwards – it's amazing.

B: What makes it move forward, then?

A: Ah well in the middle you see, between the two wheels, there are these other bits of metal and you can put your feet on these and turn them round and that makes the wheels go round.

B: Hang on – if it's only got two wheels why doesn't the whole thing fall over?

A: Well you see, um, well I'm not sure actually...

1 Explain the game, and play the Listening Model. Students guess the object being described.
   (**Answer:** a bicycle).
2 Divide the class into groups. Either give each group the name of an everyday mechanical object, or let them choose themselves. Secretly, they work out how to describe it, using *non-technical* language.
3 One person from each group describes their object to the rest of the class. They try to guess what it is.
   Suitable objects to describe are: a typewriter, a washing machine, a lift, a rifle, a polaroid camera.

COMPOSITION

> **Language:** The compositions draw on language from Units 12 and 22.

The writing can be done in class or for homework.

Unit 23 Criticising

This is the fifth in the series of units concerned with taking, initiating and commenting on *action*. It deals with language for criticising present situations and behaviour and past actions and events, and speculating about imaginary situations.

The unit falls into two sections, followed by a Reading Comprehension and Free Practice. The first section is concerned with criticising present situations and behaviour, and practises *should(n't) do* and *should(n't) be doing*, *if* + Past tense, and *keeps / is always doing*. The second section is concerned with criticising past actions and events and blaming people for what has happened, and practises *should(n't) have done* and *should(n't) have been doing*, and *if* + Past Perfect tense.

23.1 WHAT'S WRONG?
Presentation and practice of:
should(n't) be;
should(n't) be doing.

23.2 SHOULD & IF
Presentation and practice of: should(n't) do; if + Past tense... would(n't)... Practice

23.3 IRRITATING BEHAVIOUR
Presentation and practice of:
is always / keeps +-ing.
Writing

23.4 RECRIMINATIONS
Free practice

23.5 PAST MISTAKES
Presentation and practice of:
should(n't) have done; if + Past Perfect ... would(n't) have done.

23.6 EVENTS AND CIRCUMSTANCES
Presentation and practice of:
should(n't) have been doing.
Practice

23.7 CARNIVAL
Reading
Discussion
Writing

23.8 WHOSE FAULT?
Free practice

23.1 WHAT'S WRONG?   Presentation and practice

> **Language:** Criticising present situations (i.e. what there
> is / isn't and what is / isn't happening):
> i) *there should(n't) be ...*
> ii) *...should(n't) be...-ing...*

1 Look at the pictures and the examples with the class. Show how *should(n't)
be (-ing)* structures are formed by giving the situations and the criticisms:
e.g. Picture (1): The children *are* skipp*ing* near the clothes line.
          They *shouldn't be* skipp*ing* near the clothes line.
   Picture (2): *There isn't* a clear notice.
          There should be a clear notice.
Point out that *should* is always followed by an infinitive form (in this
exercise, of the verb 'to be').
2 Either discuss the pictures with the whole class, or let them talk about
them in groups and then discuss them with the whole class afterwards.

23.2 SHOULD & IF

> **Language:** Use of *should(n't) + infinitive* for criticising
> things people do / don't do.
> Use of *if + Past tense... would(n't)...* ('Second
> Conditional') for imagining alternatives.

Presentation and practice

1 Read the sentences about Colin's café.
2 Present structures with *should(n't)* and *if + Past tense* by writing
this table on the board (which gives answers to 'The windows are
filthy'):

PROBLEM AND RESULT He doesn't clean the windows, so people can't see inside.	
CRITICISM He <u>should</u> clean the windows.	
IMAGINED RESULT <u>If</u> he clean<u>ed</u> the windows, people <u>would</u> be able to see inside.	

Point out that *if + Past tense* structures do *not* refer to the past.
The Past tense and *would(n't)* are used for imagining an *unreal situation*.

3 If you think it is necessary, write similar sentences on the board for 'He overcooks everything', to show the negative structures:
   He *shouldn't* overcook everything.
   If he *didn't* overcook everything, the food *would* taste better.
4 Students make sentences about the other problems, first with *should(n't)*, then with *if*.

Practice

1 🔊 Play the example on the tape. Quickly go through the other situations and ask students to suggest possible remarks with *should(n't)* for each:
   e.g. He should work harder.
         He shouldn't go out so much.
2 Divide the class into groups of three to do the exercise.
3 As a round-up, ask individual students what *if* sentences they made.
▶ W23 Ex 1 ◀

23.3 IRRITATING BEHAVIOUR

> **Language:** Criticising people's behaviour, using:
> i) *keeps...-ing...*
> ii) *is always / constantly / continually ...-ing.*
> Adjectives and nouns for describing characteristics of people.

Presentation and practice

1 Go through the example, and make sure students understand the difference in meaning between *always does* and *is always doing* by giving examples:
   e.g. He always talks in his sleep:
         A neutral remark = he does this every night.
         He's always talking in his sleep:
         A critical remark = he does this more than he should.
2 Go through the list of words and ask students to give definitions using *keeps doing / is always doing*. Explain any new words. Point out that the words in the third column are all nouns, so we say 'a gossip', not 'a gossip person'.

Writing

Read the paragraph, and point out that *is constantly / continually doing* are alternatives to *is always doing*.
The writing can be done in class or for homework. If you like, prepare for it by constructing a few 'oral paragraphs' with the class.
▶ W23 Ex 2 ◀

23.4 RECRIMINATIONS   Free practice

> **Language:** Free practice of language introduced so far in
> this unit.
> Free practice of language introduced in Unit
> 21.

1 Divide the class into pairs. Students in each pair are either *both* A or
both B. Working together, they prepare what they will say. They should
also prepare to defend themselves against the other person's criticisms.
2 Students form new pairs, so that each pair has one A and one B. They
act out the conversation.
3 As a round-up, ask individual students what solution they found to the
situation, if any.

23.5 PAST MISTAKES   Presentation and practice

> **Language:** Use of *should(n't) have done* for criticising
> past actions.
> Use of *if + Past Perfect tense...would(n't)
> have done* for imagining alternatives in the
> past.

This is a Listening Presentation. See 'Dealing with listening' in Part 3.

A: Me, officer? You're joking!
B: Come off it, Mulligan. For a start,
you spent three days watching the
house. You shouldn't have done
that, you know. The neighbours got
suspicious and phoned the police...
A: But I was only looking, officer.
B: ...and on the day of the robbery, you
really shouldn't have used your own
car. We got your number. And if
you'd worn a mask, you wouldn't
have been recognised.
A: I didn't go inside!
B: Ah, there's another thing. You
should've worn gloves Mulligan. If
you had, you wouldn't have left
your fingerprints all over the house.
We found your fingerprints on the
jewels, too.

A: You mean...you've found the jewels?
B: Oh yes. Where you...er...'hid' them.
Under your mattress.
A: My God! You know everything! I'll
tell you something, officer – you
shouldn't have joined the police
force. If you'd taken up burglary,
you'd have made a fortune!

1 Play the tape. Students answer (1), which checks general comprehension.
   Answer: Because he stole jewels from a house and the police caught him.

2 Play the tape again. This time students note down answers to (2). Tell them they should write down only what the burglar *did* (or didn't do) and what *happened* (not 'should' or 'if' structures). Go through the answers.
Possible answers:

Mistake	*Result*
Spent three days watching the house.	Neighbours got suspicious.
Used his own car.	Police got the number.
Didn't wear a mask.	Police recognised him.
Didn't wear gloves.	Left fingerprints in the house.
Hid the jewels in his house.	Police found them.

3 Present structures with *should(n't) have done* by writing this table on the board:

> *Mistake and Result*
>
> He spent three days watching the house,   so the neighbours got
> He didn't break in immediately,   suspicious.

> *Criticism*
>
> He <u>shouldn't have</u> spent three days watching the house.
> He <u>should have</u> broken in immediately.

Point out that in these sentences, *should* is followed by the past infinitive: *have + past participle*.

4 Students look at (3). They talk about the burglar's mistakes, using *should(n't)*:
e.g. He shouldn't have used his own car.
He should have borrowed one from someone else.

5 Present 'Third Conditional' structures by adding these sentences on the board:

> *Imagined Result*
>
> If he <u>hadn't</u> spent three days
>   watching the house,   the neighbours <u>wouldn't</u>
> If he <u>had</u> broken in immediately,   <u>have got</u> suspicious.

6 Students look at (4) and talk about the burglar's mistakes using *if*:
e.g. If he hadn't used his own car, the police wouldn't have got his number.

7 Briefly discuss (5). Then students look at (6) and make sentences with *should(n't)* and *if* about the mistakes in the list:
e.g. He shouldn't have boasted about the robbery in the pub.
If he hadn't boasted about it, the landlord wouldn't have contacted the police.

23.6 EVENTS AND CIRCUMSTANCES

> **Language:**   Use of *should(n't) have been doing* for
> criticising things people were / weren't
> doing when something else happened.
> Use of *if + Past Perfect (Continuous)*
> for imagining alternatives in the past.
>
> *Note:* In this exercise, students learn the fourth
> infinitive form after 'should'. This might be a good
> point to show the four forms together:
>
> | | *Simple* | *Continuous* |
> |---|---|---|
> | *Present:* | should *do* | should *be doing* |
> | *Past:* | should *have done* | should *have been doing* |

Presentation and practice

1 Look at the example and point out that:
  i)   It is about what someone *was* (or wasn't) *doing* when something *happened* (i.e. the circumstances of an event – see Unit 12).
  ii) To criticise what someone was / wasn't doing, we use:
     – ...*should(n't) have been doing*
     – *if...had(n't) been doing...*
2 Students make sentences about the other situations:
  e.g. (1) (a) He hit the man.
         (b) He should have been concentrating.
         (c) If he had been concentrating, he wouldn't have hit the man.

Practice

1 🔊 Play the example on the tape. Ask students to suggest other criticisms:
  e.g. He should have dried his hair.
       He shouldn't have gone out that night.
2 Make sure students understand when to use *shouldn't have done* and when to use *shouldn't have been doing*.
3 Demonstrate the groupwork by doing (1) with the whole class.
4 Divide the class into groups to do the exercise.
5 Ask different groups to tell you some of the criticisms they made.
▶ W23 Ex 3, Ex 4 ◀

23.7 CARNIVAL

Reading

For procedure, see 'Dealing with reading' in Part 3.

Answers:
(1) Once a year.
(2) Because they didn't like the Carnival / because they thought it would lead to violence.
(3) An extreme right-wing political group. One of their policies is to keep black immigrants out of Britain.
(4) (a) Singing, dancing, music, street parades, people selling things.
   (b) A confrontation between a West Indian and two National Front members in a café.
(5) (a) They moved into the street where the café was, lined the streets, kept the National Front away, fought with youths, arrested more than 50 people.
   (b) They threw bottles, broke shop windows, fought with police.
   (c) They held a noisy demonstration in a nearby street.
(6) Police Spokesman: thinks police presence and action were necessary.
   Carnival Organiser: thinks police are mainly to blame for the violence because they overreacted.
   National Front Spokesman: thinks the blacks are to blame for the violence, not the National Front, and that the Carnival should have been banned.
   Local Resident: thinks the National Front started the trouble, and youths from outside the area joined in; thinks local people, black or white, aren't to blame.

Discussion

Either conduct the discussion with the whole class, or let students discuss the question in groups and ask them to summarise their conclusions afterwards.

Writing

The writing can be done in class or for homework.

23.8 WHOSE FAULT?   **Free practice**

> **Language:** Free practice of language introduced in this
> unit.

1 Introduce the activity by choosing one of the topics and discussing it with
   the whole class.
2 Either choose other suitable topics for the group discussion, or let groups
   choose their own.
3 As a round-up, ask different groups what conclusions they came to.
▶ W23 Ex 5 ▶

Unit 24   Explanations

This is the second in the series of units concerned with *explanation* and speculation about the past, present and future. It deals with various kinds of explanation: of reasons, of purposes, of causes and results, and of unexpected results.

The unit falls into two sections, followed by a Listening Comprehension. The first section is concerned with giving reasons for actions and events, explaining the general purpose of organisations, and analysing causes and results; it practises a range of structures for each kind of explanation. The second section is concerned with talking about unexpected results, and practises linking sentences with *although, even though, despite* and *in spite of*.

24.1 KINDS OF EXPLANATION
Presentation and practice of: giving reasons; explaining causes and results; explaining purposes.
Practice

24.2 GIVING REASONS
Practice of: because, in order (not) to, so that.

24.3 GENERAL PURPOSE
Practice of: 'general purpose' structures.
Writing

24.4 CAUSES AND RESULTS
Presentation of: because of, as a result of; lead to, be caused by, make + infinitive.
Practice
Writing

24.5 EXPLA- NATIONS QUIZ
Free practice

24.6 NOT WHAT YOU'D EXPECT
Presentation and practice of: 'although' and '(even) though'; despite / in spite of + noun / the fact that...

24.7 READING GAME: BECAUSE OF & IN SPITE OF
Practice

24.8 OUT OF THE ORDINARY
Free practice

24.9 SPOKES
Listening
Writing
Discussion

24.1 KINDS OF EXPLANATION

> **Language:** Structures and expressions for giving three
> kinds of explanation:
>   i) Explaining reasons – *because, in order
>   to, One of the reasons why... is...*
> ii) Explaining causes and results – *make,
>   lead to, cause, is caused by.*
> iii) Explaining purposes – *The purpose of...
>   is to..., ... exists in order to ..., ... is
>   concerned with -ing.*

Presentation and practice

1 Read the three paragraphs.
2 Ask the class (1). The purpose of this is to establish the main functions of
   the three paragraphs.
   Answer: Paragraph A explains why children start smoking.
              Paragraph B explains what diseases smoking causes.
              Paragraph C explains what the purpose of ASH is.
3 Tell students to cover the paragraphs, and ask them (2), (3), (4), which
   check comprehension and focus attention on the structures and expressions
   used in the paragraphs. Point these out as they come up, and write them
   on the board if you like, but there is no need to give detailed explanations at this point.

Practice

Either discuss the questions with the whole class, or let students discuss
them in groups and report their conclusions afterwards.

24.2 GIVING REASONS   Practice

> **Language:** Structures for explaining reasons:
>   *because*
>   *in order (not) to* + *infinitive*
>   *so that* + *would/could(n't).*

1 Go through the examples and point out that they show two kinds of
   reason:
   i) about what the person wants or doesn't want to do (e.g. saving
      money).
  ii) about the situation at the time (e.g. petrol being expensive).
   Point out that *so that* means the same as *in order to*; when talking about
   the past, it is followed by *would(n't)* or *could(n't)*.

2 Ask students to make sentences for the other situations,
   e.g. (1) ...in order to meet more people.
             ...so that she could go to the theatre more often.
             ...because it was too expensive to run.
3 Introduce the groupwork by telling the class about an important decision you made, exactly what you did and why.
4 Divide the class into groups for the activity.
5 As a round-up, ask each group to tell you the most interesting decision they heard about.
▶ W24 Ex 1 ◀

24.3 GENERAL PURPOSE

> **Language:** Explaining the *general purpose* of organisations, using:
> *The purpose of X is to ...*
> *X exists in order to ...*
> *X is concerned with ...-ing ...*

Practice

1 Look at the advertisements with the class and make sure students understand what they mean.
2 Students say what the purpose of each organisation is, using the three expressions:
   e.g. The Samaritans exists in order to help people who are lonely and desperate.
       The purpose of Shelter is to provide homes for homeless people.
       The Campaign for Real Cheese is concerned with encouraging people to eat natural cheese.
   Point out that *the purpose of...* and *...exists in order to...* are only used to talk about *general* purpose; *...is concerned with...* can also be used to talk about more specific aims. Refer back to Paragraph (C) in 24.1 for an example of this.
3 Ask students to suggest what each organisation does.
   e.g. The Samaritans have a 24-hour telephone service, they visit lonely people, and help them to meet other people, etc.
4 Either decide what organisation(s) students should interview each other about, or let them choose their own.
   Divide the class into pairs: they can either conduct a single interview, or take it in turns to interview each other. If they are discussing different organisations from those above, it may be necessary to give a few minutes' preparation time.
5 As a possible round-up after the interviews, get individual students to tell you about their organisations.

Writing

The writing can be done in class or for homework.
► W24 Ex 2 ◄

24.4 CAUSES AND RESULTS

> **Language:** Explaining causes and results, using:
> *...is caused by...*   *because of*
> *make someone do something*
> *...leads to...*   *as a result of*

Presentation

This exercise begins with a Listening Model. (See 'Dealing with listening' in Part 3.)

1 Play the tape. Students answer the questions.
   Possible answer to (3): They start fighting each other, they interfere with people, etc.

2 Make sure students understand these cause / result structures:

> X causes / leads to Y
> Y is caused by X
> Y happens because of / as a result of X
> X happens. Because of / as a result of this, Y happens.

Well, I think that this problem of teenagers getting into trouble with the law is mainly caused by unemployment. You see, because of the high level of unemployment, so many teenagers nowadays leave school and find that they have no chance of getting a job, and this obviously makes them feel bored and frustrated. And as a result of this, they're much more likely to get drunk and so on. Another thing of course is that you get groups of unemployed teenagers wandering around the streets with nothing to do, which can easily lead to trouble of one sort or another....

Practice

1. If you like, introduce the groupwork by discussing one of the topics (e.g. parents) with the whole class.
2 Divide the class into groups for the activity.
3 As a round-up, ask each group to tell you what they said about one of the topics.

Writing

The writing can be done in class or for homework.
► W24 Ex 4 ◄

24.5 EXPLANATIONS QUIZ   Free practice

> **Language:** Free practice of language introduced so far in
> the unit.

1 Either ask the questions round the class, or let students work through
them in groups, and go through the answers afterwards.
Answers: (1) (a) To help people who are being badly treated for political
reasons (e.g. political prisoners).
(b) To help motorists, especially by repairing cars that have
broken down. (See Unit 22.8.)
(c) To give money, food and other aid to starving people.
(2) (a) Sudden movements in the Earth's crust.
(b) The moon: as the moon moves it 'pulls' the sea after it.
This makes the water higher at certain times in a particular
place.
(3) It was going too fast, and hit an iceberg, which made a hole in
the side.
(4) (a) Because he wanted to prove that it was possible, and that
Polynesians might be descendants of the Incas.
(b) Because of the Watergate scandal; because people had
proved that he was involved in corruption.
(5) (a) In order to find warmer places.
(b) So that they can reach the leaves on high trees.

2 For the second part of the exercise, divide the class into groups to
think up questions. Each group then asks its questions to the rest of
the class.

24.6 NOT WHAT YOU'D   Presentation and practice
EXPECT

> **Language:** 'Concessive' structures to show that one
> event is unexpected in view of the other:
> i) *although / even though + clause*
> ii) *in spite of / despite + noun phrase /*
> *'the fact that'.*
>
> *Note: In spite of / despite can also be followed by a gerund*
> with the same subject. However, this is not practised here.

1 Go through the examples, and point out that:
i) *Although* and *even though* mean the same, but *even though* emphasises
more strongly that the event is *unexpected*. They are both followed by a
clause.
ii) *In spite of* and *despite* mean the same. *Despite* is slightly more formal.
They are both prepositions, and must be followed by *nouns*. So to follow
them by a clause, we must put *the fact that* in between.

2 Students change the sentences as in the example.
Note: Although it is always possible to think of a form with *in spite of /
despite* + *noun*, it may make the meaning less specific. Possible changes are:
(1) In spite of her (great) age, she...
(2) In spite of the cost (expense), lots of people are buying videos.
(3) Despite her parents' objections, she...
(4) Despite his deafness, Beethoven...
(5) In spite of its poor acoustics, the hall...
(6) In spite of the length of time we've known each other, we...
(7) Despite the distance of Hammerfest north of the Arctic Circle, the sea...

▶ W24 Ex 3 ◀

24.7 READING GAME: BECAUSE OF   Practice
& IN SPITE OF

> **Language:** Practice of *because of* and *in spite of*.

This Reading Game is played in the same way as the one in Unit 21.7, except
that each 'starting sentence' is read out *twice*, so there are three 'starting
sentences' and 12 'continuations'.
1 Divide the class into groups of three, and give each student a letter: A, B,
or C.
2 After going through the example, demonstrate the game by reading out
Student B's first sentence, and change it using *because of* ('Because of the
success of his book...'). Ask all Students A and C to find a suitable continuation ('...he was asked to appear on TV.'). Then say the sentence using *in
spite of* ('In spite of the success of his book...'), and ask Students A and C to
find a continuation ('... he decided not to write any more.'). If necessary, do
the same with Student C's first sentence.
3 Give a few minutes for students to read through their own section silently.
Answer any vocabulary questions.
4 Students play the game.
5 When most groups have finished, go through the answers with the class.
   Answers: (A) (1) (as in examples)
            (2) Because of his illness, he had to cancel the appointment.
               In spite of his illness, he managed to come to work.
            (3) Because of the meat shortage, everyone's living on beans.
               In spite of the meat shortage, we've managed to get a leg of lamb.
        (B) (1) (as above)
            (2) Because of the ice on the roads, there were a lot of accidents.
               In spite of the ice on the roads, he drove at 60 m.p.h. all the way.
            (3) Because of the high cost of living in Britain, there are fewer
               tourists here this year.
               In spite of the high cost of living in Britain, most people run a
               car.
        (C) (1) Because of the large crowds, we couldn't see what was going on.
               In spite of the large crowds, there were enough seats for
               everyone.

(2) Because of his foreign accent, everyone thinks he's a tourist.
   In spite of his foreign accent, we have no problem understanding him.
(3) Because of the bad condition of the house, the council demolished it.
   In spite of the bad condition of the house, they enjoyed living there.

24.8 OUT OF THE ORDINARY   Free practice

> **Language:** Free practice of:
> i) giving reasons
> ii) 'concession' structures.

1 Demonstrate the groupwork by telling the class about someone you know who lives in an unusual or surprising way.
2 Divide the class into groups for the activity.
3 As a round-up, ask different groups to tell you about the most interesting person they heard about.

24.9 SPOKES

Listening

This is a Listening Comprehension Passage. For procedure, see 'Dealing with listening' in Part 3.

A: What exactly is 'Spokes'?
B: Well, it's a voluntary organisation which has been going for the last three years or so, um it's really an action group for cyclists. And the basic purpose of 'Spokes' is to encourage cycling, especially in cities, and also to make sure that city planners are aware of the needs of cyclists and that they provide proper facilities for cyclists. Now this is very important because when plans are made for new streets in cities, pedestrians are always included because you have pavements and shopping areas and parks, and motorists are always included because you have roads and car parks and so on. But it seems to us that nobody actually thinks of the cyclists and somehow the cyclists come between the cars and the pedestrians and there aren't really any facilities provided for them. And that was really the basic reason why we set up 'Spokes' in the first place – because we felt that the cyclist ought to be represented too.

A: So what kind of facilities do you think there should be for cyclists?
B: Well, the most important thing I think is there should be special lanes for cyclists in at least some of the streets in cities where only cyclists are allowed to go – um, at the moment in most cities there's either no special lane for bicycles at all, they just share the road with all the other traffic, or else cyclists are

supposed to use the same lane as buses, which of course is extremely dangerous.

A: But wouldn't a lot of people say that there are really very few cyclists on the road compared with the number of cars, so why should so much money be spent just for them? Is it really worth it?

B: Yes we think it is worth it, for one thing because of the number of accidents that there are at the moment. Most serious accidents involving cyclists are caused by cars, and they happen because drivers assume that the road is for them and they simply don't notice that the cyclist's there – and so I'm sure special lanes for bicycles would lead to fewer accidents. And another reason it's worth having special lanes is that it would encourage more people to use bicycles. And yes of course at the moment there are very few cyclists on the roads, but that's because cycling in cities is so dangerous and so unpleasant. Now obviously if better facilities were provided for cyclists, there would be far more bicycles on the road just like there

are in Holland and Denmark, and this would be a very good thing for everybody. I think it's ridiculous that people in Britain talk so much about pollution and the energy crisis and so on, but in spite of that they don't do anything to encourage cycling, which is cheap and clean and also very good for you.

A: Now you described 'Spokes' as an 'action group' for cyclists. What exactly have you done?

B: Well, so far we've been mainly concerned with just drawing people's attention to cyclists and the needs of cyclists. So we've held meetings and we've written to newspapers and to city councils, suggesting things that can be done to help cyclists and we've held bicycle rallies in some places.

A: Do you think you've had any effect?

B: Oh very much so. I think as a result of what we've done local councils are now actually beginning to consider cyclists as another group they've got to take notice of, and in a few cities they've already started to include cycle lanes and special routes for cyclists in their plans.

Answers: (1) (a) An action group for cyclists.
      (b) To encourage cycling, especially in cities; to make sure city planners are aware of cyclists' needs and provide facilities for them.
    (2) (a) Pavements, shopping areas, parks.
      (b) Roads, car-parks.
      (c) No special facilities.
    (3) (a) Special ones for cyclists only.
      (b) Either none at all, or else shared with buses.
    (4) It would lead to fewer accidents between cyclists and cars, and it would encourage more people to use bicycles.
    (5) (a) Most serious accidents involving cyclists are caused by cars.
      (b) It's because cycling in cities is so dangerous and so unpleasant.
      (c) If better facilities were provided for cyclists, there would be far more bicycles on the road.
      (d) People in Britain talk about pollution and the energy crisis, but in spite of that they don't do anything to encourage cycling.
      (e) It's cheap, clean, good for you.
    (6) (a) Held meetings; written to newspapers and city councils; held bicycle rallies.
      (b) Local councils are beginning to take notice of cyclists; they've started to include cycle lanes in plans of some cities.

Writing

The writing can be done in class or for homework.

Discussion

Divide the class into groups for the discussion.

Activities (following Unit 24)

CONTACT

Language:	This activity draws on language from: Unit 3 (jobs and routine) Unit 11 (likes and dislikes) Unit 12 (events and circumstances) Unit 13 (leisure activities and skill) Unit 17 (similarities and differences).

Before the lesson:
1 Each student will be given one of the individual roles on pp. 210–213. Photocopy the roles and cut them up. Make sure you have enough roles for everyone in the class (the table below shows which roles to use for different class sizes).
2 Write your own name in the space provided on the detectives' cards.
3 Create an atmosphere in the classroom as much like a party as you can. The whole activity should be done standing up, with students able to move around as freely as possible.

In the class:
1 Give a role card to each student (but not in their numbered order).
2 Explain that:
  i) they are at a party
  ii) they must follow the role written on their card
  iii) their role is *secret*.
  Do not give any other information away. It is most important that no-one is sure why anyone else is at the party!
3 During the game, you can act as assistant to the host, or as an 'innocent' guest.
4 When all the criminals have either made contact or been arrested, stop the game and ask each student to reveal his role.

The roles:
1 Host
2 Diamond smuggler A
3 Diamond smuggler B
4 Detective looking for diamond smugglers
5 Innocent guest A
6 Spy A
7 Spy B
8 Detective looking for spies
9 Innocent guest B
10 Drug pusher A
11 Drug pusher B
12 Detective looking for drug pushers

13 Innocent guest C

14 Gunrunner A

15 Gunrunner B

16 Detective looking for gunrunners

17 Innocent guest D

18 Second host (same as role 1)

Which roles to use:
For a class of 18 students use roles 1 – 18; for 17 students use roles 1 – 17; for 16 students use roles 1 – 16; for 15 students use roles 1 – 13 and roles 17 and 18; for 14 students use roles 1 – 13 and role 17; for 13 students use roles 1 – 13; for 12 students use roles 1 – 12; for 11 students use roles 1 – 8 and roles 10 – 12; for ten students use roles 1 – 9 and role 13; for nine students use roles 1 – 9.

---

1 Your brother has organised a sherry party, but he was unexpectedly called away on business at the last minute, so you are acting as host at the party. You don't know any of the guests, but you want to be a good host and make the party a success. Talk to everyone briefly and make sure everyone talks to as many other people as possible. Do your best to stop the party splitting up into pairs.

---

2 You are a diamond smuggler, and have been instructed to meet your contact at a party in London. Neither of you knows what the other one looks like. You can only identify each other by the fact that you both have a strong interest in *eating in restaurants*, *walking* and *cooking*; you both know this, but so do the police, who have infiltrated the party to look for you. There are two things you know about each other that the police don't know:
  i) You were bitten by a snake while on a walking tour in Spain last year.
 ii) Your contact regularly goes to a small Greek restaurant in Soho.
You know that some of the people at the party are just guests, some are detectives, and one is your contact. Try and identify him without giving yourself away to anyone else. If you and your contact identify each other, you should make an excuse to the host and leave the party.

---

3 You are a diamond smuggler, and have been instructed to meet your contact at a party in London. Neither of you knows what the other one looks like. You can only identify each other by the fact that you both have a strong interest in *eating in restaurants*, *walking* and *cooking*; you both know this, but so do the police, who have infiltrated the party to look for you. There are two things you know about each other that the police don't know:
  i) You regularly go to a small Greek restaurant in Soho.
 ii) Your contact was bitten by a snake while on a walking tour in Spain last year.
You know that some of the people at the party are just guests, some are detectives, and one is your contact. Try and identify him without giving yourself away to anyone else. If you and your contact identify each other, you should make an excuse to the host and leave the party.

4   You are a detective, looking for two diamond smugglers who are planning to make contact at a party in London. Neither of them knows what the other one looks like, and nor do you. You can only identify them by the fact that they both have a strong interest in *eating in restaurants, walking* and *cooking*. Try and identify them without giving yourself away, either by eavesdropping or by pretending you are one of them.
As soon as you are sure you have identified one of the smugglers find an excuse to introduce him to your boss, who is at the party under the name of ...., and who will arrest him.

5   You have been invited to a party in London, at which you don't know any of the guests. You have three great interests in life – *travel, eating in restaurants* (especially Greek ones), and *folk music* (especially Irish ballads), and little interest in anything else.

6   You are a spy, and have been instructed to meet your contact at a party in London. Neither of you knows what the other one looks like. You can only identify each other by the fact that you both have a strong interest in *travel, languages* and *fishing*; you both know this, but so do the police, who have infiltrated the party to look for you. There are two things you know about each other that the police don't know:
i) You once caught an octopus with your bare hands.
ii) Your contact speaks fluent Finnish.
You know that some of the people at the party are just guests, some are detectives, and one is your contact. Try and identify him without giving yourself away to anyone else. If you and your contact identify each other, you should make an excuse to the host and leave the party.

7   You are a spy, and have been instructed to meet your contact at a party in London. Neither of you knows what the other one looks like. You can only identify each other by the fact that you both have a strong interest in *travel, languages*, and *fishing*; you both know this, but so do the police, who have infiltrated the party to look for you. There are two things you know about each other that the police don't know:
i) You speak fluent Finnish.
ii) Your contact once caught an octopus with his bare hands.
You know that some of the people at the party are just guests, some are detectives, and one is your contact. Try and identify him without giving yourself away to anyone else. If you and your contact identify each other, you should make an excuse to the host and leave the party.

8   You are a detective, looking for two spies who are planning to make contact at a party in London. Neither of them knows what the other one looks like, and nor do you. You can only identify them by the fact that they both have a strong interest in *travel, languages* and *fishing*. Try and identify them without giving yourself away, either by eavesdropping or by pretending you are one of them.
As soon as you are sure you have identified one of the spies, find an excuse to introduce him to your boss, who is at the party under the name of ....
...................., and who will arrest him.

9   You have been invited to a party in London, at which you don't know any of the guests. You have three great interests in life: *languages* (especially Scandinavian languages), *walking* (you go for walking holidays in Spain every winter) and *football*, and little interest in anything else.

10   You are a drug pusher and have been instructed to meet your contact at a party in London. Neither of you knows what the other one looks like. You can only identify each other by the fact that you both have a strong interest in *folk music*, *classical music* and *films*; you both know this, but so do the police, who have infiltrated the party to look for you. There are two things you know about each other that the police don't know:
i)   You have over 100 records of Irish folk music.
ii)   Your contact saw Woody Allen's latest film 7 times.
You know that some of the people at the party are just guests, some are detectives, and one is your contact. Try and identify him without giving yourself away to anyone else. If you and your contact identify each other, you should make an excuse to the host, and leave the party.

11   You are a drug pusher and have been instructed to meet your contact at a party in London. Neither of you knows what the other one looks like. You can only identify each other by the fact that you both have a strong interest in *folk music*, *classical music* and *films*; you both know this, but so do the police, who have infiltrated the party to look for you. There are two things you know about each other that the police don't know:
i)   You saw Woody Allen's latest film 7 times.
ii)   Your contact has over 100 records of Irish folk music.
You know that some of the people at the party are just guests, some are detectives, and one is your contact. Try and identify him without giving yourself away to anyone else. If you and your contact identify each other, you should make an excuse to the host, and leave the party.

12   You are a detective, looking for two drug pushers who are planning to make contact at a party in London. Neither of them knows what the other one looks like, and nor do you. You can only identify them by the fact that they both have a strong interest in *folk music*, *classical music* and *films*.
Try and identify them without giving yourself away, either by eavesdropping, or by pretending you are one of them. As soon as you are sure you have identified one of the drug pushers, find an excuse to introduce him to your boss, who is at the party under the name of ...., and who will arrest him.

13   You have been invited to a party in London, at which you don't know any of the guests. You have three great interests in life: *fishing* (you spend every summer octopus fishing on the Mediterranean), *mountaineering* (you went climbing in the Alps last Spring) and *classical music*, and little interest in anything else.

14 You are a gunrunner, and have been instructed to meet your contact at a party in London. Neither of you knows what the other one looks like. You can only identify each other by the fact that you both have a strong interest in *football, mountaineering* and *bird-watching*; you both know this, but so do the police, who have infiltrated the party to look for you. There are two things you know about each other that the police don't know:
i)   You once camped on Mont Blanc for a week.
ii) Your contact went bird-watching in Spain last summer.
You know that some of the people at the party are just guests, some are detectives, and one is your contact. Try and identify him without giving yourself away to anyone else. If you and your contact identify each other, you should make an excuse to the host and leave the party.

15 You are a gunrunner, and have been instructed to meet your contact at a party in London. Neither of you knows what the other one looks like. You can only identify each other by the fact that you both have a strong interest in *football, mountaineering* and *bird-watching;* you both know this, but so do the police, who have infiltrated the party to look for you. There are two things you know about each other that the police don't know:
i)   You went bird-watching in Spain last summer.
ii) Your contact once camped on Mont Blanc for a week.
You know that some of the people at the party are just guests, some are detectives, and one is your contact. Try and identify him without giving yourself away to anyone else. If you and your contact identify each other, you should make an excuse to the host and leave the party.

16 You are a detective, looking for two gunrunners who are planning to make contact at a party in London. Neither of them knows what the other one looks like, and nor do you. You can only identify them by the fact that they both have a strong interest in *football, maintaineering* and *bird-watching*. Try and identify them without giving yourself away, either by eavesdropping or by pretending you are one of them.
As soon as you are sure you have identified one of the gunrunners, find an excuse to introduce him to your boss, who is at the party under the name of ....
...................., and who will arrest him.

17 You have been invited to a party in London, at which you don't know any of the guests. You have three great interests in life: *films* (especially Woody Allen), *cooking* and *bird-watching* (you spend your holidays bird-watching in the Mediterranean), and little interest in anything else.

COMPOSITION

> **Language:** The compositions draw on language from most units in the Course.

The writing can be done in class or for homework.

JUST A MINUTE

> **Language:** This activity draws on language from all the
> units.

This is an adaptation of the radio panel game of the same name. It can be
played in two ways:
i)   as a *fluency game*, in which students should aim to 'keep going' for a
       minute, without paying attention to minor mistakes.
ii)   as an *accuracy game*, in which students should aim to speak as fluently
       as possible for a minute *without making a mistake*.

1 Demonstrate the game by talking about a topic yourself for one minute.
2 Choose one of the topics, and ask one student to begin. If he hesitates for
   a long time, or repeats himself, ask the student next to him to continue.
   If he makes a serious mistake, say 'Stop', and ask the class to tell you
   what he should have said. The first student to answer correctly continues.
3 When a minute is up, continue with a new topic.
   Scoring: The student who is talking when the minute is up scores one
   point.

ON THE ROCKS

> **Language:** This activity draws on language from:
> Unit 15 (duration)
> Unit 21 (degree)
> Unit 23 (criticising).

1 Divide the class into pairs, so that students in each pair are either *both*
   Ann or *both* Bill. Working together, they read the instructions and work
   out what they might say.
2 Students form new pairs, so that each pair consists of one 'Ann' and one
   'Bill'. They improvise the conversation.
3 As a round-up, ask different pairs what they decided to do, and why.

SITUATIONS

> **Language:** The situations draw on language from
> Units 14, 19, 21, 22, 23 and 24.

For procedure, see Activities following Unit 4.

Remedial presentation and practice

This section contains ideas for Presentation and Basic Practice of language items that are treated as 'assumed knowledge' in the units.
They are especially intended for:
i) Classes of mixed ability, where some students may be below the expected level of the course.
ii) Non-intensive courses, where students may need to revise language they have learnt at lower levels.
The items in this section should be dealt with as quickly and efficiently as possible, so as not to interrupt the 'flow' of the unit. For this reason, the practice ideas given here are limited to rapid drilling round the class of the most basic kind; there is plenty of opportunity for more elaborate and more communicative practice in the units themselves.

1.1 ROOMS AND FURNITURE

Presentation and practice of *there is / are* and *have / have got*

1 Build up these sets of examples on the board, if possible eliciting the question and short answer forms from the class:

i)

There's / There isn't a fire in the room.

Is there a fire in the room? –
Yes, there is.
No, there isn't.

There are some / There aren't any curtains in the room.

Are there any curtains in the room? –
Yes, there are.
No, there aren't.

ii)

The room has / doesn't have a fire. The room has got / hasn't got a fire.
Does the room have a fire?   Has the room got a fire?
Yes, it does.   Yes, it has.
No, it doesn't.   No, it hasn't.

2 Practice of full sentence forms. Give prompts and ask students to give sentences with (i) *there is / are* (ii) *has / has got*:

   e.g.   You: The room – a bed.
             1st Student: There's a bed in the room.
             2nd Student: The room has a bed.

             You: The garden – no trees.
             1st Student: There aren't any trees in the garden.
             2nd Student: The garden hasn't got any trees.

3 Practice of questions and short answers. Give prompts, and ask students to give questions and short answers with either *Is / are there..?* or *Does ... have? / Has...got...?*:

   e.g.   You: The room – ask about a bed.
             1st Student: Has the room got a bed?
             2nd Student: Yes, it has.

             You: The garden – ask about trees.
             1st Student: Are there any trees in the garden?
             2nd Student: No, there aren't.

2.5 MAKING MONEY

Practice of questions with *shall we?*

Tell the students what they can't decide, and ask them to make questions with *shall we?*:

   e.g.   You: You can't decide where to go.
           Student: Where shall we go?

           You: You can't decide what to buy.
           Student: What shall we buy?

Give similar prompts for questions with *who*, *when* and *how*.

3.7 ALL IN A DAY'S WORK: THE PASSIVE

Presentation and practice of *Present Simple Passive*

1 Show how Passive sentences are formed by writing these examples on the board:

	Subject	*Verb*	*Object*
ACTIVE	They	<u>pay</u>	the workers once a month
PASSIVE	The workers	<u>are paid</u>	once a month

Point out that:

i)   The Object of the Active sentence becomes the Subject of the Passive sentence.

   ii)   The Active verb becomes a Passive verb.

   iii) Passive verb form: be + Past Participle.

2 Write all the Present Simple Passive forms on the board:

I am	
He is	
We are	paid
You are	
They are	

3 Give Active sentences, and ask students to change them into Passive ones:

  e.g   You: They wake him up at seven o'clock.

         Student: He is woken up at seven o'clock.

         You: They speak English in that shop.

         Student: English is spoken in that shop.

7.1 ASKING PEOPLE TO DO THINGS

Practice of *Request structures*

1 Draw this box on the board:

CASUAL	FAIRLY CAREFUL	VERY CAREFUL

2 Point to one section of the box and give a prompt; students make an appropriate request:

  e.g. You: (pointing to 'FAIRLY CAREFUL'): Open the window.

         Student: Would you mind opening the window?

         You: (pointing to 'CASUAL'): Give me some coffee.

         Student: Give me some coffee, would you?

7.5 MAKING OFFERS

Presentation and practice of structures for *making offers*

1 Write the structures in this table on the board to show the two different types:

OFFERS (= I'll do X)	OFFERS OF PERMISSION (= You can do X)
I'll... (if you like). Shall I...? Would you like me to ...?	You can... (if you like). Would you like (to)...?

2 Give prompts, and ask students to make offers:
   e.g. You: Have something to eat.
          Student: Would you like to have something to eat?

          You: Drive you home.
          Student: Shall I drive you home?

9.1 COMPARISON OF ADJECTIVES

Presentation and practice of *comparative adjective forms*

1 Give rules for forming comparative adjectives:
   i)   Adjectives of *one* syllable: comparative formed with -*er*
        e.g. cheap*er*, nic*er*.
   ii) Adjectives with *three or more* syllables: comparative formed with *more*
        e.g. *more* beautiful, *more* interesting.
   iii) Adjectives of *two* syllables may be like (i) or like (ii); they should be
        learnt individually.
        e.g. prett*ier*, *more* careful.
2 Elicit these examples, and write them on the board:

One syllable	cheap	cheap*er*
	nice	nic*er*
Two syllables	pretty	prett*ier*
	careful	*more* careful
Three or more syllables	beautiful	*more* beautiful
	interesting	*more* interesting
Irregular:	good	better
	bad	worse
	far	further

3 Give other adjectives and ask students to give comparative forms:
   e.g. (+ -*er*):   long, short, tall, light, heavy, funny, friendly, easy, narrow,
                      wide, early, late, shallow, deep, quiet, noisy, loud.
          (+ *more*): useful, useless, careful, careless, exciting, boring, important,
                      succcessful, difficult.

9.2 SIGNIFICANT DIFFERENCES

Presentation and practice of *superlative adjective forms*

1 Give the rules for forming superlative adjectives, which are similar to those
   for comparative adjectives:

One syllable	+ -*est*	cheap*est*
Two syllables		prett*iest*
		most careful
Three or more syllables	*most*...	*most* interesting

2 Ask students to give the superlative forms of the adjectives in 9.1 above.

9.4 COMPARISON OF ADVERBS

Practice of *comparative adverb forms*

Give sentences for students to continue with comparative adverbs:
e.g. You: I work hard, but my friend...
      Student: Your friend works harder (than you do).

      You: I sing beautifully, but my friend...
      Student: Your friend sings more beautifully (than you do).

Other suitable adverbs (+ *-er*): fast, high, low, loud, late, early.
                       (+ *more*): carefully, carelessly, noisily, quickly, slowly, fluently.

14.1 SUGGESTIONS AND ADVICE

Practice of *basic advice structures*

Tell students what to advise you to do, and give a prompt to show what structure they should use:
e.g. You: Advise me to go home. 'Ought'.
      Student: You ought to go home.

      You: Advise me to have a bath. 'Why...?'
      Student: Why don't you have a bath?

17.1 DISCOVERING SIMILARITIES

Practice of *so* and *nor / neither* structures

Give a range of simple, similar remarks, and ask students to 'agree' with them:
e.g. You: I've been to France.   You: I like swimming.
      Student: So have I.   Student: So do I.

      You: I went to France last year. You: I don't like swimming.
      Student: So did I.   Student: Nor do I.

      You: I often go to France.   etc.
      Student: So do I.

Practice of *too* and *not...either* structures, with pronouns

1 Write this list of pronouns on the board:

him / her	them	
it	some	mine
one	(not) any	there

2 Give a range of simple, similar remarks, and ask students to agree with them, using pronouns from the box:

e.g. You: I've seen that film.
Student: I've seen it too.

You: I haven't seen that film.
Student: I haven't seen it either.

You: I've got a camera.
Student: I've got one too.

You: I haven't got a camera.
Student: I haven't got one either.

You: I've lost my camera.
Student: I've lost mine too.

etc.

21.3 LINKING SENTENCES

Practice of *too* and *not enough* structures with infinitives

Practice each of the three types of structure separately, by giving pairs of sentences and asking students to join them with *too* or *not enough*:

e.g. i) You: I can't see you. I'm busy. So I'm...
Student: I'm too busy to see you.

ii) You: I can't drink this tea. It's hot. So the tea is...
Student: The tea is too hot to drink.

iii) You: Grandmother can't drink this tea. It's hot. So the tea is...
Student: The tea is too hot for grandmother to drink.

Appendix A : Student's Book cassette – contents

This is a list of all material that is recorded on the Student's Book cassette.

1.1	Rooms and furniture	Listening Presentation
1.5	Asking about services	Recorded Example
1.7	Talking about amenities	Listening Model
2.1	Will & going to	Recorded Example
2.3	Changing your mind	Recorded Example
2.4	Intentions and plans	Listening Presentation
2.8	A celebration	Listening Comprehension
3.2	What's your job?	Recorded Example
3.3	Places and people	Recorded Example
3.6	Precise frequency	Recorded Example
4.8	Making puppets	Listening Comprehension
5.1	Relating past events	Listening Presentation
5.3	First experiences	Recorded Example
6.2	What are they doing?	Recorded Example
6.6	Current activities	Recorded Example
6.9	A telephone call	Listening Comprehension
7.1	Asking people to do things	Recorded Example
7.2	Getting people to stop	Recorded Example
7.4	Asking for permission	Recorded Example
7.6	Reporting offers	Listening Presentation
8.1	Making preparations	Recorded Example
8.4	The Present Perfect Continuous	Listening Presentation
8.6	Recent activities and achievements	Recorded Example
8.9	Summer jobs	Listening Comprehension
9.4	Comparison of adverbs	Recorded Examples
10.3	Remembering the past	Listening Model
10.4	Things have changed	Recorded Example
10.6	Changes of habit	Recorded Example
11.2	Responding to suggestions	Recorded Example
11.3	Preferences	Listening Model
11.5	Things that happen to you	Recorded Example
11.8	Fond of flying	Listening Comprehension
12.2	Circumstances and consequences	Recorded Example
12.4	Experiences	Listening Model
12.8	The ghost of Fernie Castle	Listening Comprehension
13.3	How much?	Listening Model
13.4	Kinds of people	Listening Model
13.6	Asking favours	Recorded Example
14.2	Alternative solutions	Recorded Example
14.3	Problems	Listening Model
14.5	Just in case	Recorded Example
14.8	Visiting Britain	Listening Comprehension

15.1	Origin and duration	Listening Presentation
15.3	Points and periods	Recorded Example
15.4	'Since' with clauses	Recorded Example
16.8	Skiing in Scotland	Listening Comprehension
17.1	Discovering similarities	Recorded Example
17.2	Similarities and differences	Recorded Example
17.3	The same thing in a different way	Recorded Example
17.6	Tastes in common	Listening Model
18.2	Doctor's orders	Recorded Example
18.6	Freedom of choice	Listening Presentation
18.7	It's up to you	Recorded Example
18.9	Coal mines	Listening Comprehension
19.1	Degrees of probability	Listening Presentation
19.2	Reassuring predictions	Recorded Example
20.2	The lost property office	Listening Model
20.4	Oneupmanship	Recorded Example
20.9	A difficult choice	Listening Comprehension
Activities (following Unit 20)		
	Call My Bluff	Listening Model
21.2	The wrong man for the job	Recorded Example
21.4	Useless possessions	Recorded Example
21.5	Faults and remedies	Listening Model
21.8	Holidays	Recorded Example
22.1	Setting a scene	Listening Presentation
22.7	Memories	Listening Model
Activities (following Unit 22)		
	Eskimos	Listening Model
23.2	Should & if	Recorded Example
23.5	Past mistakes	Listening Presentation
23.6	Events and circumstances	Recorded Example
24.4	Causes and results	Listening Model
24.9	Spokes	Listening Comprehension

Appendix B : Drills

LAB SESSION 1 (UNITS 1–2)

Drill 1 Having things done

Listen. / * Now you respond.

Are you going to alter that suit yourself?
No, I'm going to have it altered at the tailor's.

You're not going to develop those films yourself, are you?
No, I'm going to have them developed at the photographer's.*

Are you going to service your car yourself?
No, I'm going to have it serviced at the garage.

Surely you're not going to cut your hair yourself?
No, I'm going to have it cut at the hairdresser's.

Are you going to wash those sheets?
No, I'm going to have them washed at the laundry.

You're not going to repair that radio yourself, are you?
No, I'm going to have it repaired at the electrician's.

Are you going to mend those glasses yourself?
No, I'm going to have them mended at the optician's.

Surely you're not going to pull that tooth out yourself?
No, I'm going to have it pulled out at the dentist's.

Drill 2 Spontaneous decisions

Listen. / * Now you make the decisions.

Apparently that new play is fantastic. (go and see)
Mm. In that case, I think I'll go and see it.

That cake looks horrible. (have)
Mm. In that case, I don't think I'll have any.*

That car's very cheap. (buy)
Mm. In that case, I think I'll buy it.

They say that programme's not very good. (watch)
Mm. In that case, I don't think I'll watch it.

Apparently the traffic's terrible at the moment. (take the car)
Mm. In that case, I don't think I'll take the car.

There's plenty of hot water. (have a bath)
Mm. In that case, I think I'll have a bath.

Your boss is going to be at the party. (wear a suit)
Mm. In that case, I think I'll wear a suit.

I'm afraid I'm not a very good cook. (stay for dinner)
Mm. In that case, I don't think I'll stay for dinner.

It's terribly cold this morning. (stay in bed)
Mm. In that case, I think I'll stay in bed.

Part 5:   Appendices

Drill 3   Asking about intentions and plans

Listen. / * Now you ask the questions.

They're going to paint their kitchen either white or yellow.
What colour are they going to paint their kitchen?

He's thinking of going abroad either in March or in April.
When's he thinking of going abroad? *

She's planning to study either maths or chemistry at university.
What's she planning to study at university?

They're intending to spend the summer either in France or in Spain.
Where are they intending to spend the summer?

He's going to phone me either at 4 o'clock or at 4.30.
What time's he going to phone me?

She's intending to stay either with her cousin or with her brother.
Who's she intending to stay with?

They're thinking of calling the baby either Charles or Edward.
What are they thinking of calling the baby?

He's planning to invite either seven or eight people to the dinner party.
How many people is he planning to invite to the dinner party?

She's going to pay either in cash or by cheque.
How's she going to pay?

LAB SESSION 2   (UNITS 3–4)

Drill 1   Occupations

Listen. / * Now you respond.

He drives buses.
Oh, so he's a bus driver, is he?

I deliver letters.
Oh, so you're a postman, are you?*

They mend shoes.
Oh, so they're shoemenders, are they?

We smuggle diamonds.
Oh, so you're diamond smugglers, are you?

She acts in films.
Oh, so she's a film actress, is she?

He sings in operas.
Oh, so he's an opera singer, is he?

They manufacture guns.
Oh, so they're gun manufacturers, are they?

I fly jumbo jets.
Oh, so you're a pilot, are you?

He arrested 20 people last week.
Oh, so he's a policeman, is he?

She designed this building.
Oh, so she's an architect, is she?

Drill 2   Questions of routine

You are interviewing a pop star about his life. Listen. / * Now you ask the questions.

You want to know what time he gets up.
What time do you get up?

You want to know if his wife goes with him on tour.
Does your wife go with you on tour? *

You want to know how often he gives a concert.
How often do you give a concert?

You want to know what kind of car his wife drives.
What kind of car does your wife drive?

You want to know what school his children go to.
What school do you children go to?

You want to know whether he practises a lot.
Do you practise a lot?

You want to know how long he spends in the studio every week.
How long do you spend in the studio every week?

You want to know how much he
earns.
How much do you earn?

Drill 3   Things that happen

Now the pop star is talking about
some of the things that happen to him.
Listen. / * Now you're the pop star.

*Do people ever criticise you in the
newspapers? (occasionally)*
Oh yes. I occasionally get criticised in
the newspapers.

*Does someone drive you to the studio?
(always)*
Oh yes. I always get driven to the
studio.*

*Do people ever invite you to all-night
parties? (occasionally)*
Oh yes. I occasionally get invited to
all-night parties.

*Do your fans ever attack you after
your concerts? (from time to time)*
Oh yes. I get attacked after my
concerts from time to time.

*And do they ever tear your clothes?
(sometimes)*
Oh yes. My clothes sometimes get
torn.

*Do the police ever arrest your fans?
(now and again)*
Oh yes. My fans get arrested now and
again.

*Do people ever break the furniture
during your concerts? (usually)*
Oh yes. The furniture usually gets
broken during my concerts.

*Do they ever ask you to play in the
same place twice? (never)*
Oh no. I never get asked to play in the
same place twice.

LAB SESSION 3   (UNITS 5–6)

Drill 1   Events in sequence

Listen. / * Now you respond.

*Kate left university. Six months later
she moved to London.*
Six months after leaving university,
Kate moved to London.

*A few weeks after that she started
work at IBM.*
A few weeks after moving to London,
she started work at IBM.*

*Two years later she bought her own
flat.*
Two years after starting work at IBM,
she bought her own flat.

*A couple of months after that she met
Brian.*
A couple of months after buying her
own flat, she met Brian.

A year later, she married him.
A year after meeting Brian, she married
him.

A fortnight after that she sold her flat.
A fortnight after marrying Brian, she
sold her flat.

*A month later, she resigned from her
job.*
A month after selling her flat, she
resigned from her job.

*A year after that, she had her first
baby.*
A year after resigning from her job, she
had her first baby.

Drill 2   There is and there are

Listen. / * Now you respond.

*Three women are standing at the bus
stop.*
There are three women standing at the
bus stop.

Nobody's using the car today.
There isn't anybody using the car
today.*

A car's coming towards us.
There's a car coming towards us.

Is anyone using the bathroom?
Is there anyone using the bathroom?

*Some boats are sailing into the
harbour.*
There are some boats sailing into the
harbour.

No one's looking after the garden.
There isn't anyone looking after the garden.

A man's sitting on the wall.
There's a man sitting on the wall.

Some men are building a house.
There are some men building a house.

Is anyone helping them?
Is there anyone helping them?

Nobody's listening to the radio.
There isn't anyone listening to the radio.

Drill 3   The Present Continuous Passive

A police chief is checking on a gun smuggling problem with his police inspector. Listen. / * Now you answer the questions.

So they're smuggling guns into the country, are they?
Yes, sir. Guns are being smuggled into the country.

And they're bringing them in in small boats, eh?
Yes, sir. They're being brought in in small boats. *

And they're selling them in London, eh?
Yes, sir. They're being sold in London.

Hmm. And who's bringing them in? Terrorists?
Yes, sir. They're being brought in by terrorists.

You're watching the airport, are you?
Yes, sir. The airport's being watched.

And you're searching all foreign boats?
Yes, sir. All foreign boats are being searched.

And what about Davis? Are you following him?
Yes, sir. He's being followed.

But they're still smuggling the guns in. Is that right?
Yes, sir. The guns are still being smuggled in.

Hmm. I'm moving you to another case, inspector. Do you understand?
Yes, sir. I'm being moved to another case.

LAB SESSION 4   (UNITS 7–8)

Drill 1 Would you mind?

Listen. / * Now you make the requests.

Don't tell anyone.
Would you mind not telling anyone?

Can I take a key?
Would you mind if I took a key? *

Tell me your name, please.
Would you mind telling me your name?

Don't be so rude.
Would you mind not being so rude?

I can take my jacket off, can't I?
Would you mind if I took my jacket off?

Can I ask you something?
Would you mind if I asked you something?

Bring a bottle of wine, would you?
Would you mind bringing a bottle of wine?

Stop biting your fingernails, please.
Would you mind not biting your fingernails?

I don't want to come. You don't mind, do you?
Would you mind if I didn't come?

Do you think you could possibly lend me your bicycle?
Would you mind lending me your bicycle?

Drill 2 Reporting offers

Listen. / * Now you report the offers.

Here. Have an apple.
He offered me an apple.

It's all right. I'll pay for the meal.
He offered to pay for the meal.

Would you like to lie down?
He offered to let me lie down.*

Turn the TV on if you like.
He offered to let me turn the TV on.

Do you want another cup of tea?
He offered me another cup of tea.

Shall I take you to the doctor's?
He offered to take me to the doctor's.

I'll take you home if you like.
He offered to take me home.

I don't mind if you take the day off.
He offered to let me take the day off.

Would you like an aspirin?
He offered me an aspirin.

Drill 3 Is everything ready?

Everything's ready for tonight's opening performance but the producer is worried. Listen. / * Now you reassure the producer.

When are the cleaners going to clean the theatre?
Don't worry. They've already cleaned it.

I hope we sell all the tickets.
It's all right. We've already sold them.*

Where's Doris? She's got to iron the costumes.
Don't worry. She's already ironed them.

Don't forget to invite the press.
It's all right. I've already invited them.

When are they going to deliver the music tapes?
Don't worry. They've already delivered them.

The electricians have got to repair those lights.
It's all right. They've already repaired them.

I hope the photographer arrives on time.
Don't worry. He's already arrived.

I'm not feeling well. Would you phone the doctor?
It's all right. I've already phoned him.

Drill 4 Recent activities

Some time ago, Bob told some people to stop doing things, but they didn't take any notice. Now he is talking to his wife. Listen. / * Now you're Bob.

Darling, you know you told Billy not to fish in the river...
What? He's been fishing in the river again, has he?

And you asked Mrs Roberts to stop using your parking space.
What? She's been using my parking space again, has she?*

Do you remember telling the children to stop climbing through the window?
What? They've been climbing through the window again, have they?

I don't think the dog understood when you told it not to bite the postman.
What? It's been biting the postman again, has it?

And, er, that time you told Jane to stop riding on motorbikes.
What? She's been riding on motorbikes again, has she?

And you told her not to go out with Jim Smith again.
What? She's been going out with Jim Smith again, has she?

And you asked the neighbours not to light fires in the garden.
What? They've been lighting fires in the garden again, have they?

And, er, you know I promised to give up smoking.
What? You've been smoking again, have you?

LAB SESSION 5 (UNITS 9–10)

Drill 1 Comparison

Listen. / * Now you disagree.

I always think that cats aren't as clean as dogs.
Nonsense. Cats are much cleaner than dogs.

Students don't work as hard as teachers.
Nonsense. Students work much harder than teachers.*

Motorbikes aren't as dangerous as planes.
Nonsense. Motorbikes are much more dangerous than planes.

The violin isn't as difficult to play as the guitar.
Nonsense. The violin is much more difficult to play than the guitar.

Surely elephants don't live as long as people.
Nonsense. Elephants live much longer than people.

The sun isn't as far away as the moon.
Nonsense. The sun is much further away than the moon.

I always think coffee doesn't smell as good as it tastes.
Nonsense. Coffee smells much better than it tastes.

Women don't drive as carefully as men.
Nonsense. Women drive much more carefully than men.

Youth hostels aren't as cheap to stay at as guesthouses.
Nonsense. Youth hostels are much cheaper to stay at than guesthouses.

Drill 2 The past and the present

Listen. / * Now you compare the past and the present.

People used to die of smallpox.
People don't die of smallpox any longer.

Cranmore Castle is a language school now.
Cranmore Castle didn't use to be a language school.*

People used to be hanged for stealing bread.
People aren't hanged for stealing bread any longer.

There aren't a lot of wolves in Britain now.
There used to be a lot of wolves in Britain.

There used to be a Post Office in this street.
There isn't a Post Office in this street any longer.

There are rabbits in Australia now.
There didn't use to be rabbits in Australia.

India used to be a British colony.
India isn't a British colony any longer.

Oil isn't cheap any longer.
Oil used to be cheap.

Drill 3 Changes

Listen. / * Now you answer the questions.

Do they still live in Edinburgh? (move)
No, they've moved now.

Is that old hotel still there? (pull down)
No, it's been pulled down now.*

Are the printers still on strike? (go back to work)
No, they've gone back to work now.

Is he still only a captain? (promote)
No, he's been promoted now.

Is your radio still broken? (repair)
No, it's been repaired now.

Are they still engaged? (get married)
No, they've got married now.

Is your brother still staying with you? (leave)
No, he's left now.

Has your room still got that awful wallpaper? (redecorate)
No, it's been redecorated now.

Are you still looking for your keys? (find)
No, I've found them now.

Drill 4 Time comparison

An old man is being interviewed about his past and present life. Listen. / *
Now you are the old man.

Do you eat much?
Oh no, not as much as I used to.
Really?
Yes, I used to eat much more than I do now.*

Do you work hard?
Oh no, not as hard as I used to.
Really?
Yes, I used to work much harder than I do now.

Do you go out often?
Oh no, not as often as I used to.
Really?
Yes, I used to go out much more often than I do now.

Do you drive fast?
Oh no, not as fast as I used to.
Really?
Yes, I used to drive much faster than I do now.

Do your children visit you regularly?
Oh no, not as regularly as they used to.
Really?
Yes, they used to visit me much more regularly than they do now.

Do you sleep well?
Oh no, not as well as I used to.
Really?
Yes, I used to sleep much better than I do now.

LAB SESSION 6 (UNITS 11–12)
Drill 1 Likes and dislikes

Listen. / * Now you talk about the woman's likes and dislikes.

Shall we play cards? (love)
She loves playing cards.

Don't touch me! (loathe)
She loathes being touched.*

I'm not making the beds. (don't like)
She doesn't like making beds.

Are you going to give me a present? (adore)
She adores being given presents.

Don't interrupt me! (hate)
She hates being interrupted.

Let's visit a museum. (like)
She likes visiting museums.

Well, I'll drive if you like. (don't mind)
She doesn't mind driving.

Kiss me! (enjoy)
She enjoys being kissed.

Shall we dance? (fond)
She's fond of dancing.

Don't expect me to write you a letter. (hate)
She hates writing letters.

Don't lie to me. (can't stand)
She can't stand being lied to.

Drill 2 Events and circumstances

A lot of things went wrong for Martin last week. Listen to his complaints. / * Now you say what happened.

Why does the sun always go in when I'm sunbathing?
Martin was sunbathing when the sun went in.

How is it that whenever I'm watching television there's an electricity cut?
Martin was watching television when there was an electricity cut. *

Why does the phone always ring when I'm having a bath?
Martin was having a bath when the phone rang.

It's terrible the way the boss always walks in when I'm reading the newspaper.
Martin was reading the newspaper when the boss walked in.

How is it that whenever I'm washing up I break a plate?
Martin was washing up when he broke a plate.

*It's always the same. Whenever I'm
entertaining friends my mother turns
up.*
Martin was entertaining friends when
his mother turned up.

*Why does it always start to rain when
I'm sitting in the garden?*
Martin was sitting in the garden when
it started to rain.

*How is it that the postman always
knocks when I'm shaving?*
Martin was shaving when the postman
knocked.

*Why does the alarm always go off
when I'm having a nice dream?*
Martin was having a nice dream when
the alarm went off.

Drill 3   Hearing things

Last night you didn't sleep very well.
Here are some of the things you could
hear happening and some of the things
you heard happen. Listen. / * Now you
say what you heard.

(Sound of dogs barking.)
I could hear some dogs barking.

(Man: 'Be quiet'.)
I heard a man say 'Be quiet'. *

(Sound of people walking.)
I could hear some people walking.

(Sound of door shutting.)
I heard a door shut.

(Sound of wind blowing.)
I could hear the wind blowing.

(Woman: 'Goodnight'.)
I heard a woman say 'Goodnight'.

(Sound of people laughing.)
I could hear some people laughing.

(Sound of window breaking.)
I heard a window break.

(Sound of woman crying.)
I could hear a woman crying.

(Sound of woman's sudden scream.)
I heard a woman scream.

LAB SESSION 7   (UNITS 13–14)

Drill 1   Skill

Listen. / * Now you respond.

I'm fantastic at skiing, you know.
Yes, I know. You're a fantastic skier.

You're a useless dancer, you know.
Yes, I know. I'm useless at dancing.*

*I'm quite good at playing backgammon,
you know.*
Yes, I know. You're quite a good
backgammon player.

*You're not a very good footballer, you
know.*
Yes, I know. I'm not very good at
playing football.

I'm terrific at cooking, you know.
Yes, I know. You're a terrific cook.

*You're pretty hopeless at playing cards,
you know.*
Yes, I know. I'm a pretty hopeless
card-player.

*I'm very good at taking photographs,
you know.*
Yes, I know. You're a very good photographer.

You're a useless horseman, you know.
Yes, I know. I'm useless at riding horses.

*I say – your spoken English is quite
good.*
Yes, I know. I'm quite good at
speaking English.

Drill 2   Giving advice

Jack's worried about his weight. Some
friends give him some advice. Listen. /
* Now you give the advice.

Don't eat so much. (if)
If I were you, I wouldn't eat so much.

Join a slimming club. (try)
Have you tried joining a slimming
club?*

Give up eating butter. (ought)
You ought to give up eating butter.

Go jogging every morning. (if)
If I were you, I'd go jogging every morning.

Don't eat any more chocolate. (better)
You'd better not eat any more chocolate.

Take slimming tablets. (try)
Have you tried taking slimming tablets?

Don't drive so much. (ought)
You ought not to drive so much.

Start doing some exercises. (better)
You'd better start doing some exercises.

Don't worry about it. (if)
If I were you, I wouldn't worry about it.

Drill 3   Giving advice with a reason

Listen. / * Now you give the reason.

Take an umbrella – then you won't get wet. (so that)
You'd better take an umbrella so that you don't get wet.

Wear a raincoat – it might rain. (in case)
You'd better wear a raincoat in case it rains.*

Tie a knot in your handkerchief – then you won't forget. (so that)
You'd better tie a knot in your handkerchief so that you don't forget.

Have a sandwich – they might not give you anything to eat. (in case)
You'd better have a sandwich in case they don't give you anything to eat.

Take your passport – the police might stop you. (in case)
You'd better take your passport in case the police stop you.

Wear your red shirt – then he'll recognise you. (so that)
You'd better wear your red shirt so that he recognises you.

Don't go in – they might be busy. (in case)
You'd better not go in in case they're busy.

Leave work early – then you can do the shopping. (so that)
You'd better leave work early so that you can do the shopping.

Take a compass – it might get foggy. (in case)
You'd better take a compass in case it gets foggy.

Practise this language – it might come up in the test. (in case)
You'd better practise this language in case it comes up in the test.

LAB SESSION 8   (UNITS 15–16)

Drill 1   It's still going on

Listen. / * Now you respond.

I arrived two days ago.
So you've been here for two days, have you?

Mary moved to London in April.
So she's been living in London since April, has she? *

I met Ethel five years ago.
So you've known her for five years, have you?

Ted bought his hi-fi last Christmas.
So he's had it since last Christmas, has he?

He became Prime Minister in January.
So he's been Prime Minister since January, has he?

John was taken ill a week ago.
So he's been ill for a week, has he?

Angela started playing the piano half an hour ago.
So she's been playing the piano for half an hour, has she?

They got divorced in 1980.
So they've been divorced since 1980, have they?

I started playing chess 20 years ago.
So you've been playing chess for 20 years, have you?

Drill 2 Ever since

Listen. / * Now you respond.

Soon after she met Pierre, she had her first French lesson.
She's been having French lessons ever since she met Pierre.

Soon after he got his new hi-fi, he got his first complaint from the neighbours.
He's been getting complaints from the neighbours ever since he got his new hi-fi. *

He read his first detective story while he was in hospital.
He's been reading detective stories ever since he was in hospital.

Soon after he left school, he started looking for a job,
He's been looking for a job ever since he left school.

Soon after he was mugged, he went to his first judo class.
He's been going to judo classes ever since he was mugged.

Soon after leaving England, she wrote her first novel.
She's been writing novels ever since she left England.

Immediately after they got married, they had their first argument.
They've been having arguments ever since they got married.

Not long after being sacked, he sold his first used car.
He's been selling used cars ever since he was sacked.

Drill 3 Location

Listen. / * Now you respond.

The house has got a study. (front)
There's a study at the front of the house.

The car's got a bullet hole. (side)
There's a bullet hole in the side of the car. *

The pool's got a statue. (middle)
There's a statue in the middle of the pool.

The street's got a post office. (end)
There's a post office at the end of the street.

The room's got a bookcase. (corner)
There's a bookcase in the corner of the room.

The cinema has got two emergency exits. (back)
There are two emergency exits at the back of the cinema.

The bucket's got a hole. (bottom)
There's a hole in the bottom of the bucket.

The country's got some mountains. (north)
There are some mountains in the north of the country.

The town's got a lot of nightclubs (centre)
There are a lot of nightclubs in the centre of the town.

The caravan's got a skylight. (roof)
There's a skylight in the roof of the caravan.

LAB SESSION 9 (UNITS 17–18)

Drill 1 Discovering similarities

Listen. / * Now you respond.

I've had my car serviced.
So have I.

I don't like doing night duty.
Nor do I.

I should go.
So should I *.

I haven't got any money.
Nor have I.

I used to be a brilliant pianist.
So did I.

I wasn't at home.
Nor was I.

I'd better have a wash.
So had I.

I'd love a cup of coffee.
So would I.

Sorry, I wasn't listening.
Nor was I.

I don't think I'll tell him.
Nor will I.

I haven't flown before.
Nor have I.

I'm going swimming tomorrow.
So am I.

My room was broken into last week.
So was mine.

My brother can't drive.
Nor can mine.

Drill 2   Have to and allowed to

A man is talking about his schooldays.
Listen. / * Now you respond.

They made us wear a uniform.
What? You mean you had to wear a
uniform?

They let us copy in exams, though.
What? You mean you were allowed to
copy in exams? *

*They didn't let us play in the play-
ground, of course.*
What? You mean you weren't allowed
to play in the playground?

*But they didn't make us do any
homework.*
What? You mean you didn't have to do
any homework?

They let us smoke in class, too.
What? You mean you were allowed to
smoke in class?

*And they didn't make us buy any
books.*
What? You mean you didn't have to
buy any books?

*But they did make us clean the class-
rooms.*
What? You mean you had to clean the
classrooms?

And they didn't let us have long hair.
What? You mean you weren't allowed
to have long hair?

*On the other hand, they didn't make
us do lab drills.*
What? You mean you didn't have to
do lab drills?

Drill 3   Freedom of choice

Listen. / * Now you respond.

Who can I bring to the party?
You can bring whoever you like.
Really?
Yes, I don't mind who you bring.

How late can I stay up?
You can stay up as late as you like.
Really?
Yes, I don't mind how late you stay
up. *

When can I leave?
You can leave whenever you like.
Really?
Yes, I don't mind when you leave.

How many books can I borrow?
You can borrow as many as you like.
Really?
Yes, I don't mind how many you
borrow.

How long can I keep them?
You can keep them as long as you like.
Really?
Yes, I don't mind how long you keep
them.

What shall I tell him?
You can tell him whatever you like.
Really?
Yes, I don't mind what you tell him.

LAB SESSION 10 (UNITS 19–20)

Drill 1   Probabilities

Janet's going to fly for the first time next week. She wants to know what it'll be like. Listen. / * Now you respond.

'Will the stewardess give me some magazines?'
'She might if you ask nicely.'
If you ask nicely, the stewardess might give you some magazines.

'Will I be sick?'
'Probably not, unless the weather's bad.'
Unless the weather's bad, you probably won't be sick. *

'Will I see some mountains?'
'I expect so, if it's not cloudy.'
If it's not cloudy, I expect you'll see some mountains.

'Will they let me speak to the captain?'
'Certainly not – unless you hijack the plane.'
Unless you hijack the plane, they certainly won't let you speak to the captain.

'Will the plane be crowded?'
'I doubt it, if you fly at night.'
If you fly at night, I doubt if the plane will be crowded.

'Will there be a film?'
'I should think so, if it's a long flight.'
If it's a long flight, I should think there'll be a film.

'Will I get a window seat?'
'Probably – unless the plane's crowded.'
Unless the plane's crowded, you'll probably get a window seat.

'Will I have to pay for my drinks?'
'You may – if it's a cheap flight.'
If it's a cheap flight, you may have to pay for your drinks.

'Will the plane crash?'
'I shouldn't think so – unless there's a bomb on board.'
Unless there's a bomb on board, I shouldn't think the plane'll crash.

Drill 2   Will be doing and will have done

Diana's ill in hospital, but she'll be better by next week. Listen. / * Now you talk to Diana about next week.

I do want to recover.
Don't worry. You'll have recovered by next week.

I want to play tennis again.
Don't worry. You'll be playing tennis again next week. *

I wish I could leave hospital.
Don't worry. You'll have left hospital by next week.

I like cooking my own meals.
Don't worry. You'll be cooking your own meals next week.

I'd love to go back to work.
Don't worry. You'll have gone back to work by next week.

I like sleeping in my own bed.
Don't worry. You'll be sleeping in your own bed next week.

And I really miss sitting in my garden.
Don't worry. You'll be sitting in your garden next week.

I want to go home.
Don't worry. You'll have gone home by next week.

I want to forget all this.
Don't worry. You'll have forgotten it by next week.

Drill 3   Describing objects: relative clauses

Listen. / * Now you respond.

I need a pair of boots. I want to wear them for hillwalking.
I need a pair of boots that I can wear for hillwalking.

I'd love one of those cookers – you know, they light themselves.
I'd love one of those cookers that light themselves. *

I want to buy a shirt. And I don't want to have to iron it.
I want to buy a shirt that I don't have to iron.

Have you got a small camera? I want to be able to carry it in my pocket.
Have you got a small camera that I can carry in my pocket?

I'm looking for a car. It mustn't cost too much to run.
I'm looking for a car that doesn't cost too much to run.

I want a small car. I want to be able to park it in a small space.
I want a small car that I can park in a small space.

I'd like to buy a watch. It must give the day and date.
I'd like to buy a watch that gives the day and the date.

Could I have a brush? I want to use it for cleaning the steps.
Could I have a brush that I can use for cleaning the steps?

I need some of that stuff – you know, you use it for cleaning saucepans.
I need some of that stuff that you use for cleaning saucepans.

I'm looking for a sofa. It must turn into a bed.
I'm looking for a sofa that turns into a bed.

LAB SESSION 11 (UNITS 21–2)

Drill I   Too and enough

When Frances joined the army, she found that life was harder than she expected. Listen. / * Now you're Frances.

You can sleep on this bed. It's a bit hard, I'm afraid.
Oh no. It's much too hard for me to sleep on.

Here, eat this. It's not very hot, I'm afraid.
Oh no. It's not nearly hot enough for me to eat. *

Drink this tea. It's rather strong, I'm afraid.
Oh no. It's much too strong for me to drink.

You have to wear this uniform. It's not very warm, I'm afraid.
Oh no. It's not nearly warm enough for me to wear.

Climb over this wall. It's a bit high, I'm afraid.
Oh no. It's much too high for me to climb over.

Lift these weights. They're rather heavy, I'm afraid.
Oh no. They're much too heavy for me to lift.

Use this knife. It's not very sharp, I'm afraid.
Oh no. It's not nearly sharp enough for me to use.

Time to get up now. It's a bit early, I'm afraid.
Oh no. It's much too early for me to get up.

Hit that target. It's not very big, I'm afraid.
Oh no. It's not nearly big enough for me to hit.

Hope you pass the exam. It's rather difficult, I'm afraid.
Oh no. It's much too difficult for me to pass.

Drill 2   So and such

Frances is telling a friend about life in the army. Listen. / * Now you respond.

My bed's terribly hard – I sometimes lie awake all night.
Her bed's so hard that she sometimes lies awake all night.

They serve really bad food – I can hardly eat it.
They serve such bad food that she can hardly eat it. *

They make me do a lot of exercise – my
body hurts all over.
They make her do such a lot of exercise
that her body hurts all over.

The tea's incredibly strong – it tastes
like soup.
The tea's so strong that it tastes like
soup.

My uniform's really thin – it doesn't
keep me warm at all.
Her uniform's so thin that it doesn't
keep her warm at all.

I have to carry really heavy weights –
my arms nearly drop off.
She has to carry such heavy weights that
her arms nearly drop off.

And I get up terribly early – it's still
dark outside.
She gets up so early that it's still dark outside.

They pay me a really poor salary,
too – I can't afford to go away at the
weekends.
They pay her such a poor salary that
she can't afford to go away at the
weekends.

It's a hard life in the army – actually,
I'm thinking of leaving.
It's such a hard life in the army that
she's thinking of leaving.

**Drill 3   Past states and previous
actions**

Philip was ready for his journey.
Listen. / * Now you say what Philip
had done.

His suitcase was packed.
He had packed his suitcase.

The lights were all switched off.
He had switched off all the lights. *

The newspapers and milk were cancelled.
He had cancelled the newspapers and
milk.

The washing-up was all done.
He had done all the washing-up.

The house was locked up and the
windows were closed.
He had locked up the house and closed
the windows.

His suitcase was in the boot of the car.
He had put his suitcase in the boot of
the car.

He was wearing a thick coat.
He had put on a thick coat.

His tank was full of petrol.
He had filled his tank with petrol.

His passport and tickets were in his
pocket.
He had put his passport and tickets in
his pocket.

The engine was running.
He had started the engine.

LAB SESSION 12   (UNITS 23–4)

Drill I   Should and shouldn't

Listen. / * Now you respond with
criticisms.

The children are playing in the road.
Well they shouldn't be playing in the
road.

Paul didn't do his homework yesterday.
Well he should have done his
homework. *

Angie stays out till midnight sometimes.
Well she shouldn't stay out till midnight.

They broke a window yesterday.
Well they shouldn't have broken a
window.

They were playing football in the
garden.
Well they shouldn't have been playing
football in the garden.

Paul isn't wearing his coat.
Well he should be wearing his coat.

He wasn't wearing it yesterday either.
Well he should have been wearing it.

I don't mind what they do, really.
Well you should mind what they do.

I do believe they're laughing at you.
Well they shouldn't be laughing at me.

Drill 2   Conditional sentences

Listen. / * Now you respond.

'I feel ill.' 'That's because you don't eat properly.'
If you ate properly, you wouldn't feel ill.

'I've lost my address book.' 'That's because you didn't put it away.'
If you'd put it away, you wouldn't have lost it. *

'He doesn't like me.' 'That's because you criticise him.'
If you didn't criticise him, he'd like you.

'I've burnt the toast.' 'That's because you weren't watching it.'
If you'd been watching it, you wouldn't have burnt it.

'They laugh at me.' 'That's because you shout all the time.'
If you didn't shout all the time, they wouldn't laugh at you.

'I didn't pass my test.' 'That's because you drove too fast.'
If you hadn't driven too fast, you would have passed your test.

'Sorry, I didn't hear you.' 'That's because you weren't listening.'
If you'd been listening, you would have heard me.

'I keep getting headaches.' 'That's because you watch TV all day.'
If you didn't watch TV all day, you wouldn't keep getting headaches.

'I'm bored.' 'That's because you're not trying.'
If you were trying, you wouldn't be bored.

Drill 3   In spite of

Listen. / * Now you respond.

It was dark, but I could see them.
I could see them in spite of the darkness.

He's strong, but he couldn't break the door down.
He couldn't break the door down in spite of his strength. *

The houses are old, but they're in good condition.
The houses are in good condition in spite of their age.

She was wearing a disguise, but I recognised her just the same.
I recognised her in spite of her disguise.

They behave badly, but I like them.
I like them in spite of their bad behaviour.

He was unhappy, but he managed to smile.
He managed to smile in spite of his unhappiness.

The theatre's popular, but it doesn't make much money.
The theatre doesn't make much money, in spite of its popularity.

It was hot, but she was shivering.
She was shivering in spite of the heat.

The explosion was big, but it didn't kill anyone.
The explosion didn't kill anyone in spite of its size.

It was a long book, but we got through it.
We got through the book in spite of its length.

Appendix C : Guide to test answers

These notes are intended as a guide to marking (and going through in class) the answers to the Progress Tests and the Final Achievement Test. The answers given should be treated as a guide only, since many of the test questions allow a fairly wide range of 'correct' answers. In some cases (e.g. the Sentence Rewriting sections) the student needs to keep very close to the answers given. Where a larger range of answers is possible, the answer given is preceded by 'e.g.' to show that it is only one of a number of possibilities. Answers are not given for the Composition sections: these should be judged on how successfully the student uses appropriate language to talk about each topic.

PROGRESS TEST UNITS 1-4

1 Sentence rewriting
2 marks for each answer

(1) There are 30 beds in the hospital.
(2) I usually have my car serviced at/by Monkton Garage.
(3) She often gets sent to the United States (by her employers).
(4) Keep on/carry on, etc. until you reach/get to the chemist's and then turn right.
(5) The company publishes a report twice a year/two reports a year.

2 Asking questions
2 marks for each answer

(1) e.g. How often do you clean your shoes?
(2) e.g. Is there a desk in the room?
(3) e.g. How long does it take you to drive to work?
(4) e.g. What kind/make/type of car are you going to buy?
(5) e.g. Excuse me. Could you tell me the way to the hospital?
(6) e.g. What do you have for lunch?

3 Gap-filling
1 mark for each answer
(1) on
(2) sometimes/now and again/occasionally, etc.
(3) again/then
(4) past
(5) which
(6) up to
(7) out of

4 Vocabulary
1 mark for each answer

(1) Landlord/landlady.
(2) (a) Road sweeper.
   (b) Optician.
   (c) Architect.
(3) (a) e.g. Takes and gives out money in a bank.
   (b) e.g. Mends gas and water pipes.

(4) (a) e.g. Theatre, museum.
     (b) e.g. Funfair, zoo.
     (c) e.g. Hotel, guest house.

5 Composition   *4 marks for each paragraph*

PROGRESS TEST UNITS 5–8

1 Sentence rewriting   *2 marks for each answer*

(1) I didn't visit France until/till I was 30.
(2) Would you mind not talking in the library?
(3) Medical supplies are being flown into the war zone by the Red Cross.
(4) Fiona asked Paul if she could borrow his camera.
(5) He hasn't found a flat yet.
(6) There isn't anybody/is nobody using the kitchen at the moment.
(7) Beryl offered to let Ken use her telephone.

2 Making sentences   *2 marks for each answer*

(1) Henry was born at 4 o'clock in the morning on Tuesday, 18 May/the 18th of May/
     18th May.
(2) The church was designed by Sir Thomas Woolley in the Middle Ages.
(3) His first novel was published at the turn of the century.
(4) A year after leaving/she left college, Mona emigrated to Australia.

3 Making requests and offers   *1 mark for each answer*

(1) e.g. Give me that newspaper, would you?
(2) e.g. Do you think you could help me carry this luggage?
(3) e.g. Would you mind if I gave a party?
(4) e.g. Could I use your phone?
(5) e.g. I'll give you a lift if you like.
(6) e.g. Would you like me to collect that parcel for you?

4 Recent activities and achievements   *(1) and (3): 1 mark The others: 2 marks*

(1) Peter has been trying to find a job.
(2) He has been looking at the advertisements in the newspapers and so far he has
     applied for six jobs.
(3) But he has not received any replies yet.
(4) He has also been visiting/has also visited (some) local factories over the past few
     days.
(5) Yesterday he had an interview at a shoe factory, but he was not/has not been
     offered a job.
(6) Now he has decided to put an advertisement in the newspaper himself.

5 Composition   *4 marks for each paragraph*

PROGRESS TEST UNITS 9–12

1 Sentence rewriting   *2 marks for each answer*

(1) He goes to the theatre (much) more often than he used to.
(2) He prefers spending money to earning money.
(3) I love having my photograph taken.
(4) I heard the news while I was having breakfast.

2 Comparison   *1½ marks for each answer*

(1) Poodles can't/don't run as fast as greyhounds.
(2) India has a (much) larger population than Saudi Arabia.
(3) Nurses don't earn as much money as doctors.
(4) Corner shops are (e.g. friendlier) to shop at than supermarkets.

3 Changes   *1½ marks for each answer*

(1) It's been turned into an antique shop.
(2) They've been cut down.
(3) It's been pulled down.
(4) It's been resurfaced.

4 Likes and dislikes   *1 mark for each answer*

(1) He doesn't mind writing letters.
(2) e.g. He hates being laughed at.
(3) e.g. He loathes doing housework.
(4) e.g. He adores eating garlic.
(5) e.g. He loves waking up late.
(6) e.g. He enjoys playing golf.

5 Gap-filling   *1 mark for each gap*

(1) e.g. speak a bit louder
(2) e.g. walking as fast as
(3) like to
(4) e.g. whispering
(5) e.g. he was knocked down
    e.g. he was crossing the road
(6) e.g. collecting me
(7) the highest mountain
(8) did you use
(9) e.g. was washing up the teapot
(10) e.g. live with her parents any more
(11) e.g. as I earn/as my brother does/as I used to

6 Composition   *4 marks for each paragraph*

PROGRESS TEST UNITS 13–16

1   Sentence rewriting   *2 marks for each answer*

(1) If I were you, I'd/I would have it repaired.
(2) He does quite a lot of mountain climbing/mountaineering.
(3) She suggested that I took/should take/take an aspirin.
(4) She's quite good at playing the piano./She's quite a good pianist.
(5) I'm better at driving than you (are).
(6) I've been living/I've lived in this house (ever) since I got married.
(7) It's ages since I last saw them.

2   Giving reasons for advice   *1 mark for each answer*

(1) (a) e.g. Otherwise you might not get a seat.
     (b) e.g. in case the train's full.
(2) (a) e.g. so that you have enough money for the weekend.
     (b) e.g. Otherwise you may run out of money over the weekend.
(3) (a) e.g. in case someone tries to rob you.
     (b) e.g. so that you can protect yourself.

3   Location   *(1)–(6): ¹/₂ mark; (7)–(9): 1 mark*

(1) at
(2) at the top/back/side of
(3) next to/beside
(4) in the side/roof/door
(5) on
(6) opposite
(7)–(9) e.g. Town A is at the foot/edge of the mountains. Town A is 20 miles from town
     B. Town A is southwest of town C on the A356. Town A is between towns B and C.

4   Gap-filling   *1 mark for each answer*

(1) e.g. you ever been kicked by a horse?
(2) e.g. Have you tried counting sheep?
(3) you had it?
(4) have you been going (to them)?
(5) cleaned it/washed it/had it cleaned since
(6) e.g. Do you do (any) yoga?

5   Vocabulary   *¹/₂ mark for each answer*

(1) (a) A compass. (b) Boots. (c) An anorak. (d) The weather forecast.
(2) An au pair girl.
(3) (a) A level crossing. (b) The Equator. (c) A border/frontier. (d) The mouth/estuary.
(4) (a) e.g. chess, backgammon.
     (b) e.g. jogging, playing tennis.
     (c) e.g. pottery, knitting.

6   Composition   *4 marks for each paragraph*

PROGRESS TEST UNITS 17-20

1 Prediction   *1 mark for each answer*

(1) I should think John and Mary will get married soon.
(2) I expect you'll get on very well together.
(3) I doubt if you'll have to work very hard.
(4) They definitely won't offer him the job.
(5) The miners will probably go on strike.
(6) He might try to borrow some money.

2 Similarities   *1 mark for each answer*

(1) e.g. I've got one too; So have I.
(2) e.g. I can't either; Neither/nor can I.
(3) e.g. Mine is too; So is mine.
(4) e.g. I went to it too; So did I.
(5) e.g. Mine wasn't either; Neither/nor was mine.

3 Obligation   *1 mark for each answer*

(1) don't have to/needn't/don't need to
(2) aren't allowed
(3) must/have to
(4) don't have to/needn't/don't need to
(5) can/are allowed to; must/have to

4 Definitions   *1 mark for each answer*

(1) e.g. Football boots are boots you wear for playing football.
(2) e.g. A waterproof coat is a coat that keeps you dry in the rain.
(3) e.g. An automatic cooker is a cooker that turns itself on and off.
(4) e.g. A waiting room is a room you sit in while you are waiting to see the doctor or the dentist.
(5) e.g. A bread knife is a knife you use for cutting bread.

5 Gap-filling   *1 mark for each answer*

(1) I'm going to
(2) will be collecting/am collecting
(3) Neither......nor
(4) e.g. you use for correcting typing mistakes
(5) either
(6) whoever/anyone you like
(7) one with/one that's got
(8) don't make you

6 Vocabulary   *marks as shown*

(1) *1 mark* (a) Coal (tin, copper, etc.). (b) Coffee.
(2) *1 mark* They're both insects.
(3) *2 marks* (a) e.g. on a bag/watch. (b) e.g. on a clock. (c) e.g. on an electric fire.
            (d) e.g. on a bread knife.
(4) *4 marks* (a) e.g. waste-paper; shopping.
            (b) e.g. chess; bread.
            (c) e.g. tea; flower.
            (d) e.g. paint; tooth.

7 Composition   *4 marks for each paragraph*

PROGRESS TEST UNITS 21–24

1 Sentence rewriting   *2 marks for each answer*

(1) The water wasn't warm enough (for us) to swim in.
(2) It was such an easy examination that I left after 20 minutes.
(3) 'Spokes' is concerned with improving conditions for cyclists.
(4) She's a very ordinary person, in spite of her strange appearance.
(5) By the time/When I arrived, everyone in the house had woken up.

2 Criticising   *(a) 1 mark and (b) 2 marks for each answer*

(1) (a) Albert shouldn't eat such a lot/so much.
    (b) If he didn't eat so much, he wouldn't be so fat.
(2) (a) Felicity should put things away.
    (b) If she put things away, she wouldn't lose things.
(3) (a) Sid should have (remembered to) set his alarm. (or 'shouldn't have forgotten to...')
    (b) If he had (remembered to) set his alarm, he would have caught the train. (or 'If he hadn't forgotten to...')
(4) (a) Cynthia shouldn't have been throwing bricks at passing cars.
    (b) If she hadn't been throwing bricks at passing cars, she wouldn't have been arrested.
(5) (a) Anthony should have been watching the milk.
    (b) If he had been watching the milk, it wouldn't have boiled over.

3 Describing a scene   *1 mark for each answer*

(1) e.g. The cat was up the tree, hanging off a branch.
(2) e.g. There was a ladder leaning against the tree.
(3) e.g. The fireman was half way up the ladder, trying to reach the cat.
(4) e.g. The neighbours were standing by the fence, pointing.
(5) e.g. There were two dogs by the tree, barking and jumping up at the cat.

4 Gap-filling   *1 mark for each answer*

(1) keeps biting/is always biting
(2) faced
(3) had left/gone
(4) The purpose of ASH
(5) to/in order to
(6) e.g. the level of unemployment
(7) e.g. of the rise in the price of petrol
(8) e.g. I had spoken to him

5 Composition   *4 marks for each paragraph*

Part 5: Appendices

FINAL ACHIEVEMENT TEST

1 Multiple choice
1 mark for each answer

(1)(b)	(6)(a)	(11)(c)	(16)(d)
(2)(b)	(7)(d)	(12)(a)	(17)(b)
(3)(a)	(8)(d)	(13)(a)	(18)(c)
(4)(c)	(9)(c)	(14)(c)	(19)(c)
(5)(b)	(10)(a)	(15)(c)	(20)(d)

2 Sentence rewriting
2 marks for each answer

(1) The children are being looked after by the au pair girl.
(2) I used to be better at swimming than I am now./I used to be a better swimmer than I am now.
(3) You can stay as long as you like.
(4) There wasn't enough room in his cell (for him) to lie down.
(5) I haven't had my eyes tested since 1967.
(6) I suggested that he complained/complain/should complain to the police.
(7) If you had been paying attention, you would have heard what I said.
(8) Would you mind not blowing smoke in my face?
(9) I prefer giving presents to being given presents.
(10) I doubt if you will be paid very well.

3 Writing a letter
2 marks for each answer

(1) We are now in Turkey, and will probably arrive in Istanbul tomorrow.
(2) We are both very tired as we have been travelling non-stop for three days.
(3) Perhaps we shouldn't have driven so far in such a short time.
(4) Yesterday we were too tired to concentrate properly, and we nearly had an accident.
(5) It happened while we were driving along an empty road on the north coast of Greece.
(6) A lorry suddenly came out of a side turning in front of us.
(7) Richard braked as hard as he could and we stopped on the grass at the side of the road.
(8) If the brakes had not worked/had not been working properly, we would have gone straight into the side of the lorry.
(9) We were both so scared that we decided/have decided to sell the car.
(10) We are continuing/are going to continue our journey to Istanbul by train!

4 Gap-filling
1 mark for each answer

(1) e.g. How often do you have your car cleaned?
(2) e.g. How long is it since you (last) went to London?
(3) turned/converted into
(4) e.g. cleaned your teeth regularly
(5) e.g. Would you like a lift?
(6) still looking for one?
(7) e.g. have been working very hard
(8) e.g. (that) you can put
(9) e.g. I should think he'll turn up
(10) e.g. it might get/be stolen.
(11) e.g. grown such a long beard
(12) e.g. all those TV programmes about smoking

244

5 Vocabulary   *¹/₂ mark for each answer*

(1) (a) Buy papers/magazines. (b) Ask for something you've lost. (c) Make a telephone
     call.
(2) (a) A roof rack. (b) A lawn mower. (c) A chessboard. (d) A mousetrap.
(3) (a) A window cleaner. (b) A guitarist. (c) Clumsy. (d) Vain/self-centred.
(4) (a) Crawl. (b) Interrupt. (c) Jog. (d) Hitchhike. (e) (Re)decorate.

6 Composition   *5 marks for each paragraph*